"Bregman has once again brought her experience to bear upon the weighty topic of death, dying, and the afterlife. Clear, concise, and accessibly written, this book will doubtless be of interest to a wide audience."

—Christopher M. Moreman, Assistant Professor of Philosophy, California State University, East Bay

PREACHING DEATH

The Transformation of Christian Funeral Sermons

—Lucy Bregman—

BAYLOR UNIVERSITY PRESS

Cover Design by Nicole Weaver, Zeal Design
Cover Image © iStockphoto.com / Frank Vinken

Library of Congress Cataloging-in-Publication Data

Bregman, Lucy.
Preaching death : the transformation of Christian funeral sermons / Lucy Bregman.
p. cm.
Includes bibliographical references and index.
ISBN 978-1-60258-320-7 (pbk. : alk. paper)
1. Death--Religious aspects--Christianity--History of doctrines. 2. Death--Biblical teaching. 3. Funeral sermons. 4. Funeral rites and ceremonies. I. Title.
BT825.B735 2011
236'.1--dc22

2010052531

Printed in the United States of America on acid-free paper with a minimum of 30% pcw recycled content.

Table of Contents

Part IV
What Might Have Been

Part V
Conclusion

Acknowledgments

This book's themes took shape gradually. I am indebted to the Collegeville Institute, where I was a resident scholar back in 2000–2001, and to the following individuals: Judith Buck-Glenn; Al Dueck; Dennis Klass; Thomas Long, Chris Moreman, and the Death, Dying and Beyond Consultation; Greg Schneider; Gerard S. Sloyan; Virginia Sloyan; and the family of the late Sara Thiermann ("Gigi").

I am also indebted to the staff at the Lutheran Theological Seminary of Philadelphia, colleagues and students at the Temple University Religion Department, and fellow parishioners of St. Stephen's Church, Norwood, Pennsylvania.

Some of this material has been presented at meetings of the Association for Death Education and Counseling and the American Academy of Religion. All of the quotations from the Bible are taken from the New International Version (NIV) unless otherwise indicated.

Part I

What Christians Used to Say about Death

1

A Changeover of Messages and Images

Martha answered, "I know he will rise again in the resurrection at the last day."

Jesus said to her, "I am the resurrection and the life. He who believes in me will live, even though he dies; and whoever lives and believes in me will never die."

—John 11:24-26

Christians have been fascinated with death, with imagery and ideas surrounding it, since the time when Jesus taught, suffered, and died. The enigmatic pairing of resurrection and life, with death and in opposition to death, has been intrinsic to Christian faith from the beginning. All die, or "never die," or both. Yet this does not mean that Christians have simply echoed an eternal unchanging message, nor that one era's words have or will suffice for the next. Sometimes the changeover from one set of images and ideas is slow, while more recently it was abrupt. Yet the shift, however real and dramatic, has gone almost unnoticed. That changeover is the subject of this book: what Christians not very long ago used to say about death, and what they stopped saying, and what they say now. Also, to complete the story, what they might have said at the time of transition, but did not.

That is why we need another Christian book about death and dying. There are shelves full of pastoral care textbooks, historical and theological studies, and manuals for clergy on how to perform funerals. There are many sermon anthologies that make up the primary texts on which our study is based. But this book tells the story of now-obsolete words for dying, death, and grief as has not been done before. It is a truism that Christians have always had something to say about death and afterlife. But in this book, we examine how that "something" was in fact many things, some gone and no longer even remembered. This book describes and explains a change, a momentous shift from what Christians used to say about death, and what they say now. The older language, ideas and images, had a long history, and persisted in full force through the early decades of the twentieth century. Then this language faded, losing its hold over the collective religious sensibility of American Protestantism. This in-between period is what we and many others now look back upon as the age of "silence and denial," in regard to death. Then, suddenly, in came a brand-new language, drawn from the modern death awareness movement, whose imagery and preoccupations were radically discontinuous with what Christians had once said so frequently and forcefully. This new language has continued to hold sway for approximately the past four decades. And the most amazing thing about this change: no one seemed to notice it. The change happened under the radar of public or media attention.

Certainly, the switchover in Christian death language was never a battle between old and new, a lineup of adversaries with one side entrenched in the past, while the other claimed the role of "progressives" heading into the future. Such a model misses one basic point of our study, which is that there was no direct conflict, no public controversy, and no attention to what had been lost once the new language entered the scene. Instead, what grew up was the belief that prior to the 1970s, "nothing" had been said about death. American society's denial of death was a vacuum, one that our current, recent language and understanding has now filled. The conventional way to label this is to say that "American society denies death," and that only now are we emerging from an era of silence and denial.

The lack of overt, direct conflict is all the more astonishing since on other issues some Christians lined up to battle against "secular humanism" and its inroads into traditional Christian perspectives on family, sexuality, gender, and many other issues. Simultaneously, the old battle between "science" and "religion" was revived, and debates over creationism and intelligent design raged as here and there school boards voted down textbooks that taught evolution. But on death, the conflicts were over medical ethics issues, not the basic beliefs and images for death, dying, and afterlife that had served Christians for so long, and yet had been so quietly abandoned and forgotten.

So it is the task of this book to look backward, to discover the neglected ways Christians in North America encountered, understood, and imagined situations of dying, death, and bereavement early in the twentieth century. This before the period of silence and denial that came mid-century, and so also before the contemporary death awareness movement of the 1970s and beyond. Then we shall see how the Christian message about death has been irrevocably changed by the death awareness movement, the model of understanding based on a psychological framework, and assumptions such as "death is a natural event." This movement's impact is widespread, affecting health care, education, and psychotherapy and creating new professions such as hospice nurse and grief counselor. For Protestant Christians, the subjects of our study, the new language reshaped pastoral care and the hospital chaplain's role and even, as we shall see, drastically revised the Christian pastor's understanding of the purpose of funerals. Indeed, a great deal of pastoral energy went into supporting the newer perspectives on dying, death, and bereavement, and in critiquing American society's silence and denial on these topics.

Lack of public, media-promoted conflict may be why the story we will tell remained relatively obscure. The death awareness movement promised a meaningful and realistic stance toward death and dying. Unlike with the abortion debate or legalization of physician-assisted suicide, no protesters took to the streets or to the front doors of churches. Popular media never spotted how new views of bereavement were incorporated into worship, or when older standard sermon motifs vanished from funerals. In fact, many of these had vanished or faded decades before the 1959 publication of *The Meaning of Death*, the title of a groundbreaking anthology edited by Herman Feifel, ever appeared.

With the full arrival of the death awareness movement in the late 1960s, very few Christian thinkers really questioned whether its model of "death as a natural event" was truly in tune with what Christians had believed and still wanted to affirm. Because there was widespread support for the movement's practical programs, such as hospice, many pastoral caregivers and chaplains went overboard in agreeing that Christianity taught "acceptance" rather than "denial of death." If older approaches were mentioned at all, it was to lambaste these for supporting "denial" rather than realistic acceptance. Accusers targeted pastors who ignored the human plight of the hospital patients in order to read the Bible at them, or otherwise betray defensiveness and denial rather than empathy. A first generation of pastoral care books might well have been subtitled *Kübler-Ross for Chaplains*. (See Bane, *Death and Ministry: Pastoral Care for the Dying and Bereaved*, and Kübler-Ross' *Death: The Final Stage of Growth* anthology, two 1975 anthologies that exemplify this model.) For the many Christians committed to the work of hospice, for example, it was important to show that such a philosophy of dying as hospice advocated was indeed fully compatible with the best insights of Christian faith (as Paul Irion's *Hospice and Ministry* did).

Even today, when a far more critical and analytic stance toward the psychological framework of the death awareness movement is possible, one finds little or no interest in looking at what it replaced. Pastoral theologian Thomas Long's recent and excellent *Accompany Them with Singing: The Christian Funeral* is highly suspicious of the recent redesigning of funerals, including what we will term "the triumph of the biographical." But he is even more dismissive of the mistaken "Platonism" that he finds at deep odds with the authentic Christian view of persons (Long, 22–27). While "Platonism" became a term of insult for theologians mid-century, this stance effectively severs Long from a true appropriation of the earlier era's messages. He does not turn to the recent past in order to reclaim a new and better future for Christian understandings of death.

Meanwhile, the religious and cultural changes with which this book deals happened under the radar, and brought with them a more or less standard account of the present in relation to the past. The tale goes as follows: Once, back in the relatively recent past, people lived in rural communities, where death happened often and was considered natural, a part of life. Everyone learned to accept death. Religion was a resource; it helped by providing a framework of shared understanding of death, and it helped by binding the community together in shared ritual activity. In this view, the specific doctrines of religion were rarely the focus. Yes, unquestioned belief in an afterlife and some understanding of suffering as "God's will" may have been what religion taught. But what really mattered was the "homelike" quality of dying and death. The contrast, of course, is with today's high-tech hospital environment, which is presumably the way the majority of us now will experience dying. And along with this new environment for dying came an era of silence and denial, when *nothing* could be said publicly about death. Again and again, in contemporary writings about death and dying, one finds these two contrasting situations pictured, together with the moral lesson they reveal. Embedded in the agenda of the death awareness movement is the theme that although modern medical advances are marvelous, some important human dimension of dying was sacrificed along the way. Christian pastors, chaplains, and counselors supported this agenda, accepted this critique of the American present, and had no interest in questioning the historical or religious accuracy of the rhetoric.

Such a portrait of the past, steeped in nostalgia, is suspiciously hard to fix chronologically. Kübler-Ross placed her scene of "traditional dying" in the Swiss village of her childhood (1968, 5). By now, that would have been almost ninety years ago. Americans from rural or small-town roots often report memories of similar scenes, if they are at least middle aged. Even within the past ten years, I heard a nurse remark, "I don't think the people I work with have a problem facing and accepting death." She then added that her patients were the elderly residents of a Catholic nursing home in extremely rural Stearns County, Minnesota. "They just say their rosaries, and wait for God to call them," she explained. They do not need "death education," or any special "spiritual care" beyond what they already learned over the course of long, traditionally devout lives. They are the people for whom "traditional dying" is "natural," "a part of life."

But Stearns County is, symbolically enough, the original site of "Lake Wobegon," the celebrated fictitious American small town created by Garrison Keillor, where the women are all strong, the men are good looking, and all the children are above average. . . . For purposes of rhetorical contrast, "then" versus "now," this conventional nostalgic portrait of the past is one of the popularized features of the death awareness movement, just as Lake Wobegon is part of the middle-class mainstream American nostalgia for a heartland that was innocent, peaceful, and secure. For the death awareness movement, nostalgia's primary function is not as an accurate description of the early twentieth century, but as a critique of high-tech dying, and our own more recent attitudes toward death. Without denying the truth of the Stearns County rosary-saying elderly and their "acceptance of death," we need to denostalgize what was going on that made such activities and attitudes—and their Protestant counterparts—more fully visible.

First, let us be less nostalgic and more clear about the chronology of this "recent past." Suppose we want to know when the era of "death is natural" ended, and the era of "silence and denial" began. If we have it in for high-tech medicine, the answer to these questions is found in the 1950s–1960s developments of intensive care, life support, and other biomedical innovations. Journalist Marilyn Webb, writing on *The Good Death: The New American Search to Reshape the End of Life*, accepts this chronology (34ff.), just as she contrasts "traditional" versus "modern" dying in the same manner as Kübler-Ross did. Webb's locale for "traditional dying" is Ireland, but the pointed critique of contemporary dying is identical.

> "This is how people die in Ireland," Sister Martina later said. "No machines. Surrounded by family and people saying prayers. But here it is very unique." (Webb, 284)

So "silence and denial" caused by high-tech hospital dying seems a reasonable connection. But it is misleading. Our inquiry suggests that these medical technologies seem to follow rather than initiate a shift in language and imagery. A book published in 1936, Cabot and Dicks' *The Art of Ministering to the Sick*, whose authors are a pastor and a doctor, reveals a situation basically identical to that discovered by Kübler-Ross and Webb more than thirty years later, and indeed one that remains the same today. Dying had become the province of medical specialists. In the hospital, disempowered, helpless dying patients struggled on their own to find meaning. Cabot and Dicks argued that ministers to the sick therefore are not "religious specialists" but must see their role as "patient advocates," trying to restore a sense of human presence in an environment where specialists' technical expertise rules. "Religion has always been an antispecialist force," they declare at the start (Cabot and Dicks, 3), and therefore is meant to become a counterforce to the triumph of technical expertise that diminishes the experiences of the sick and dying. It is worth mentioning that this book was written not only before the development of modern medical technology, but even before the role of "hospital chaplain" had been firmly defined. Yet whatever had changed—from "death is natural" to "silence and denial"—had already begun long before the age of today's high-tech medical miracles.

So to find the real start of the era of "silence and denial," we can seek another landmark. Leo Tolstoy's classic story "The Death of Ivan Ilych" was written in 1884, and here the problem of meaningful dying and the hero's spiritual emptiness is laid out in such strikingly contemporary terms that it is hard to place the tale in nineteenth-century Russia, and not in today's hospitals. Ivan had lived an externally successful life, but he learns right before his death that it has also been a false and deceptive life, "a huge deception" that hid both life and death (152). Tolstoy may already have spotted silence and denial, even in a culture that by and large represented the earlier era of "death is natural." (The peasant servant Gerasim in the story symbolizes that attitude, and becomes the spokesman for Tolstoy's own nostalgia.) Significantly, this story is the only piece of nineteenth-century literature frequently cited by today's death and dying authors; virtually everything else from that era of great English novels and fine poetry is missing. This disappearance is an intrinsic and telling part of our story.

But Tolstoy was certainly the exception, and in 1884, and up through the early decades of the twentieth century, the American Christian language for death and dying seemed to be present as it was not for Ivan Ilych. The problem of dying was not that of Ivan, nor of Cabot and Dicks' or Kübler-Ross' hospital patients. There was a lot to say about death's meaning, and it was said and repeated often at funerals. Death's meaning was proclaimed in songs, poems, and sermons. While discontent and disillusion may have seethed under the surface, funerals of 1899 were not exercises of silence and denial. Nor were funerals of the 1910s, the 1920s. . . . But, as the decades of the twentieth century passed, certain things did change. For one thing, infant mortality dropped dramatically between 1870 and 1920, and this shift carried with it certain consequences for religious messages about the universality, omnipresence, and unavoidability of death. When a preacher of the 1920s reminded his congregation that one-third of all humanity dies in infancy, he was already behind the times, at least for white North Americans. Moreover, in the post–World War I era, enormous political and international catastrophes reached out to link Americans to events in Europe, not to mention the Great Depression at home. Ironically, while theological leaders tried to respond to these crises with new statements of Christianity's large-scale relevance, what was said about personal individual death remained relatively unchanged. Yes, there were theological challenges to the traditional messages, but the prevalent pattern was that the motifs of personal death and heavenly afterlife seemed too small scale to matter. And so the older images lingered, then faded, rather than anything more dramatic.

The death awareness movement popularized the idea that Americans mid-century had no words at all for death. Society simply repressed death, period. After all, the 1950s was off the scale in denial about lots of things, so it is no surprise that it had no words to speak about death. Countless autobiographies and memoirs depicting that era have reinforced this sense that nothing was said about death, that death, dying, and bereavement were experiences to be silenced until *Someday* (Andrew Malcolm's title about his elderly mother's dismal, unprepared-for dying) when it was in fact too late. Yet in spite of this, that mid-century era still did have some words, leftovers from earlier. The meanings of such words were by then stretched and thinned, "like butter scraped over too much bread." These words of the hobbit Bilbo (from Tolkien's *Lord of the Rings*), whose unnaturally prolonged life is becoming a burden to him, might well describe the theologies, images, and pastoral preaching about death available to mainline Protestant Christians mid-twentieth century.

Our task in this book is to examine what ideas and images for death were used and were still vigorous before their fading out. We will look at them unavoidably but not solely through the lenses of the ideas that eventually replaced them (the era "after silence and denial"). We want to discover the staying power of religious motifs that seemed permanent, static, and uninvigorated for a relatively long time, yet were then very rapidly overrun by the newer language that we have now. Let us look carefully at what was once said, what was lost, and make an attempt to evaluate it. Inevitably, we will ask if anything from this relatively recent past could become a "resource" for us, and if so, how could we use it wisely. There will, I promise, be no quick and easy answer to this question.

Moreover, under that deceptively cozy first-person plural of "us" and "we" lies concealed the multiplicity of who "we" are. Not just are now, in the age of pluralism and diversity, but once were. The present study is based on anthologies of funeral sermons preached by mainline Protestant clergy. These pastors saw themselves as central, representative, normative for their faith communities and for American society. Their congregations saw themselves this way too, and those who did not quite fit in went unnoticed in the stories and anecdotes that fill the sermons. The sermons deemed good enough to be anthologized were the cream of the crop, and undoubtedly useful as models for other preachers' efforts at the time of other deaths. In this sample of several thousand sermons, there appears to have been a relative uniformity for mainline Protestant Christians and their clergy, on the topic of death. For instance, images of heaven were genuinely common ground for them; there was no "Methodist heaven" versus "Baptist heaven," nor were regional differences noticeable that I can detect in any of the sermons preached at funerals.

The divide between Protestants and Roman Catholics is another matter. Back when Protestants and Roman Catholics did not see one another as "sundered brethren" but as adversaries representing false and distorted understandings of Christian faith, it is unspoken that the others remained "other." If there was a level of piety that both groups could share, Protestant clergy never spoke of it. Remember those elderly Catholic Minnesotans and their rosaries; here we are telling a distinctively Protestant story, filled with Bibles and hymns but no rosaries or Sacred Heart devotions. It is also a very white story; as African Americans are invisible, and even missionaries' pious Hindu converts are more present in the preachers' stories than are the local African Methodist Episcopal (AME) congregations. While chronology is the obvious divider for our topic—then vs. now—other divisions cannot be completely discounted. However, familiar and recent lines some of us now expect, such as between "liberal" and "conservative," "mainline" and "evangelical," or even between "Christian" and "New Age," may not be valid when applied to the topic of death one hundred years ago.

In this study, I assume that ideas matter, theology matters. How Christians read and respond to the Bible matters. How the church as a community visions, believes, and hopes matters. The religious aspects of the story are not just by-products of cultural and sociological forces at work, they must be treated as having their own internal meanings, significance, and importance for those who lived them. Even as "religious practices" are what people do, how they think about what they do is vital to the complete picture of their piety. One very vivid strategy to get at this part of our story is to look directly at particular biblical passages, once used frequently as the primary texts for funeral sermons, and reflect on the divergent ways these are now heard. (Assuming they are "heard" at all, since several of these are no longer preached at funerals, nor used for any other public occasion today.) Although John's "many mansions" promise by Jesus (John 14:1-2) continues as a standard funeral sermon text (and probably will for the foreseeable future), this is not the case for other passages from Scripture. For many of the favorite preaching texts of eighty years ago would not be considered relevant to death, or important for any other reason, even by the most devout. Listening to the texts that spoke meaningfully to persons in the past, but no longer to us (at least no longer for the same occasions and purposes), will help us grasp and grapple with the religious ideas that dominated the era before silence and denial.

Curiously, an important part of the story is the supplementing of biblical texts by other, literary ones, in the context of words about dying and death, even in the setting of funeral preaching. To gain access to the images from that era before silence and denial, one must be prepared to hear lots of Victorian poetry. Only a fraction of this represented the words to hymns; much of it was "poetry," not intended for church use by its authors. It is high quality poetry, but is now read for English and American literature survey courses, rarely by ordinary persons for personal inspiration, and certainly not recited by the pastor in church. "Before silence," when words were still abundant, might also be described as the golden era of recitable poems. A 1926 *Funeral Cyclopedia* anthology for preachers featured large sections of "quotable poetry" because this was assumed to be integral to a Christian funeral. Most of the poems dealt allegorically with death and the transition to afterlife, employed a wide range of images that captured what persons who read and recited these hoped would be fitting for Christians' imaginative hopes. The poems depended upon rhetorical devices long-standing in Western arts and literature, such as personifications (as when death becomes Death and is addressed by the poet, or addresses mortals in his own speeches). The presence and abundance of such devices, absent from the creative work of twentieth-century persons, intensifies the sense of an era long gone, whose sensibilities and styles are far in the past and unrecoverable by us. In contrast, when today a poem is read at a funeral or memorial service, it is usually authored by family members, about or addressed to the deceased. "Thank you, Gigi," written and read by a young granddaughter at the memorial service for her grandmother, has replaced Tennyson and Wordsworth. Penned for the occasion, these new poems are personal tributes, part of "expressive ritual" but without any claim to literary quality or universal scope regarding death. We will discuss this shift in the final section of this book.

Moreover, the profusion of those mostly Victorian poems at religious occasions early in the twentieth century—and undoubtedly before that—raises in me a suspicion all of the preachers and congregations of that era would have vehemently denied. Namely, that these people found the Bible lacking, its resources (as they understood them) insufficient to express their deepest, most fervent intuitions regarding death. I might even intimate that the clergy and their congregations were already secretly New Age (similar to what Long and others call "Platonist") but thought they were still Protestant Christians. Victorian poetry, however Christian on the surface, was really heading in a direction that eventually led to *Life After Life* and other New Age eschatologies, and away from Jesus' death and resurrection. But this standard is unfair and anachronistic, as superficial as the nostalgia for "death as natural." More charitably, one of the twists of this story as a whole is redefining boundaries. Metaphors and allegories and poems considered perfectly legitimate expressions of Christian hopes in 1920 were eventually discarded and would today be labeled "sub-Christian" by many pastors and others with theological training.

In any story of "what gets lost" and "what replaced it" there is the possibility that the replacement went awry, failing to reflect the intentions of those who eagerly first proposed it. In this case, the older imagery and ideas had faded before the newer were introduced, so there was never an active head-on collision between them. But we can ask if what replaced the older images and ideas always expressed the hopes and aims original death awareness movement advocates desired. Other possible new images for dying and death were proposed to overcome silence and denial, but were unsuccessful, and never caught on. Some really excellent ideas just did not fly. Since we are dealing with human appropriations, meanings, and aspirations, rather than with fixed laws of nature, it is always intriguing to wonder what alternatives Christians might have explored or adopted, as the older imagery faded. We will look at the case for turning Christian funerals into occasions for "lament," an excellent instance of this "might have been." Another "lost" possibility was to explore more fully and daringly the negativity of death, no longer "Platonized" as a gentle friend, but neither transformed into neutral "natural event." Neither of these possibilities penetrated into the contemporary mainline Christian funeral sermon, and today they seem even further from what funeral-goers expect than they did when first proposed a generation ago.

This study hopes to accomplish three things relevant to how persons today understand and reflect upon religious ideas from the past.

1. It breaks through a monolithic view of "tradition," the assumption that what Christians taught about death has always and everywhere repeated the same eternal truths. Because God does not change, and the Bible does not change, nor does church traditional teaching change (according to this mind-set), therefore core religious themes on a topic as important as death could not have changed. What is very evident is that this view is wrong; ideas have changed, and none of the sermons preached in 1910 could be repeated today.
2. This study also questions the now-popular idea that the past—tradition—can serve as a "resource" for the present, a repository of possibly useful ingredients for our meaning making today. While this is an improvement over the "timeless tradition" model of Christian faith, the subtitle for this book might well be *The Past Is NOT a Resource*. Or rather, we had better be much more careful as to how we use this idea. Sometimes it is important to learn the reasons why

ideas and imagery from the past were discarded. No matter how hungry we may be for "resources" there are aspects of "tradition" that should remain neglected, faded out, or replaced. We do not endorse a linear model of "progress" in religious insights, but those hungry for "resources" will be frustrated when they discover how different the needs and sensibilities of persons in the relatively recent past really must have been. What "resources" they used will just not suit us.

3. But to forget the past makes one more likely to repeat its mistakes, as well as to miss out on what it could, perhaps, still be saying to us. The nostalgia model of "death as natural event" is comforting, just as Lake Wobegon is comforting and feels familiar even to those of us who never grew up in small towns. But nostalgia can actively interfere with what the voices of the past were trying to say, with the story they tell. When we turn to earlier voices, we can hear something very disturbing, very unlike what we hope from them. This disturbing quality cannot be discounted, or ignored. And perhaps the most disturbing fact is that in spite of our emphasis on transition and change, a few of the older ideas about death linger on, in places well away from formal public occasions such as Christian funerals. Greeting cards and memorial websites preserve some of the most dismal themes and images, those long since discarded from any preacher's storehouse of Christian teaching on death.

I can place these three concerns in the wider underlying context not just of past and present but of the future. This looks to the needs of the future generation of Christians, asking what messages and meanings for death and bereavement they will be given and be able to receive. Surely they deserve something better than silence and denial, and also something other than "death is natural and we should accept it." Some among these younger generations of Christians are the students I teach in a college course on "Death and Dying." They have by now the legacy of the death awareness movement, so that terms such as "denial" and "the grief process" and "closure" come naturally to them. They have a Christian background or education and in some cases, real and strong faith. But the Christian ideas they have been taught or absorbed are a mush of the less theologically thoughtful emphases, a kind of New Age hope for contact with the dead (born of Hollywood, or merely expressed by it?) and an unshakable Platonism so that "the soul" and its afterlife are really what religion is, they assume, all about. While for life and living, they are not Platonists—for they take both bodies and clothes as essential expressions of inner identity!—when it comes to anything religious, they are at a loss for dealing with death except through these hodgepodge ingredients. They are in some ways still heirs of the legacy of before silence and denial, even as the other language, of the death awareness movement, is what most of them use day to day. Perhaps, just perhaps, if American Christians can discover how we got to this place, we can see it more clearly and find ways to move beyond it.

2

What Is a Christian Funeral?

We need to know what a funeral is, and why have one. At a funeral, many things can happen, it can serve many functions. Some purposes are focused on the social and psychological needs of the family, community, or attendees, some are focused on the existential yearning to confront death and say *something*. By the era of silence and denial, these various and sometimes conflicting purposes and expectations could be discussed freely, along with intensive debates over the costs of funerals. We refer to the latter as the "consumerist" perspective.

But for a Christian funeral, the primary purpose is to worship God. So say at least five generations of clergy writing "how-to" manuals for other clergy about Christian funerals. That there should be funerals is not a point of debate among Christians, especially not one hundred years ago. The debates raged, however, over what kind of funeral, and how to separate Christian practice and beliefs from inherently "pagan" customs. The latter excited wrath and disgust on the part of clergy.

This early twentieth-century debate over funerals took shape right along with the solidification of the modern pattern of embalming, viewing, and professionalization of body preparation. Even before the University of Michigan started the first program in mortuary science in the 1920s, the practice of preparing the body had become a business for specialists. Embalming and a formal "viewing" became the ideal (if not the statistical norm) by the 1890s. Earlier, before the Civil War, embalming had been perceived by ordinary persons as gruesome and mutilating. It was the need to embalm the dead soldiers in order to ship them home that began to make this practice seem humane and compassionate (Laderman, 1996, chap. 9ff.). The first fully embalmed on-display individual in American history was President Abraham Lincoln, whose funeral train provided a traveling public viewing experience for thousands of persons. The embalming job was horrible by modern standards, but at the time people were enormously impressed by it. It permitted mourners to say their last good-byes, facing a Lincoln who—while not alive—looked "lifelike" enough so that he resembled the person he would have been in life (Laderman, 1996, 157–63). This, according to American religion historian Laderman, is the true purpose of "viewings," which are not intended to deny that the person is dead, but are meant to give the visitors a sense of encounter with someone whom they remember. Thus, embalming and viewing met psychological and social needs, customers desired these practices, and so this is how Americans became accustomed to what earlier generations would have found cruel and repulsive. Meanwhile, clergy could depict certain aspects of this funeral pattern, particularly its focus upon the body of the deceased, as "pagan" and objectionable and sub-Christian (Blackwood, 76). Yet what is most remarkable is that a pattern set as the norm by 1890 has continued as the norm, for this is what the phrase "traditional funeral" has meant for the mainstream Americans of the twentieth and twenty-first centuries. Although a standard news story today is of "innovative" and "nontraditional" funerals, these are set against a universally agreed upon standard, which surprisingly has endured for well over one hundred years.

It is well to recall what preceded this professionalized "funeral industry" model. The realities of "home-based" funerals were still close to many persons in the late nineteenth and early twentieth centuries, including a firsthand familiarity with what a mess these could be. The family did the body preparation, and the only professional on hand was the pastor, who held the service in the parlor, not at the church. People raised on this pattern were therefore less nostalgic, and more grateful that difficult and unpleasant tasks could be delegated to trained specialists.

Some of the risks of a preprofessionalized death ritual were gruesome. A fascinating glimpse of this is found in James Chrissman's *Death and Dying in Central Appalachia*, a close look at an area of the country so "backward" that the 1880s practices did not arrive there until after the 1940s. The situation for Appalachians can indeed be understood as the authentic American equivalent of Kübler-Ross' Swiss village death from her childhood. Chrissman tells how "preprofessional" body preparation was done, and some of the problems typically encountered in the age before refrigeration and easy transportation. The dead person required a vigil all night in the home, not just out of respect but because cats would eat the fingers off an unguarded corpse (70). Bodies left in coffins a little too long in hot summer weather exploded before burial (72). In winter, the ground froze and no one could be buried until spring thaw. When the American funeral industry finally came to this remote rural area, inhabitants embraced it; there was no resistance to abandoning these inconvenient and occasionally repulsive situations. The urban and more affluent practices charted by Laderman had long since thoroughly triumphed elsewhere, and no wave of nostalgia gripped anyone. (Some of my immigrant students come from places where "old-style Appalachian" patterns still exist, such as rural Ukraine, and their families too embraced the American funeral practices with relief, rather than with much sense of loss for home-based body preparation.)

However, this amazing triumph and continuity of a pattern new in the post–Civil War era did not mean that funerals were without public controversy and debate. Early in the new century, the consumerist critique of prevailing practices mobilized, and has continued ever since. The argument was that funerals, embalming and viewings included, are too expensive. They are a waste of money lavished on the dead, when the living could use the cash. Funeral directors are businessmen, unlike doctors or clergy; they are likely to rip off their customers (who are not patients or parishioners) since the latter are vulnerable at the time of a death. Even if there is no actual dishonesty, or intention to defraud, the reality of death as a business enterprise makes for tension (Laderman, 2003, 53ff.). The consumerist argument often goes further: to spend money on display for the dead is wasteful, irrational, wrong. Especially criticized were the opulent funerals by and for the poor, those who could least afford it but who wished to receive respect and show devotion through a fancy, extravagant ceremony.

Protestant clergy occasionally joined in this part of the consumerist argument. It seemed to them that a true "social gospel" message should include a plea to curtail this kind of "wasteful" and "pagan" display, especially because the poor seemed to suffer disproportionately from the obligation to give the deceased the proper ceremonial send-off. Feelings of guilt, or the desire to "do right by" the deceased, overcame ordinary financial prudence often enough for this to be mentioned as a problem. In the best by far of the earlier generation of "how-to" manuals by and for clergy, Presbyterian Andrew Blackwood's 1942 *The Funeral: A Source Book for Ministers*, the author addresses this concern (18). Blackwood complained that the conventional funeral focused all attention on the body, obscuring the proper Christian emphasis on the soul (76). Ironically, the manuals by pastors often take for granted that good personal and professional relationships between clergy and funeral directors are the norm, but the "consumerist" critique endures. The charge that American funerals are extravagant and wasteful gains strength from other, deeper, and more philosophical arguments that in some ways support the ethos of silence and denial that came later in the twentieth century. We will look at this issue more closely later, in chapter 8.

Blackwood's assumption was not just a dualist anthropology of body and soul. His view was that the real focus of funeral activity should be on something other than just "saying good-bye" and providing memories for the bereaved viewers. A Christian funeral is about the transition from this life to the life beyond, it is not about what is being left behind, but about what lies ahead for the deceased. Such a future-directed understanding makes much of the conventional American pattern not just irrelevant and distracting (let alone too expensive) but repulsively inappropriate. In spite of massive evidence of mutual goodwill between clergy and funeral directors, as fellow professional specialists, the proper task of the Christian funeral was not just to help friends and family say good-bye, nor to linger on the occupation and hobbies and family life of the deceased (Daniels, 32ff.). Something more, something different, was required.

Here we enter into the realm of what Christians had to say about death and its meaning—or rather, what professional spokesmen for Christianity had to say at the most formal occasions, in regard to their public role as presider at funerals. The underlying and most basic purpose of the Christian funeral is worship of God. The role of the minister is to turn the congregation's attention away from anything less than this, and neither the dead person nor the pastor is to take center stage. "Comfort" is the aim of the funeral, but this is achieved when our hearts touch God's, and not through direct psychological consolations. From this starting place, it is clear why "pagan" practices, such as viewings, may be a part of American life, but potentially subvert the authentic Christian aims of a funeral.

We may wonder if this is harsh, unrealistic, or a case of denial about the actual motives and feelings of those present. All of these doubts, so real to many of us, do not seem to discomfort early twentieth-century pastors and preachers. Their anthologies of funeral sermons reveal a deep commitment to a God-centered, worshipful funeral service. It is very clear that they could be good pastors, that they were used to dealing with "problem funerals" (although these were defined somewhat differently from how contemporary pastors would find helpful) and that they were not trying to be intentionally haughty or disconnected from those they served. These preachers were just trying to lay down a principle for what a Christian funeral is really supposed to be about.

We find this claim for a fundamental theological purpose that overwhelms social and psychological discourse periodically repeated in similar manuals by clergy, and in their funeral sermons during the age before silence and denial. Just as "[l]ife is to be subordinated to one great end—so to please God as to have the testimony that we are accepted" (Ketcham, 146), so the funeral should subordinate all else to worship of God. In an outline of basic Christian theology useful for preaching, from a large anthology, we find,

> What is implied in dying . . .
> Death implies a separation of soul and body.
> How do the living know that they shall die?
> The living know, by the appointment of God, that they shall die.
> What improvement should we make of this important subject?
> We should sit loose upon the world. (Ketcham, 114–16)

Sermons that centered on these ideas were always appropriate, always on target, and always clearly Christian and not distracting or "pagan." The "Doctrinal Sermons" of Daniels' 1937 manual focus on "Varieties of Immortal Hope," "Reasons for Our Faith," and "The Nature of the Future Life" (70–93).

> Our faith in immortality may be likened unto a seed which we plant in the ground. As we put the seed into the ground, so do we bury the bodies of our loved ones under the sod. As the body of the seed decays, so does our physical body return unto the dust from which it was made. But as life blossoms new from the dead body of the planted seed, so shall that in us which is deathless continue beyond the grave. (Daniels, 71)

We will turn in a later chapter to examine this specific imagery, but as a sample of a properly focused funeral message, this reveals why preoccupation with the prior life and interests of the deceased is to be discouraged: it is just like a focus on the decayed husk of the seed underground.

The earlier generations of Protestant pastors would have all agreed in principle with such a message, but then most of them would have allowed a "yes, but. . . ." Yes, but this theological norm needs to be tempered to the expectations and emotional state of the congregation. Yes, but there are times when the faith of the person being funeralized is uncertain, or known to God alone, and when it may nevertheless be permissible to perform a Christian funeral. Yes, but. The "yes" is evident in the religious content of the sermons preached at funerals, hundreds of which have been collected into anthologies used by other pastors and preachers. The "yes" is evident in the basic definition of the Christian funeral as worship, and of the gathering as a congregation. Whatever the social and psychological purposes of the funeral, for Christian clergy the primary purpose lies beyond these, even when these are not explicitly excluded; the ideal funeral happens in the church, where the Christian nature of the gathering is made obvious. Some funerals happen at the home of the deceased, Blackwood notes, and these are acceptable, but the worst are those that are performed in the funeral parlor. Even when minister and funeral director have a strong, positive professional relationship, it is less than fitting for anything Christian to be staged in a place that ultimately reeks of a pagan preoccupation with bodies and material display.

And, yes, because at the funeral itself there is no avoiding the reality of death. Preaching death is where a Christian funeral must begin. The congregation is, above all else, the future dead. "Today we bury him. So you, too, may die. Are you living under the power of the world to come?" (Ketcham, 18). This stark question, from an anthology of 1899 funeral sermons, can act as point A in our journey from the past into the present. Definitely before silence and denial, the whole point of a funeral sermon is to lay out explicitly and publicly Christian doctrines of salvation, eternal life, divine judgment. To shirk the task of reminding those present that they, too, will die—some suddenly and/or soon, some lingering on for decades, but all eventually—would be to miss the whole point. It would betray the vocation of the minister, whose purpose on this and other occasions is to remind everyone (including himself, of course) that ultimate realities such as God and salvation through Christ should outweigh everything else (Daniels, 70). So, "If the death angel should come soon, if he were to knock today at your door, would he find your house in order? Would he find you trusting in the crucified Son of God?" (Schuh, 1918, 45). We are all, always, the future dead; a funeral is the time of truth when even the least spiritual person is faced with this reality. The emotional vulnerability of the congregation is an opportunity to present them with the gospel, the doctrines of faith, which they desperately need to hear.

> Let not the call of God be heard in vain. Some of you are evidently halting between two opinions. The world and the flesh with their temptations have beset you, and you are saying, "Not now, not now. Some other day when I have a convenient season. . . ." If the death of this young man should make you more thoughtful . . . or win you away from the world and its service and direct your feet heavenward, then both his life and his death would have been a blessing. . . . May God grant it! (Schuh, 1925, 112)

While the businessman funeral director sells his customers expensive funerals they do not really need, and takes advantage of their emotional fragility, the preacher *must* proclaim and teach what will really save those who hear and respond.

"Are you living under the power of the world to come?" Death is not an ending in the sense of annihilation, and it is not, in its ultimate meaning, a loss. It is a transition from one world to that which is to come, the world of salvation and heaven. That world's power should be at work in us now, delivering us from sin and also from the distractions of everyday life. The man at whose funeral these words were preached had been, one week before, at work in his office, immersed in this world even though his soul had been inwardly focused on the world to come. But now he is wholly there; what is for us still "to come" is now for him an eternal present. Two places, two worlds, and on which should our attention be fixed? Such a question is not just perfectly normal in the sermons of one hundred years ago, it forms their backbone and reason for their being preached.

We need to ponder this aim, and the wording of the question, before moving on. Note that in this case, what made the questions so vivid for both preacher and congregation was that the death was a sudden one. One week here among us, the next gone—and it could be any one of us whose funeral is the following week. This theme is not just a nineteenth- and early twentieth-century motif; it has a long, long history. Prayers to deliver us from "dying suddenly and unprepared" (Episcopal Church's *Book of Common Prayer*, Litany, 149) have been continuous since ancient times. What may strike the contemporary reader as odd is that the preacher in 1899 could still deal with this situation as normal, as ordinary, as part of what everyone might reasonably expect. A sudden death showed God's providential timing, it was not disruptive of the order of this world. While the congregation continues to be addressed as "the future dead" long into the century, within a very short time the expected "normality" of sudden death disappears from Protestant funeral sermon anthologies. We do not find quite this stark a reminder that "any of us could go at any time" by the 1930s and by Blackwood's 1942 manual for clergy. Whatever the statistical occurrence or shifts in favor of long-lingering dying over sudden death, it is the perception of "last week here, now we bury him" as no longer normal that truly represents a shift.

To most of the pastors and preachers, the issue of sudden versus prolonged dying would not have been of ultimate importance. Their theological answer would have been, that whether slow and painful and lingering death, or sudden, "Are you living under the power of the world to come?" now, in this life, is just as valid a question. The manner of death, including traumatic deaths such as in mining accidents, is not ultimately significant (the exception is suicide, of which more later). Indeed, even age is not an ultimately significant factor, since the same doctrines hold true when the occasion is the death of a child as for an adult. "Doctrinal sermons" are far more appropriate on all occasions than "biographical" (which focus on the individual who died, not on God) or than "occasional" sermons, which distract by centering on circumstances surrounding the death. These categories are Daniels' (1937), but the preference and reasoning behind the preference were widely shared. When these criteria were rigidly imposed, then truly "one size fits all," and there would have been no need for more than a few standardized funeral sermons. Fortunately, the clergy who produce manuals and anthologies are too skilled as pastors to obey this principle. Their anthologies are indeed divided into sections by age, profession, and even manner of death. Sermons preached at funerals for children are different, and legitimately so, from funeral sermons for the elderly, or for those in especially dangerous occupations. The theology ultimately does not vary, but there is much more adaptation to circumstances than the theological "doctrinal sermons" criteria suggest.

Yes, the congregation gathered for the Christian funeral is the future dead, and their hearts are to be directed to God and "the power of the world to come." This is a universal purpose, making no distinction between family members and casual or even accidental attenders. The assumption is that a worshipping community is present, related to God but not necessarily bound to the deceased by close personal, emotional ties. For this reason, it is entirely appropriate to hold some sort of funeral, however brief, for a friendless person, a vagabond found dead on the street. Such an anonymous corpse may have had faith known to God alone, just as God alone knew the details of his life and why he ended up as he did. Although the only ones in attendance may be the city employees whose task will be to bury such a person, the Christian meaning of death is just as relevant to this case as to those where the church fills up with relatives and friends of the deceased. Theologically, *all* are the future dead. *All* are in need of salvation, and *all* may repent and receive it. In the norms for early twentieth-century funerals, one did not need a special "altar call" at a funeral, an explicit invitation to the unsaved to step forward and receive Jesus Christ as their Lord and

Savior. Although this sometimes happened, the basic purpose of the Christian funeral included, implicitly, the open invitation to all, equally, to begin to live under the power of the world to come.

But some persons may have objected to funerals. The consumerist critique is addressed to the "pagan" practices of viewings and showy coffins, but from Christian perspectives there is never a doubt that a funeral itself is valid and valuable. Perhaps another level of criticism lurked beneath the consumerist/rationalist critique that American funerals cost too much. Perhaps there was a suspicion that this life was the totality of human existence, and that no "world to come" beyond it existed. That death, decay, and the grave were the fate of all, no matter what the preacher told his hearers. Rhetorically, this is sometimes portrayed as the alternative—a grim alternative—to the Christian view of death. Maybe someone in the congregation silently thought this way, and maybe he or she voiced doubts in private with the pastor. Protestant clergy must have heard this view, and tried to respond with reasons for their faith. Such a "this-worldly" view would make virtually everything said at a Christian funeral false, so a rebuttal would have been required.

The funeral director had heard this doubt about a "world to come" so often that the self-promotion of the funeral industry, from early on, has included a "humanistic" defense against this line of thought. Look at ancient Egypt, look at all the great civilizations of the past. Do we really think we know better? Can we really emotionally afford to forget the dead? If we disregard "the world to come," we still need not dismiss funerals, for to forget the dead is a sign of heartlessness, not progress (Laderman, 2003, 10). Such a response would have been shared up to a point by Protestant clergy, for whom the human personality was often referred to as "sacred" and of ultimate value. Except that the mention of ancient Egypt would have reminded them that "pagan" customs are alive and well. Not all ways to remember the dead are fully Christian, and the emphasis on family and memory is subordinate and potentially distracting from the true purpose and grandeur of the funeral, which is to place this life and bodily death within the larger context of eternity.

We may ask if this skeptics' "death is the end" view was even a possible position to which clergy needed to reply. The collected sermons from this era do show some evidence of such ideas, lurking in the background, so to speak. Perhaps the unspoken problem was that for such skeptics in the pews funerals were "morbid," because they deal with death. The real, under the surface rejection of them was that any attempt to deal with death was unthinkable and too threatening. But this is much more typical for the era of silence and denial, as we shall see in detail in part II. Clergy such as Blackwood were not there yet, and they do not seem to have spotted this cloud on the horizon. Instead, they would reply, that although pagan death practices may indeed be morbid, Christians' funerals are filled with hope. Yes, there are morbid and unhealthy ways to mourn the dead; Blackwood cites a few and considers this a minor problem. But to be focused on death, for Christians, is a different matter. The power of the world to come enters and suffuses the atmosphere at the funeral of a devout Christian, so that only those without such hope for eternal life as Jesus promises would find death truly a time for despair. This explicitly Christian reference, and not arguments about psychological denial of death, forms the core of the response by early twentieth-century pastors, to a view that many of them sense is "out there," and probably secretly held by at least some members of the congregation present.

Funerals are morbid; no, Christian funerals are hopeful. When set out in this simple and abstract manner, the terms of the argument look clear. The key is the real belief in the world to come, an afterlife in heaven. Without that, it is assumed by all, death is terrifying, and it is unsurprising that we would like to avoid it entirely. With it, death is an occasion for Christians to remind ourselves that our Savior has promised us that "whoever lives and believes in me will never die." He promised a home with him, in the "many mansions" of his Father. Mansions, homes, and several other allegorical images of hopeful transitions are the heart of the message of Protestant funeral sermons up through the 1970s. The question of "denial of death," so very prominent in the death awareness movement and echoed by those in the funeral industry, does not appear in the Christian preachers' answer of an earlier era. "Denial of hope" or "denial of the power of the world to come" would have been their worry.

But hope is itself a relative category. A contemporary reader, even one accustomed to reading books about death, will find the volumes of older funeral sermons incredibly dreary and depressing. Even when "hope" prevails, it is hope set amid a field of possibilities so different from what today's funeral or memorial service includes, that the effect is disturbing and not consoling. The preacher's call for all the future dead to live now under the power of the world to come is "hopeful" by his standards. If we go by the funeral sermons believed worthy of being anthologized, there is no expectation that "hope" meant joyous exuberance. There is none of that in the sermons and other worship texts from before silence and denial, not among mainline mainstream American Protestants. Nor is there the kind of folksy humor and familiarity that may have actually played a role in how clergy related to their flocks, but which would have seemed drastically out of place at funerals back then.

We can imagine those congregations of the not-too-distant past, sitting stiffly in their formal, dark outfits, listening to preaching about death. They did not make noise and their children did not fidget during the sermon. Mainline Protestants were expected to keep stiff upper lips, and their hopes were to be expressed as moderately and with as much self-control as their grief. Excessive grief was not only a mark of weak faith, but "ungenteel" and lower class. Perhaps as the future dead, they were trained to sit silently and stolidly, thinking soberly of the world to come, and their own eventual transition to it. If they shed tears, these were very private—although part of the "stiff upper lip" demeanor is to project an air of true inward grief. Perhaps in reality they did not think of any of the things in the sermon, but focused attention on the fine-quality casket, or the number of persons in the congregation (and on those who should have come but did not!). Perhaps too they loved their pastors, admired their preaching and their mostly taken-for-granted faithfulness and kindness to the family at the time of death. The pastor was available twenty-four/seven, and so he was called in as death approached, and saw the family through the entire funeral process. Moreover, he had known them for years, as in most Protestant denominations the minister stayed put with his congregation and became a public fixture among his community's leaders. This loyalty between parishioners and clergy, rather than any of the formal doctrines of salvation and eternal life, may have been what mattered and made a successful and unmorbid (although solemn) funeral. Perhaps a few funeral-goers, even in the early part of the twentieth century, hated the whole experience, and wished for a world where nothing connected with death was the norm. But none of those present expected to enjoy themselves, and "hope" did not include a celebratory atmosphere when death was preached.

We can imagine those congregations, and attribute to them, perhaps wrongly, the thoughts and feelings that now invade us in similar situations. At a particularly painful and depressing memorial service for a colleague, I wondered, "How many of these am I going to have to sit through?" And then, following quickly on that thought, the knowledge that no matter how many colleagues' memorials may happen in the future, there is one that I know I will *not* have to sit through: my own. A Christian funeral, in the days before silence and denial, began from this insight that we are all the future dead. It did not have to arrive there, privately and independently of what was going on. It was the heart of why to have funerals at all.

3

FUNERAL THEOLOGIES OF DEATH

Once again men and women of ripe old age will sit in the streets of Jerusalem, each with a cane in hand because of his age. The city streets will be filled with boys and girls playing there.

—Zechariah 8:4-5

Distinguished church historian Jaroslav Pelikan once gave a series of lectures that became a short book, *The Shape of Death*. His topic was ancient theologies of death, and his point was that there need not be any *one* Christian view of it. There were, among the ancient Christian intellectuals, those who represented death as enemy, while others were happy to adopt Hellenistic Neoplatonism and make only minor adaptations to express the Christian gospel. Pelikan's thesis was not that anything goes, or that theological relativism is inevitable. It was just that death is one of those topics where among Christians there can be a certain spread of views and ideas. These he represented by different "shapes," such as parabola, an imaginative device to persuade those who hoped to discover "*the* Christian view of death." The biblical materials of the New Testament and all of the later materials used by Pelikan have a great deal to say about death, but perhaps because of this, there is no one "biblical theology of death." There are, instead, many diverse possibilities.

Pelikan's wise stance serves as the opening for our discussion of the early twentieth-century Protestant theologies of death. Although they come from the past one hundred years, not the past sixteen hundred as did his materials, these theologies express ideas of Christ, salvation, death, and afterlife that would make contemporary clergy, either liberal or conservative, cringe. Early twentieth-century ideas depend on a network of assumptions about how to read the Bible, how to discern its central doctrinal contents, and how to proclaim these on occasions where death is already on everyone's minds.

Depending on denominational affiliation, too, these theologies are intended to re-present the traditions of Lutheran confessions, for example, or of Calvinist systematic thought. They explicitly hark back to the Reformation. However, it is always the Reformation as understood and reappropriated by those living in North America in the first half of the last century, which is not the same Reformation already being "rediscovered" in Europe during this same era. Moreover, even Luther and Calvin take a back seat to anecdotes from Germany or Scotland that the preacher heard from his immigrant grandfather, perhaps also a preacher; these stories convey a definite vision of the meaning of death for Christians. Although "doctrinal" sermons were preferred for funerals, for reasons discussed in the previous chapter, the use of stories and poetry made these concrete and emotion filled, although some of the emotions evoked were not the ones we might expect.

Even Pelikan could not really persuade those who hold a "changeless tradition" view of the Bible, theology, and the Christian church, and a few more examples cannot be successful here either. But I can find no better way to begin a challenge to this view of Christian faith as an immense edifice of timeless doctrinal truth than to turn to the passage from Zechariah, our epigraph for this chapter, and use this as an entry point into the words that Christians used to speak about death. We can all read it today and decide what it is about. To me, it appears to be a promise made at the end of the Babylonian exile, that a renewed and repopulated Jerusalem will once again be a safe and blessed place to live. The dependent, both elderly and children, can relax because peace reigns, because the Lord once again watches over his people, from his home base in the temple. From this point, there are at least three possible contemporary interpretations, each dependent on a view of how

Christians should apply biblical prophecy. These three (and I am sure there might be others) are

1. This is a prophecy about what God wants for the whole human community; it is a vision of multigenerational harmony, a people able to enjoy the goodness of life, even of urban life. Long life is a natural good, and this is what God wants for all humans, just as God wants childhood to be free from cares, fears, and pressures to perform labor in the adult world. This may be dubbed the "liberal" interpretation, and yet it is less allegorical and more literal than either of the others. However, it is also so universal that the city cited in the original text might just as well be Philadelphia.
2. This is a prophecy about the renewal of the Christian Church, the new Jerusalem. Allegorizing as did Paul in Galatians 4:26, "the Jerusalem from above" is what matters to Christians, and all references to the city may be applied to the Christian community. Particularly appealing to those of all eras who wished to purify and "restore" the church to its Spirit-filled beginning, this interpretation will suggest a revitalized joyous community of believers. They are inhabitants of a restored city, healed or in the process of healing, and filled with hope for what God is doing now and will do even more completely in the near future. This version of Zechariah is the "charismatic" reading of the prophecy, and a group such as the Vineyard, born in the 1970s and 1980s in California, gravitated to many passages such as this. Their brochure featured a whole series of "restoration" texts, together with lovely photographs of a dry, yet blooming landscape. Was it Israel or southern California? For this reading of the text, it is unimportant where on earth the photos were taken; the real land in bloom is the church.
3. This is a prophecy about the end times, and it deals with the Middle East. God will establish his rule in modern Israel, right at the heart of the same place where he was worshipped in Zechariah's time. Peace in the land of Israel, and in Jerusalem, also means the destruction of Israel's enemies,

> as indeed chapter 9 of the biblical book makes abundantly clear. This reading is not necessarily more "literal," but it is far more particularistic than the others. For those who chose this, it does make a difference that Zechariah is not talking about Philadelphia or California. He weighs in on politics in one of the troubled regions of the world. Although I personally resist this approach to biblical prophecy, which we can label "dispensationalist," this kind of interpretation has plenty of contemporary advocates.

But what none of the above three views ever accounts for is that this same passage was frequently used as a preaching text at Christian funerals. For preaching at funerals for children, particularly, it was a favorite. The Jerusalem of the text was heaven, and the children who played in its streets were always in the company of Jesus.

> The city shall be full of boys and girls playing in the streets thereof. . . . What a beautiful, peaceful, joyous scene! Every child delights in such enjoyment. . . . The boys and girls who are good are safe. They are in the streets of a city walled and eternal. . . . How full of gladness and freedom will be the streets of that Heavenly Jerusalem. (Hallock, 46–47)

They were safe, totally safe, as they had not been here on earth. Had they remained on earth, and grown into adults, they would have been in continual danger from sins and temptations.

> Their holiness is perfected. . . . Every thought and desire and action is in perfect harmony with the mind of the Holy One of Israel. . . . Their happiness is consummated. . . . They sin no more and so they do not suffer any more. They are as happy now as they can be. . . . They are so happy that they are forever singing. If they ever pause, it is to draw in a larger inspiration for a more melodious burst of praise. . . . Who would bring them back? (Hallock, 33)

Here is another exposition of this state of "perfected children," and the message for parents,

> Your babe has been delivered from the pains of disease . . . from the ingratitude of men, their base treachery, their fickleness and deception.

> It has been delivered from the fierce struggle of existence, taking place all around with brutal intensity. But this is not all. The foes mentioned are trivial in comparison with those who threaten the soul and its peace with God. . . . Let the significance of your tears be not only grief over a vanished life, but also gratitude, because the angel of death has delivered your child from the inevitable ills of human life, and above all, from the possibilities of sin. (Schuh, 1925, 23–24)

Or, in the words of an anonymous poet,

> *Weaned*
>
> Sweetly thou didst expire; thy soul
> Flew home unstained by its new kin;
> For ere thou knewest how to be foul
> Death weaned thee from the world of sin. (Hallock, 64)

So the message of Zechariah becomes a message of consolation for bereaved parents: your child is much better off now in heaven than he or she ever was on earth with you. This is exactly why these verses, with their references to "playing children," were so often the primary sermon texts at funerals. (Note: This is also why pastoral theologian Thomas Long's contemporary hope to use this Zechariah passage to spur social improvements for children here on earth would never have worked; it ignores the basic contrast between "there" and "here" on which the older preachers depended [128].)

Note what has to happen for the early twentieth-century message to work. First, all references to the Middle East are automatically ignored, since every reference to Jerusalem is eschatological. But it is not the eschatology of "end times," cosmic consummation, and divine judgment. It is an afterlife eschatology, a timeless eternal nonearthly realm to which individuals move when they die. This is never argued, it is simply assumed by those who preached from this text, until it fell out of the funeral repertory in the 1940s. This heaven is what the Bible is about, this is what Christians hope for, and this is what salvation must center upon. We enter it as individuals at death, we need to remember it long before our own death, and at every occasion when others die. Therefore, not only are references to the Middle East irrelevant, but the identification of Jerusalem with the church, the collectivity of the faithful people of God, is not there either. The church is on the scene here, gathered for the funeral. But the church here is an earthly rather than an eternal, heavenly reality. At any rate, the basic communal-collective referent of our second contemporary interpretation is altogether missing. Equally absent is the assumption behind the first, most "liberal" reading of today; early twentieth-century preachers could never equate the life of a Christian, child or adult, with our natural, this-worldly human life cycle. It was not that this life was bad in itself, but heaven was just so much better by comparison. And heaven was what the Bible points us toward, throughout the Old and New Testaments.

We have here an extremely important and revealing example of the gulf between now and the relatively recent past. The death awareness movement's nostalgia looked backward to the days when "death was natural." But to the preachers at Christian funerals, "nature" was not a category, at least not as this term is now meant. Certainly, the sheer "otherworldliness" of the Christian message outweighed any sense that natural embodied life has a built-in finite span. Those who today opt for today's first interpretation will find such a message in Zechariah's original text, which seems to them a promise that God will respect that span and make a full life cycle possible for all. But no funeral sermons that used this text ever considered such an idea of "natural lifespan," anymore than they doubted when they substituted "heaven" for "Jerusalem." *Otherworldly*; the funeral sermons actively embrace this choice to focus on the power of the world to come, and as we will see, they search not just the Bible but a wide range of extra-biblical sources for texts to support this.

These same preachers did not mean that they believed this world and this life to be bad. They did not preach contempt for these, or for the body that belongs so irrevocably to this world of earth and nature. While this world should sit "loosely" on the Christian, there is no accompanying exhortation to despise physical matter, the body, or life "in the world" as normally lived. In wistful imagery the pastor who preached at his brother's funeral voiced this "here" versus "there" contrast, minus all gnostic or ascetic contempt for the life shared by the two men:

> Brother, farewell! We have lived many years together in our earthly father's house. Here are the rooms where the loved ones used to gather. I see the trees under whose shade we sat. . . . Today thou art in

> thy Father's house above. I am still on earth. Some day I will meet thee there. (Schuh, 1925, 185)

Rooms and trees are good, the relationships among people are good. Yet when confronting death, pastors challenged their congregations: "Are you living under the power of the world to come?" As we will see, trying to find the right imagery to express the relationship between this world and that one, between life in time and life eternal, was a continuous challenge to them. The Bible itself was not sufficient to do justice to all they wanted to say. But we can be clear that in this context, "otherworldly" did not mean "world denying" or ascetic. They were not really wondering about the goodness of this life, but about the superiority of heaven. The clergy who preached at funerals through the first half of the twentieth century would never have accepted a more recent agenda in which these issues become paramount, anymore than they would have accepted "death is natural." Their reading of the Bible simply did not include what the first interpretation assumes. By contrast, their whole task was to remind and encourage people to yearn for a timeless disembodied "Jerusalem," for a world to come without pain, loss, and sorrow.

We may argue whether this shift from automatic otherworldliness is a loss, a gift, or a sign of progress or of the triumph of secularism and materialism. Somewhat later in the twentieth century, theological challenges to the earlier view take up such evaluative questions, in attacks on the perceived "Platonism" of previous conventional interpreters. But in documenting the theologies of death proclaimed at early twentieth-century Protestant funerals, the implications of this allegorization of "Jerusalem" into "heaven" need to be spelled out. One deals with "history." If all references to Jerusalem are actually references to heaven, then we are not speaking of a place that can be rebuilt or reinhabited. It is a realm equidistant from everywhere on earth, with no special links to physical geography or particular political or military events that happen in specific places. No one ever argued this, it was just assumed, intrinsic to the meaning of Christian heaven, especially when the "place" imagery was so central to its use, as we have seen.

Here, even someone who distrusts the third contemporary interpretation (apocalyptic dispensationalist "end times") must allow that the recent history of the Middle East might matter. With the founding of the modern state of Israel in 1948, something changed for Christians as well as, obviously, for Jews. Retroactively, the easy earlier forgetfulness about the geography of the Middle East that permitted "heaven" to be substituted so routinely for "Jerusalem" now seems either a luxury or an example of complicity in a long history of Christian anti-Judaism. To the preachers and funeral-goers of the 1920s, the Middle East was "the Holy Land" to which pious pilgrims and other travelers might go, but it was awfully far away. Nothing had happened there since the time of Jesus, as far as most Protestants knew or cared (the Crusades were something that Catholics had been responsible for—had anyone even raised this question). As for the peoples living there now, no connection could possibly hold between them and the people addressed by Zechariah. By 1948, the Zechariah text had dropped from the repertoire of those used for funerals, as mid-century sermon anthologies reveal. Its playing children in heaven had faded as the era of silence and denial replaced older messages.

However, eventually modern Israel's existence and modern Jerusalem's political and military significance truly sank into the consciousness of Christians in America. They could no longer use the terms "Israel" and "Jerusalem" without some distant echoes from an important, troubled area of the world. Revealingly, in sermons on death no preacher explicitly took up this controversial issue directly at all. They did not disclaim references to modern Israel, nor did they justify continuing to allegorize "heavenly Jerusalem." By the late 1940s, silence and denial had set in, and the use of Zechariah at funerals was a thing of the past, for other reasons. But the older allegorized stance would have had to become far more self-conscious. After all, it required a particular understanding about how one interprets the Bible, where and how Christians "supersede" the old covenant, and so on. (For a good recent discussion of these issues, see Sarah Pinnock, "Atrocity and Ambiguity: Recent Developments in Christian Holocaust Responses.") No trace of that appears in any of the sermons, and instead "heavenly" readings of "Jerusalem" are quietly abandoned. At any rate, the Middle East went from a place where nothing had happened since the time of Jesus, to one at the top of the news. It therefore lost its utility for automatic "otherworldly" allegory, even if anyone had wished to restore the wholesale substitution of "heaven" for "Jerusalem" when preaching on death.

When we turn to the early twentieth-century sermons and search directly for their "theology of death," we find less clarity and unanimity than we might expect. Perhaps this is the same situation Pelikan outlined for ancient church thinkers, perhaps the mainline preachers among American Protestants were heirs of a long tradition, whose multiple "shapes" continued to coexist. For they used a range of imagery, which we will explore in the next several chapters. Yet we can declare that to ask "Is death a 'natural event'?" is to ask a wrong question, although there will be more to say on "natural" as a category later on. In sharp contrast, it makes sense to wonder if they still held that death is "a punishment for sin," an idea that all of the Reformation theologies accepted. If so, then death is essentially negative, because human death is terribly and irrevocably marked by guilt, and thus remains even for Christians a sign of God's wrath.

This idea of death as intrinsically punitive is deeply repugnant to many contemporary pastors and seminary-trained counselors, let alone members of their congregations. They are utterly estranged from "death as punishment for sin," and immediately associate the whole idea with neurotic guilt and cruel judgmentalism. Let me explain briefly that "death as punishment for sin" takes us back to Augustine, to the doctrine of the fall, and to a long and deep tradition of reflection on the human universal tendency toward sin. The link between death and punishment says nothing about particular deaths, with special instances where the manner or timing of death seems to suggest God's direct vengeance upon disobedient sinners. For the Augustinian view, death universally is both sheer mortality and also rejection of God in favor of the idols of the heart, and to separate the two into "physical" and "spiritual" death only confuses what those who advocate this Christian theme want to keep bound together. The "juridical" language of punishment also links to the theme of "justification," whose imagery also derives from the courtroom where the judge decides a verdict and the accused is declared "righteous." In this theological cluster, terms such as guilt, vindication, punishment, and justice all cohere, with death as the punishment borne by Christ on our behalf, but experienced nevertheless by each of us. The sorrow of death is one's own guilt—residual after Christ's redemptive sacrifice—of facing a penalty one deserves to suffer. We will return to this topic when we discuss mid-century theological challenges to the earlier "before" view of Christian death.

We can admit that such a motif as "death is punishment for sin" is not entirely absent from early twentieth-century funeral sermons. Yet, remarkably, in Ketcham's 1899 sternly theological collection of sermons and reflections on death, the idea barely appears. Death is certain, and ordained by God, yes—but the specifically juridical language is absent (Ketcham, 20–21). Such imagery seems to hold sway particularly among Lutherans, even down to mid-century. " 'The wages of sin is death.' This explains it all" (Schuh, 1918, 97), and the sermon goes on to elaborate why death, sin, and God's universal curse all answer the question, "Why death?" Lutherans showed more "doctrinal" focus during funerals than did other mainline Protestants. Or maybe there was something not quite "mainline" about Lutherans. They were still partially an immigrant church, their sermons were published by the German Literary Board in 1912 (Neumann, *Sowing in Tears, Reaping in Joy: A Collection of Funeral Sermons by Lutheran Pastors in America*) even if written out in English rather than German. Hence Lutherans could be expected to preserve some of the "old world" preoccupations, including a doctrinal focus, especially at the funerals for their elderly members. Remember, however, that all sermons were, ideally, "doctrinal," for preachers in all denominations. Still, death as punishment for sin could not be said to control the preaching even of the stodgiest, most backward-looking German Lutheran pastor. It was one of several very traditional ideas, yes—but note the title of the anthology. Allegorized restoration hope from the Old Testament prophets trumps the theme of punishment, divine wrath, and even justification by faith. When preaching on death, the congregation needed to hope that death could be set over against "the power of the world to come," and juridical language and imagery were already foreign to this message.

If death is not necessarily a punishment for sin, then it might have been a force, an active power, an enemy of God, in these early twentieth-century sermons. Here, the answer is decisive: this is not a premier theme for the era before silence and denial. Even the Lutherans are pre–Gustav Aulén, the influential Swedish theologian who rediscovered and publicized the ancient Christology of *Christus Victor*. Certainly, there are some references to ideas such as Christ's battle against death in the earlier sermons, but these are not thematized and focused in the way that, thanks in part to Aulén, they later became. Once again, this particular theological challenge lies ahead in our story.

What does appear, as a carryover from traditional treatments, is the personification of death into Death. *When Death Speaks* is the title of another anthology. Death spoke all the time in the era before silence and denial, Death was addressed in prose and poems, and Death answered back. Rather than as an Enemy, or the punishment for a divine verdict of human guilt, Death is a dialogue partner in the early twentieth century. This is different from what persons today anticipate, and even in the translations of our Bible the possibility for this is lost or made more difficult. When Paul cited Hosea to cry out "Where, O death is your victory?" (1 Cor 15:55) he never expected an answer, for he was not holding a conversation. In the New International Version translation, "d" in death is not capitalized, and there is therefore no sense of addressing a named being, a personification. This is in keeping with contemporary perspectives, as well as being an accurate apprehension about the meaning of the original Hosea passage, where the NIV editors also use only lower-case letters. But in the King James Version, which is what English-speaking pastors would have used in 1920, the preceding verse goes, "Then shall be brought to pass the saying that is written, Death is swallowed up in victory" (1 Cor 15:54). It may be an accident that an older translation was more free with capital letters, yet from at least the Middle Ages on, Death had been a conversation partner for Western Christians, and this tradition continues well through the first half of the past century. But, as we shall see, what Death says when he speaks is not what Aulén or other later theologians would have expected.

Let us return to the world of sermons based on the Zechariah passage, which taught Christians to look forward to heaven, not to focus exclusively on death or Death. Remember that this particular passage was used especially at the funerals of children. The vision of one's child playing in the streets of Jerusalem, with Jesus as protector and companion, consoled those whose child was gone from their lives now. But since the people at the Christian funerals of 1920 were not "present mourners," but the "future dead," this is the wrong emphasis. The right direction to look is toward how the hearers could be absolutely certain that the power of the world to come outweighs the grief they now feel. They must live now, so as to be assured that they will one day rejoin their children in a heaven that will also be something like a reconstituted home. When Death speaks, these are the questions he (Death personified is always, unquestionably male) will answer. Meanwhile, the task of the preacher is not to deny grief, sadness, or death, but to shrink and eclipse such temporal and partial realities into insignificance when attention is redirected to what really, eternally matters.

The first strategy here is to invoke and make as vivid as possible the benevolent and safe environment of heaven. We will look at the range of images used for this in the next chapter. Note that the "safety" theme would have been particularly important because at the start of the twentieth century, infant and child deaths were still common, and childhood was assumed to be an especially vulnerable period of life. During the early decades of the century, this was to change, until death became linked with the aged, not the very young. But deaths of children were frequent, not the kind of disruptive anomalous events they are assumed to be today. The causes of these deaths were illnesses, presumably unpreventable, although there is a lot of indirect evidence parents felt guilt over them. "You did not keep your child safe," the preacher's sermon might be interpreted by such a parent. "Jesus will do a better job at this than you." And, indeed, such is exactly the message of those many sermons that use the Zechariah text.

But just as there is no longer a threat of disease in heaven, there are other dangers from which children who now play there are spared. No, not gun violence and gangs; this is the early twentieth century, not the early twenty-first. I have found no example of a funeral for a murdered child, in any of the earlier anthologies. A small number of children died by accidents, such as drowning, but none by malice. So the dangers from which child inhabitants of heaven are now spared are of a different kind. These may be described as the dangers of adult life, and so, adult sins. Children who die before puberty are spared any experience of sexuality (this is pre-Freud, naturally), and they are also spared from other sins such as drunkenness, criminal behavior, and shiftlessness. The sins of adult self-indulgence, of lack of discipline or control over one's impulses, will never touch the dead child. These sins are the ones mentioned repeatedly, not sins such as ruthless ambition, abuse of others, or hypocrisy. The latter more complex sins are compatible with social success and accomplishment, and perhaps even to mention them would have been to evoke in parents a sense of loss for their child's unfulfilled possibilities. To imagine him a wastrel or drunkard—had God not called him to play with Jesus in heaven—minimized this problem. All told, "That child, so young, so bright, so full of promise, will never be old, wan, tearful, withered. This is one of the sources of consolation in the death of children" (Hallock, 48).

This earlier era's assumption of the child's basic innocence made funeral sermons for children's deaths easy to preach. Astonishingly (to us!) this is the decisive verdict of those pastors who performed this duty early in the twentieth century, and who authored and edited the sermon collections from that era. Such a situation, however sad for the bereaved family, is very easy for the pastor. There is no doubt that the dead child plays now in the streets of Jerusalem. There is no doubt that every child belongs there. No attention to doctrines of original sin, or questions about infant baptism, really enter this picture. Although once again Lutherans seemed slightly more likely to at least refer to the idea of a universal need for salvation (Schuh, 1918, 3ff.), this is not what they or any other Protestant minister will stress at the funeral of a child. St. Augustine, the theological champion of "original sin," stressed in his *Confessions* that babies do not lack evil desires and intentions, only the physical strength to carry these out (book I, 7). Augustine would not have been welcome at an early twentieth-century funeral for a dead child. Instead, the child of Christian parents is now safe and secure. There are no sinful, or even nasty children. We may wonder how long did one remain a "child" within the worldview of these sermons. The drowned boy who went fishing was fourteen years old, yet his funeral sermon was focused on these same "child" themes even if in some social classes he might have been already in the workforce rather than innocently still playing here by the river (Neumann, 26–30).

In very sharp contrast to these "easy" child funeral sermons, the minister who must frequently preach at funerals finds that the "difficult cases" are the ones where ample evidence exists that the deceased had both evil desires and strength to act on these. Again and again, in manuals for clergy who preside at funerals, there are sections on "problem funerals," and what to do for them. As Blackwood comments, "In a case where the minister can find no cause for Christian comfort, he is fortunate if he is not expected to speak" (136). Daniels points out, "It will be a sobering thought for the minister to remember . . . that he will be speaking to people who know intimately the life of the deceased"

(28). Because a funeral sermon was the norm, and becoming a requirement even in dubious cases, examples of funerals for prostitutes ("fallen women"), for suicides, for other "visibly sinful" deceased, find their way into the anthologies. One suspects that, for some of these cases, many clergy would refuse the request to preside at the funeral, or to have anything to do with one. But on the whole, the authors of manuals reject this path. Because all persons have some relation with God, however negative or broken or hidden, the preacher may reiterate that message alone, even without the false or presumptuous assurance that the deceased's relation with God was a secure and happy one. In an early example of a funeral for a suicide, the message is a threat against wasted lives and missed opportunities for salvation (Neumann, 131–33). Once again, this is as always addressed to all the "future dead," and not the bereaved and distraught family. It is measured against the alternative of these "problem funerals" that the funeral sermon for a child seemed "easy."

In addition to the consolation of safety from adult sin, the preacher who used the text of Zechariah for his sermon could assume that a prophecy, by definition, is a "Thus says the Lord." This is how God wants things to be, and God's wants are not just empty desires, they are his firm, abiding will. To mourn is human, it is not a sin in itself. To mourn excessively is. And to accept God's will with "Christian resignation" is the unquestioned ideal, held up by the preacher even in times when human sorrow risks dominating Christian hope. Here is another sharp contrast between past and present, one we will discuss in much more detail later. Mourning as mourning is of no religious interest for these preachers, for "the Lord's will" overwhelms any other considerations.

Among the more optimistic preachers on death, there was also the assurance that a dead child strengthened the Christian's existing link to heaven, the world to come. For instance, Shepfer, in a 1937 collection of his sermons/meditations on death called *When Death Speaks*, concentrates on this idea. Those whose children have gone before them into heaven—including the author himself—feel themselves connected more closely to God, since the child becomes a link. In the words of an anonymous poem in one anthology,

Heaven's Nearness

It seemeth such a little way to me,
Across to that strange country, the Beyond;
And yet not strange, for it has grown to be
The home of those of whom I am so fond;
They make it seem familiar and more dear,
As journeying friends bring distant countries near. (Hallock, 182)

We should be clear, however, as to what kind of link this "nearness" does and does not provide. We do not find the very recent contemporary part-Hollywood idea that the bereaved can actually see and converse with the recently dead. Such an expectation, by now made familiar to us through movies such as *The Sixth Sense*, would have been utterly strange within the formal Christian context of a Protestant funeral sermon. Shepfer's idea is instead that a close personal tie to anyone now residing elsewhere makes one interested in that place, which no longer seems so far away or unreachable (Shepfer, 13–14). Whether heaven or Japan, a relative in residence there makes that place a focus of interest and excitement. There is nothing spooky or supernatural about such a claim, and Shepfer is far from the only pastor who voices it. Nevertheless, there may be more than this at work. It may be that the power of the world to come is nearer, more personal, made more immediate, through the love of parents for their dead child. Remember, though, that this is a mainline Protestant Christian view of the relation between the living and the dead: no spiritualism, no necromancy, no intentional contacting of the dead, and no intercessory prayers to or for the dead child are directly advocated. The same Protestant pastors who preached "easy" funerals for dead children would have recoiled from any of these possibilities. In their world, Death could speak, but the dead, children or adults, do not any longer speak directly to us. At least not in any of the public, official texts where normative Christian theologies of death are on display.

For the other world of heaven is *other*. It is not a hidden facet of this world. It is not so near as contemporary fascination with continuing bonds to the dead would require it to be. It is a world of God, salvation, Jesus: mysterious and yet familiar, another world and yet simultaneously "heaven, our home." There are no Jacob's ladders that automatically can connect us to it, or that offer its inhabitants an easy chance to descend and ascend. Indeed, there is a remarkable restraint on such imagery, especially given recent flamboyant use of it in New Age spirituality. (Although as we will show, the boundaries between Christian and New Age are far more flexible and time dependent than most persons realize.) Heaven is really absolute, too. It is not an intermediate state such as the Tibetan *bardo* realm (versions of which have today percolated into Americans' imaginations). There is no transition out of or beyond heaven. Whatever was known of reincarnation beliefs, there is no trace of these, or space left for anything like this, in the personal afterlife imagery of the mainline Protestants of one hundred years ago.

Just as "Jerusalem" is not in the Middle East, so there is a need for symbolic, allegorical distance even when the images for heaven are sometimes homelike and folksy. To go more deeply into what these were, and how they were used, requires a move beyond a catchall and dismissive term such as "otherworldly." There are a variety of otherworldlinesses, just as there are multiple "shapes of death."

4

Heaven as Home

Let not your heart be troubled; ye believe in God, believe also in me. In my Father's house are many mansions: if it were not so I would have told you. I go to prepare a place for you.

—John 14:1-2, KJV

This text, unlike that of Zechariah, is still a favorite one for Protestant—and indeed all—Christian funerals. For many Christians it still comes closest of all the promises in the Bible to their own personal feelings and aspirations about what an afterlife is meant to be. The wise preacher, past and present, knows this, as the following story from an anthology attests:

> [A preacher] was once asked by letter to preach on hell, so that the writer might be kept from committing a great sin. Instead he preached on "In my Father's house are many mansions," and said in his sermon that if that verse would not save the man, nothing would. (Hallock, 238)

The questions discussed in this chapter hinge to some extent on the use of this biblical passage about the "house" of the Father, and "mansions" within it, in the context of Christians' imagery and expectations about death.

Notice that although "Heaven as Home" is our title, this leaves ambiguous something the biblical text itself does not suggest. Heaven is the "home" for both Father and Son; in the fourth Gospel, there is no doubt about that. Jesus the Son comes from God, and knows he will return to God, where he will go to prepare a place for his followers. But the sermons insist that it be *our* home. And if it is, then the preacher must state what makes it so "homelike" and how is it related to the "home" we, not Jesus, started out from and now remember fondly. Such questions seem never to have interested the author of the fourth Gospel, while they are central to the use of this passage in early twentieth-century Christian funerals.

For example, a home is where all the inhabitants know and love one another. "Heaven is represented as the home of the good, and is called 'our Father's house,' and surely the children will all be acquainted" (Hallock, 158). It will be filled with profound restoration of a bygone time of happiness on earth, with "[r]emembered smiles, a heartease from the hand of one who loved us, and a child's pure kiss" (Hallock, 184). It will be familiar and dearly loved:

> Lord, our lives we give to thy tender keeping
> Let not our footsteps roam;
> And stay the torrent of our bitter weeping,
> With foretastes of our Home.
> There where no change, nor death, can make us sever,
> May we our dear ones meet. (anonymous poem, Schuh, 1918, 14–15)

These ideas are repeated, with the assumption that what was home for Jesus will be home and homelike for us as well. Sometimes, Jesus' experiences are imagined to mirror ours when we are far away from our homes.

> Jesus spoke of death as a GOING TO THE FATHER. . . . Jesus felt that He was away from home, a traveler in a foreign land, a voyager. He had lived amidst the glory of the eternal throne. When He came to earth how frequently his thoughts must have journeyed back to the land from whence He came, and forward to the land to which He was soon to return. Undoubtedly, He like all travelers, suffered at times from homesickness. (Shepfer, 42)

A homesick Jesus will help us envision a heaven so homelike for us that it will make the transition of death smooth, safe, and reassuring to anticipate. This chapter unpacks the imagery of such sermons.

First, let us dismiss one possible meaning of this imagery from the start. The transition from death to heaven, from this life to the realm of eternal Jerusalem, is never a kind of "eternal return" to a metaphysical "higher level" from whence we all descended at birth. Such an idea, however intriguing, includes the nonmaterial "preexistence" for all of us in a world of souls. From such a realm we travel downward in order to be born, and our hearts yearn unceasingly for that sphere above during life here below, in the realm of time and matter. Throughout our embodied, time-bound existence, we are exiles from our true "home" above, lost wanderers in a world where we were never meant to feel comfortable. This Neoplatonic metaphysical vision may have pleased Origen in the second century C.E. and some medieval Jewish mystics, but it is absolutely *not* the sense of "home" in any of the Protestant twentieth-century funeral sermons, no matter how vivid their portraits of "homesick Jesus." Indeed, such ideas continue to be alien to conventional Christians today, sounding vaguely New Age to many.

Instead, the "home," which is heaven in these funeral sermons' imagery, is strikingly a return to the first homes we remember from earth, from this life, from childhood. When a poem cited in a sermon claims that "[d]istant heaven seems more like home" (Shepfer, 64) home is that place of "one who loved us," and "a child's pure kiss," whose domestic imagery we will examine in this chapter. It is this meaning of "home" that countless sermons early in the twentieth century rely upon, and that endless anecdotes and poems repeat and elaborate.

It is hard to overstate the enthusiasm for this image of heaven as "home." All of the preachers who used it believed that this "heaven as home" theme was biblical, and their understanding of the Johannine text was guided by this assumption. "Heaven is a HOME and death a Homegoing" (Shepfer, 43) represents an idea with which virtually all of the contributors to the earlier anthologies would have agreed. Preachers had a lot of other things to say about heaven and the transition to it, but this "home" motif is the most pervasive, and for them the least problematic. "Heaven as home" does not appear to have created any doubts, questions, or ambiguities at all for Christians in the 1920s, in church for funerals when pastors such as Hallock preached and recited the poetry that reinforced this idea. These pastors knew about "problem funerals," they knew of deaths tragic and sad, needing all the resources of Christian hope to be overcome; but in this context, "heaven as home" was a certainty.

In order to embark on an analysis of this theme, let us begin with one matter that seems on the surface to be ludicrously trivial, but which ultimately is not. I have kept with the King James translation of the text above, which is what Protestant preachers and their congregations would have used throughout the first half of the twentieth century. In this version, although the "house" is the Father's, the individual dwelling places are "mansions," while in more recent translations such as both the RSV (Revised Standard Version) and NIV (New International Version) the word is now "rooms." There are plentiful humorous stories of simple-minded and literalistic folk who hated this precise change because they felt cheated. Hoping for a "mansion," they are now merely promised a "room"! Invariably, those who tell this anecdote assume they know better, that this is a silly concern betraying the misguided materialistic minds of other Christians.

Ironically, however, anger over this switch in translations may not be so silly as those who tell the stories believe. Normally, all of us do think that a "room" is a downgrading from a "mansion," and while "room" may be far more accurate as a translation of an ancient Greek word, it makes less plausible many of the associations between "heaven" and "home" that fueled an era's hopes for an afterlife. Because this passage is so important for Christians' quest for appropriate imagery for death and what lies beyond, we cannot avoid this kind of concern, even though I too may be accused of literalism. Images and words matter, and religionists know that the quality and range of symbolism, biblical and otherwise, is important to take seriously.

So, let us be literalistic. A room, in any era, is a part of a total house, one restricted space within it. Whether "a room of one's own" necessary for a woman writer in a house presumably owned by her husband, or the partial "room" in a hospital that will likely be the last room many of us will inhabit, a room is not the whole house. By contrast, a "mansion" is a luxurious self-standing house. We cannot imagine any earthly mansion as a subunit within someone else's house, although Jesus' words here suggest exactly that. The house is God the Father's; its subdivisions, however grand, are all included within it. Whatever the connotations to the original readers and hearers of John's Gospel (no doubt, to most of them, the privacy and wealth of "a room of one's own" was already an incredible luxury!) what matters here is how the American Protestants from mainline denominations of one hundred years ago received and assessed these two terms.

For them, a self-standing owner-occupied home was a central part of the American dream. This living arrangement appears as the norm in most of the sermons. Correspondingly, God's home would be both enormous in itself, and somehow contain enormous self-standing units for all the inhabitants.

> How magnificent must that house be which is the residence of the infinite Creator and Governor of all worlds . . . (with) ample accommodations . . . the sources of felicity will be numerous and diverse. (Ketcham, 190–91)

To move from our house here to the Father's house would be to exchange "a cottage to a mansion" (Ketcham, 61). Clearly, these preachers took "house" imagery very seriously.

We may ask about the poorer members of their communities, those whose lifestyles fell short of even a cottage of their own. Those who lived in "rooms" may have been in boarding houses, or squeezed into filthy crowded tenements, both sad downgrades from the middle-class ideal. Another group for whom "rooms" would have been normal were servants. The homes they inhabited belonged to others, while they lived in rooms in the servants' quarters, often sharing. For them too the dream of a home of one's own remained a dream. These are persons, by the way, whose funeral sermons remain by and large unanthologized; although "occupation" may not have been a deciding factor when all those at the funeral are the future dead, whenever the work life or vocation of the deceased is mentioned, it was never as maid, housekeeper, groom, or farmhand. Yet we can guess that the traditional translation of "mansion" would have resonated deeply with all of these groups: a home that was a house but grander and more spacious. Warmer and cleaner, too. Perhaps with a garden in front, or trees and paths and a stream . . . a home where there was room for the extended family of several generations, in peaceful domestic bliss. Above all, a home that was one's own. None of this would have been as possible had the King James Version word been "rooms." And so, the specific word mattered, and far from being a silly concern, the precise promised dwelling is actually a good introduction into a whole set of imagery and ideology about "home," family, and the sacred.

By this route, we enter the territory of what has become known as "the cult of domesticity," a term so derogatory today that its origins in the nineteenth century as a model of praise for "true womanhood" have been turned upside down. The home may have been important in Protestantism even from the days of Luther, but the real flowering of home imagery comes later. Home imagery proliferated in the early nineteenth century, especially linked to religious hopes. Recent discussions of this development focus on social class, power, and gender roles, and on the kind of material objects with which advocates of "the cult of domesticity" filled their homes. These approaches touch on eschatology and death as extensions of such this-worldly dynamics. According to this approach, of which feminist historian Ann Douglas' *The Feminization of American Culture* (1977) is an outstanding example, the cultural ideology of nineteenth-century domestic piety made "home" and "family" into sacred spaces and realities, just at a time when the large-scale public sphere of business became detached from the family as economic productive unit. Paid work more and more took place outside the home, in alien places such as factories, while "home" became the site of consumption and culture, altogether a "haven" from the heartless world of business competition.

In the home, women were the special guardians and caretakers, while the world of commerce and industry was the realm of men. The cult of domesticity was an ideology that proclaimed the higher spiritual value of the former, over the crude materialism of the latter. While farms remained productive units where both genders contributed, the emergent urban ideal designated two separate and opposing spheres. Once this happened, the ideal of "pure womanhood" could develop so that the ideas about gender, and women's exalted role in "civilizing" and "culturing" was intrinsic to domesticity. A woman was expected to be the one who guided children, and her husband, toward the finer things of life: music, literature, and art, but also occasionally philanthropy and mission work (Douglas, 94–139).

Because home became a central, sacred place, childhood too became a special, crucial site of spiritual significance. In middle-class urban families, children were not producers; they had no farm chores, nor did they do factory work. But they were to be trained, educated, and disciplined, so as to become the kind of persons whose funerals (if they lived to adulthood) were not the "problem" kind. The family here was not quite the nuclear family of the mid-twentieth century, but it was smaller and much more intimate than in earlier centuries. To celebrate this new style of intimate family, new holidays were needed. Not yet "Mother's Day," but this was the time when family Christmas gift giving was created as an American tradition, when the new figure of Santa Claus emerged from whatever folklore of the European past, to become the familiar grandfatherly gift bringer of Clement Moore's poem. Allied with department stores, themselves a new invention, a world of consumer goods, family ties, and private happiness was celebrated in American popular culture. (See Nissenbaum's *Battle for Christmas* for a wonderful look at how quickly this pattern assembled, and how "nontraditional" it really is.)

Religion changed when the family unit became detached from the wider world of economic production, politics, and male dominance. Religion, or a certain type of middle-class religion, allied with the "domestic," and so rendered faith private, ahistorical, and sentimental (Douglas, 197–239). This happened in the first half of the nineteenth century for mainline Protestants, whose leaders saw their own institutions legally "disestablished," and newly severed from the normal masculine world of work and war and making money. Thus, culture and especially religion became "feminized," in Douglas' scathing account of this development. Although feminists subsequently objected to the implication that "real" religion is always "masculine," by and large today's accounts of the "cult of domesticity" follow her lead in understanding this ideology and its impact on religion. Douglas treats the whole development as the outcome of a more or less conscious alliance between clergy, newly disempowered, and middle-class women, who sought outlets in religion for their lack of public and economic power. Flattered by clergy into belief in their own superior spirituality and sensitivity, they created a tissue-paper imaginary realm of hopes, consolations, and compensations.

Douglas is particularly merciless when she shows the link between "domestic piety" and death. Here was one topic that remained a monopoly of religion, and religious leaders made the most of it. For advocates of domestic piety, the sacred spaces of home and family on earth were anticipations of the blessed realm of the dead, for "heaven our Home" became a major theme for those immersed in domestic piety's set of beliefs and images. What Douglas refers to as "The Colonization of the Afterlife" (265) is the process of elaborating a "homelike" domestic vision of life after death, in a country where imagination rules.

> No matter how genuine the need and belief of its proponents, the new domestic heaven was unquestionably the earliest—but in some sense the most perfect—"pseudo-event" in American history: totally fabricated, yet uncontestable. (257)

Conveniently for those who advocated "heaven as home," "they did not have to win over or subdue a hostile populace; their new supporters were just like themselves, their new country was home" (271). While the West was being "won," with effort and bloodshed, heaven was the domestic colonization project for those who stayed at home in this life. Douglas' final verdict: domestic piety transformed earlier Christian eschatology into a "celestial retirement village" (272).

Douglas takes as her case in point Elizabeth Stuart Phelps' *The Gates Ajar*, a post–Civil War bestseller, which was followed by a long stream of sequels. *The Gates* of the title are, of course, the gates of the traditional Christian heaven, but when Ms. Phelps opened them, the landscape within was anything but standard tradition. This book stressed the analogy between pleasant things and activities here on earth, and what the afterlife would include for those blessed to dwell there. "Heaven as home" meant that in imaginative anticipation, people were encouraged to take it all, take everything with them. Would there be pianos in heaven? Of course. . . . Although during the nineteenth century there was a widespread "anthropocentrizing" of traditional ideas of heaven (McDannell and Lang, chap. 8). Phelps' heaven was easy to satirize. According to Mark Twain it resembled western Massachusetts (Douglas, 268). The problems with this exorbitant and unrestrained reliance on "home" as the image for the afterlife were apparent, but the power of the imagery continued to appeal. To the credit of the early twentieth-century

Protestant pastors, the excesses and sentimentality of Phelps' outlook would have been disturbing and no longer credible to them. Their generation of clergy may have grown up when this stuff was new and popular, but in none of their funeral sermons is any attention devoted to typical Phelps' questions about pianos. The theme of "heaven as home" did not translate into detailed material descriptions of a "celestial retirement village," although naturally they would have resented Douglas' sarcastic treatment of the whole topic. For it seems from their anthologized sermons that no pastor could avoid or safely challenge the basic image of "heaven as home." Their theological imaginations remained uncritically committed to its power and emotional appeal, and so risked inclusion of all the most sentimental and shallow themes of domestic piety.

The preachers' theology avoided pianos, but stressed family ties, familiarity, and unconditional love as the key features of "home." These themes curbed, sort of, the excesses of a previous generation for concretized "western Massachusetts"–style heaven. The early twentieth-century sermons kept heaven accessible, so that in stories, poems, and hymns there is ample space left for a "homelike" small-scale personalized and private-sphere eschatological vision. This is no model of "celestial retirement village," and not just because in 1900 there were not yet retirement villages, or because young children still made up a sizeable proportion of the funeralized dead. Home was HOME, our own dear starting point in this life. A "retirement home," no more than a "funeral home," could possibly substitute for the real thing.

One key point where their vision diverges from not only Douglas' portrait, but from all traditional hopes of an afterlife was on the matter of "work" versus "rest." While "Rest in Peace" remained a traditional tombstone motto, this as the consummation of gospel promises seemed sadly incomplete. For the dead, there will be peace but never idleness. Activity and work will continue, for these are what fulfill personality, what make humans dignified and noble:

> That is precisely what our blessed dead are doing now; they are not only resting from their labors in the beautiful home beyond, they are not only enjoying the happiness and beauty of Jerusalem, their happy home . . .—but they are serving their Lord, as they served him on earth. (Schuh, 1918, 14)

Learning and growth will continue, for "that life is not one of idleness." God is always active, and "He could not tolerate creatures around him that do not revel and delight in activity" (Schuh, 1918, 76). The emptiness of an eternity of unending "rest" bothered many of the pastors. These ideas may have been influenced by the social gospel movement, where desire to build God's kingdom here on earth generated such ideas about work and human dignity. Or they express what we call the "Horatio Alger" myth, where the hard work of a poor youth is rewarded by material success, while the leisure of those born to riches proves morally disastrous. The preference for effort versus idleness was part of the Swedenborgian legacy to eschatology, as religion scholars McDannell and Lang in their study *Heaven: A History* believe (chap. 7). It is impossible to separate the strands that went into suspicion of mere "rest" as the goal of Christians' hopes, but on this ground alone Douglas' sarcastic portrait looks skewed. Not a "celestrial retirement village," but a kind of eschatological continuing education program, complete with internships, would be the this-worldly model of early twentieth-century heaven. This emphasis on "growth" and "learning" eschatologized by Christians of all stripes in the first half of the twentieth century, as a corrective to traditional themes of "rest," may seem weird today. By the end of the century, such imagery had gained a reputation as New Age, part of an alternative spiritual worldview now dropped from Christian imagery and funeral sermons altogether.

So instead of "rest" and "retirement," the "home" that heaven most resembled was not housing for the elderly but the first home, the place of mother, security, and innocence. Here is the key to the image's meaning, and it incidentally opens up the possibility of a different and less hostile interpretation than that of Douglas. A heavenly "home" was something like the home presided over by the gentle Christian mother, from whom the now-deceased adult had once learned the right path of life, and also received his or her religious instruction.

> I prefer my mother's translation of the Bible to any other version. I mean that my mother has translated the Bible into the language of daily life for me ever since I was old enough to understand it. (Hallock, 226)

Beyond the role of religious teacher, the mother is a sacred figure who provides the nourishment of invisible divine love; she is therefore a "shrine" or a manifestation of the sacred even for the grown-up child.

> How the true mother holds her heart-sway even when the children are grown! . . . And there is this consolation for all who have known what it was to worship and find help at the shrine of a fond mother's heart. It was God in the mother's heart that drew the adoration. Her fond bosom was the inlet into which the great tide of divine love surged and kept it always full. (Hallock, 228)

Christian fathers seldom appear in this imagery, as one might expect from the legacy of "domestic piety," even when in other parts of the sermon the role of the father may be mentioned. Stories of "old-time" farm life, sometimes located by the preacher in the congregation's own hometown, and sometimes in the "old country" of Scotland or Germany, place the home in a past, not so different from Kübler-Ross' Swiss village, but probably much closer to the actual memories of the congregation. But the emphasis is not on the whole community, but on the mother's simple piety, her devotion to God and her family, her hard work and patience in the face of adversity. Sermons at the funerals for such mothers were obviously among the "easiest" to preach for the pastors, since the Christian mother's salvation was so secure, and so visibly recognized. But even when the deceased had been male and long gone from this original rural home, the imagery is evoked, time after time. This picture is far less middle class and consumerist than Douglas' view of domestic piety would render it. Yet it must have been recognizable as the place from which "we the future dead" started. It then becomes the hidden treasured remembered holy place, serving to foreshadow that ultimate eternal home in John's Gospel. For instance, just as the mother taught the children to sing her favorite hymns with her, so the role of music and family intimacy will be rediscovered after life in the wider and more dangerous world is over.

We may ponder what it meant to hear this message at a funeral in, say, 1920. The person funeralized, and his or her age cohort, would have remembered a world much more rural, slower paced—and yet still trying to heal from the Civil War. This generation had lived through another war, "over there" in Europe, and a society of major social and moral changes. We should take an alternative perspective to Douglas' sarcastic stance, and speculate that in a world of such rapid change, when persons contemplate death they also must go on inner quests for retrieval of what is now gone. The funeral sermons extolling "home," "mother," and simple rural piety prompted hearers to engage in their own versions of the *Remembrance of Things Past*. While Marcel Proust's multivolume introspective autobiographical novel would not be to their taste, funeral sermons focused on home, childhood, and mother helped everyone who listened begin such a life review, a nostalgic attempt to revisit and reclaim a past now gone forever from the visible public world. In eternity it never dies, never disappears, and never alters for those who as Christians set their hopes on heaven as home. In this sense, to go to heaven is to go "back," an eternal return not to a disembodied realm of souls, but through a Proustian quest through time and memory.

And yet, the early twentieth-century "home" imagery was profoundly pre-Proustian and so even more profoundly pre-Freudian. The home was not a source of ambivalence and ambiguity, or of repressed violence and sensuality, nor of loss or betrayal, as it certainly is for both Proust and Freud. Never, at least in the public imagery available to preachers, and evoked endlessly by them in the context of death. Nor can one find a theme that has become commonplace in later writings on "return to the beginning place": namely, that we first know the place only in our return to it. Here, the mystery is of a past we only thought we knew, which is discovered truly later on (by the adult narrator or psychoanalytic patient). This is such an important element in Freud, Proust, detective novels, and later spiritual writers' perspective, that its absence in the earlier American funeral sermons is one of the dividing lines between "them" and "us." For "them," home was a place you were at before things started to go wrong, and you "strayed far from home," where life suddenly became evil and complicated. For us—and this would include all those who live in the ages after "before silence and denial"—"home" can be complex and mysterious, and is often anything but innocent and idyllic. When it comes to "home," we have lost our "first naïveté."

To take this approach one step further, the exorbitant use of "heaven as home" images was a solution to the problem of what to say about death and the world to come that would make sense and concretize the Bible's promise of "mansions" somewhere beyond. It seems perverse to dismiss this project, as Douglas and many others have done, to treat it as nothing more than a smoke screen for failure to achieve influence and power in this world. Death is not, in itself a "pseudo-event," and to wish to say something about it is not absurd, for its alternative is silence and denial. In the era of preaching death before silence and denial set in, the best response is to ask how far could such imagery go without undermining other more basic Christian motifs. Saying or shouting "heaven is a HOME" could do damage to other messages about the transition through death to something beyond. In the passage from John, the house of heaven is and remains the Father's, and preachers never entirely forgot that even in their enthusiasm for the mother-dominated visions of "first home" back on the farm or the small town. As we shall see in the next chapter, they supplemented this imagery with others, more daring and even less tied to the Bible, for an afterlife that was truly "other."

Is heaven still a "home"? We will examine the contemporary imagery and ideas for death and what follows, in the final section of this book. But it is clear that the answer to this question is, "Not in the way it was for the preachers and their congregations of one hundred years ago." This imagery is gone from contemporary funeral sermons, almost entirely, and it is much more likely that the references to "home" in these are to the broken, devastated homes of the survivors, who find their dwellings and their hearts suddenly empty. And yet . . . a better answer to this question can be found in the contemporary religious autobiographer, Joseph Cardinal Bernardin, writing his final statement as he faced death, *The Gift of Peace*. The book was completed only two weeks before his death from cancer. Very little of the story deals with what lies ahead for him, but in response to others' concerns, he includes about a half page on his personal imagery for what will come after life in Chicago.

> The first time I traveled with my mother and sister to my parents' homeland of Tonadico di Primero, in northern Italy, I felt as if I had been there before. After years of looking through my mother's photo albums, I knew the mountains, the land, the houses, the people. As soon as we entered the valley, I said, "My God, I know this place. I am

> home." Somehow I think crossing from this life into life eternal will be similar. I will be home. (Bernardin, 152)

Bernardin's heaven is not truly like northern Italy. Unlike Elizabeth Phelps and her devotees, Bernardin knows perfectly well he is dealing with imagery and allegory. Nor is heaven based on his own real childhood home. That link also is no longer of use to him, a fact that separates him from the abundant use of the same imagery before silence and denial. But heaven is somehow like a foreign country, seen and known in photographs and stories from the past. It is both strange and "home," and this ambiguity places Bernardin post–Proust and separates him from those who proclaimed so loudly "heaven is our HOME," earlier in the past century. However, to express a similar ambiguity of strangeness/familiarity, of "foreign" places that are somehow recognized as "home," the preachers from the past needed a different set of images.

5

Heaven as Journey

Instead, they were longing for a better country—a heavenly one.

—Hebrews 11:16

Because funeral preaching centered upon an intense focus on heaven, pastors invested much creative energy in its depiction, in making heaven real to those who were the future dead. While "heaven is a HOME" was the most frequently cited and emotionally vibrant image in the funeral sermons of the early twentieth century, other images supplemented and to some degree counteracted it, all during the period before silence and denial set in by mid-century. These are images of travel and even adventure—not back to a once-familiar "home" of long ago, but to someplace new, better, and exciting rather than soothing. In a sample sermon outline from Ketcham's anthology, the heavenly country is better, "more exalted," "more healthful," happy, and abiding. Believers are travelers, looking to become permanent residents, and they "seek the company of heaven-bound travelers" (106–8). The new country of heaven was the destination for pilgrims, in another sermon in this collection, drawing for its imagery on the favorite devotional classic by John Bunyan, *The Pilgrim's Progress* (Ketcham, 178ff.). Or, in Shepfer's words,

> Jesus spoke of death as an EXODUS. . . . The word decease is here used in the sense of an exodus, a going out. It seemingly has reference to Israel's exodus from Egypt, the land of bondage, to Canaan, the Promised Land. . . . The same thought was expressed by Paul when feeling that "the time of my departure is at hand. . . ." The word "departure" literally means "to pull up anchor and set sail." He felt he would sail away home led and borne by angels, to some fairer clime. (39–40)

When this image of new and exciting destination is used, the process of dying and preparing for death is filled with hope and anticipation. It fits sermons preached at the funerals for the middle aged and aged, whose lives could more easily be construed as journeys than could the lives of youths or children.

Here, however, we encounter a problem that never seems to have troubled any of the preachers who prepared funeral sermons. They preached from the Bible, they firmly and unquestionably believed that what they preached was *in* the Bible, and not an imaginative extrapolation of their own, unrelated to the basic Christian message. They sought imagery in the Bible for a peaceful and hopeful transition to a marvelous existence in "a better country." But we may question that the images and examples they longed for can truly be found in the Bible itself, at least as applied to an individual's death. The Zechariah passage shows just how flexibly the Bible's resources were used by those certain that all of its hopes and promises dealt with personal death. The Johannine promise of "mansions" in the Father's house was an important pathway to the motif of heaven as "home." But let us look again for accounts of biblical peaceful and hopeful transition-and-journey deaths. The Hebrews verse is an extended comparison of the "faith" and anticipation of the heroes of Hebrew Scripture, with the fulfillment available through Christ. No one individual's death is actually depicted there; that is not what the passage is, literally, about. Let us start to search for actual literal depictions of such deaths understood in the biblical texts themselves as hopeful departures. Raise the question this way, start looking, and a startling fact emerges: very few can be found.

Once we start to look at human examples, and abandon the allegorical use of texts so intrinsic to traditional preachers, the story is stark and striking. The ancient patriarch Jacob died and "was gathered to his people" (Gen 49:33). King David "rested with his fathers" (1 Kgs 2:10).

These "good deaths" may have satisfied the ancient Hebrews, but every Christian pastor recognized that this is NOT the Christian hope for eternal life with Jesus, nor do these Old Testament deaths invoke any "exodus" model of transition. Moreover, a good amount of biblical language was dismal and negative, much more than hopeful.

> I am set apart with the dead,
> Like the slain who lie in the grave,
> Who you remember no more,
> Who are cut off from your care. (Ps 88:5)

The threat of "going down to the Pit" where the dead existed far from God appears in the Old Testament, but could never have been drawn upon by Christians who wished to say something when a fellow Christian died. The evocative end to the book of Ecclesiastes might have served them, for this shows frailty, failing, and decay ("before the sun and the light and the moon and the stars grow dark"; Eccl 12:2), and a final end when "the dust returns to the ground it came from, and the spirit returns to God who gave it" (12:7). Yet not surprisingly, this passage was never listed by anthologists as suitable for a funeral text, and there are no sermons in the collections that draw on it, although it at least includes the idea of a "return to God" and deals explicitly with personal death.

Here as with the Zechariah passage, the ideas of contemporary scholars on all these examples bear little or no relation to the theological assumptions of the first half of the twentieth century, such as Shepfer's. The more recent majority scholarly view is that the people who wrote and edited the Hebrew Bible were not very interested in personal death, were content to focus on the "collective personality" of the people of Israel and their history of salvation (exodus, conquest, and so forth). The references to Sheol ("the Pit") show how the ancient Hebrews shared a common ancient Near Eastern view of the grave, where the fate of the dead was to become "shades" flitting around a giant underground cave like bats. Therefore, "Most of the scholarly world agrees that there is no concept of immortality or life after death in the Old Testament" (Mendenhall, 68). To put this more positively, contemporary scholars argue that life and livingness were such positive goods for these people that death is always a negative, even when it is assumed as a given for all *nepheshim* (living beings). While there are "good deaths" such as

Jacob's, and "bad deaths" such as Korah's, who was swallowed by a sinkhole into the earth as punishment for insolence (Num 16:32), there is no major concern with personal death, let alone afterlife, in the canonical Hebrew Bible.

Turn to the New Testament, and we do find very explicit death scenes of important persons. Jesus' of course, and Stephen's, the first martyr. Preachers at funerals did not use these as reference points, nor do the stories from the Gospel's Passion Narratives provide the text for funeral sermons. None of the anthologies, manuals, or cyclopedias where long lists of "suitable texts" are provided would include texts that cover the actual dying of Jesus or Stephen. Not only are both deaths violent, but there are other insurmountable problems. Jesus as world Savior dies to redeem the world, but he is not, in the sermons from this era, a role model for the dying, nor for the future dead. Jesus' own dying is followed by resurrection, of course, but this takes place "offstage," and is separated by three days. This is clearly not what pastors wanted to stress when they preached on heaven, the likely immediate abode of the person they funeralized. Even Jesus' promise to the good thief, "Today you will be with me in paradise" (Luke 23:43) would have been unsuitable for the funeral of a faithful Christian, since it was addressed to a repentant criminal; this verse too was not used for this context at all.

Let us turn to the death of Stephen, an explicitly "Christian death" and filled with imagery of hopeful departure. Stephen dies triumphantly, with a vision of Jesus "standing at the right hand of God" (Acts 7:54-60). He forgives his persecutors, following Jesus' own example in Luke's Gospel, and then, using the euphemism of the New Testament, "fell asleep." Yes, this scene has heaven as the ultimate destination. But Stephen and his martyrdom must have been unusably distant from the main purpose of early twentieth-century Protestant funeral preachers, which was to help their listeners envision a future that was different, glorious, and yet somehow a believable destination for each one of them. Stephen's gruesome death narrative would have dramatically disrupted the purpose and the mood of an early twentieth-century Protestant funeral. So, although there is an abundance of materials that deal in some way with death in the Bible, the irony is that there are no appropriate "death scenes" that can be used directly as a model, given the needs of funeral preachers.

The funeral preacher's agenda, aimed at the future dead, was to make Christians contemplate their own deaths with a certain attitude. Hopeful, serious, aware that "the power of the world to come" would impinge on their lives one way or another, sooner or later. "Home" imagery did work for the part of this task that would console and reduce anxiety, but lacked the other meanings: departure, radical transition, a sense of awe and mystery. No one would have said, "The Bible fails to provide adequate source material," but it appears that when the message about heaven as destination was to be communicated, alternative sources gave the best and most vivid examples. As we shall see, nineteenth-century poetry became the primary resource here, used and overused, long into the twentieth century. Victorian poetry was supplemented by more recent but decidedly lesser examples of the same basic genre, until this too was silenced by mid-century.

To a contemporary person, it certainly seems as if the profusion of suitable poems and hymns on the topic of death as a journey to heaven demands some explanation. If we follow Douglas' argument about domesticity and the afterlife, we will suggest that heaven was a realm ready for "colonization," and therefore needed publicity, a brochure advocating its charms and advantages. The revision of previous eras' relatively sparse descriptions was part of a change in spiritual sensibility that started in the eighteenth century, flowered during the nineteenth, the period examined by Douglas, and continued unabated up through the first portion of the twentieth century. What the Bible did not provide, was amply filled in by other voices.

A reader may object. "Are you truly saying that the Bible is defective, imperfect, incomplete when it comes to imagery for death and afterlife?" On the surface, this seems an absurd charge. But remember church historian Pelikan's wise caution: there is no *one* Christian "shape of death." A much better way to proceed draws attention to the difference between the biblical authors' own priorities and concerns, and those hopes that dominated the imaginations of early twentieth-century pastors and their congregations. "Defective" and "incomplete" are loaded words; we might more fairly say that the New Testament is vigorous and eloquent about what mattered to those who wrote and worshipped with its texts. Furthermore, attention to the biblical texts can reveal how defective and incomplete our vision and imaginative capacity has been.

A clear instance of different priorities is Paul's magnificent extended vision of 1 Corinthians 15, "For as in Adam all die, so in Christ all will be made alive" (20). And

> I tell you a mystery: We will not all sleep, but we will all be changed—in a flash, in the twinkling of an eye, at the last trumpet. For the trumpet will sound, the dead will be raised imperishable, and we will be changed. For the perishable must clothe itself with the imperishable, and the mortal with immortality. (51-53)

This is definitely death as transition, it is filled with hope, and it is universal, sublime, and mysterious. He uses images of seeds into plants, "physical" into "spiritual body," and death as enemy "defeated." No Protestant pastor one hundred years ago would have argued against Paul, or considered the apostle "sub-Christian." But he might have worried whether Paul's passionate hope for transfigured "spiritual" eternal existence answered to the needs of his funeral congregation. For what the Corinthians passage does *not* do is try to offer congregations a picture of where dear old Mrs. Jones is right now, or where they as the future dead can expect to be. Indeed "where" is not even a Pauline category, and his "when" is at the end of time, "at the last trumpet," rather than immediately after an individual's death. The passage depicts the final consummation when God will be "all in all" (1 Cor 15:28), and beyond this nothing is said about the personal state or experiences of those who will be resurrected. Pauline eschatology will fascinate theologians whose ideas we will discuss in Part II; they eventually challenge the worldviews of the earlier generation. For those of the age before silence and denial, "where" more than "when" was what they needed to picture. The "when" of direct interest at funerals is the personal time of death, not the last day of Pauline universal eschatology. Just so, heavenly Jerusalem or that "heavenly country" was more appropriate to these hopes than what Paul anticipated. The Bible left room for more personal eschatological preoccupation if all of the "restoration" passages were read as the Zechariah text was, with all its place language read allegorically as heaven. The heavenly country sought by the patriarchal nomads (in our Hebrews verse) could easily be assimilated into this picture.

Place language mattered. Therefore the preachers of an earlier era created and borrowed from everywhere abundant references to departures, travel, transitions, and arrivals. This spatialized imagery was much more suitable for them than Paul's "perishable into imperishable" since it allowed for a huge range of very practical analogies. Dying was like starting on a journey, a ship setting out to sea, a plant growing into a new space, and a cultivated bush "transplanted" to a better spot. In all of these, space matters. These people were not literalists, they were *less* literalistic than many of us today, and they could therefore freely and imaginatively explore the possible "destinations" of the journey out of this life into somewhere else. It is this imagery that poetry expresses and elaborates, while "home" was best presented via anecdotes about the "old country" or the simple rural family life.

Destinations, departures, journeys: this is the stuff of adventure. The nineteenth century was indeed a century of exploration and colonization, from the point of view of white European Americans. Those who did not stay home to enjoy the consolation of "domestic piety" ventured forth to find new lands and wealth, to subdue native populations, and probably to escape from the stifling world depicted by Douglas as "feminized." Let us not overstress gender, because lots of women as well as men had traveled or dreamed of exciting journeys. Moreover, from the stories and references in the earlier collections of sermons, the immigrant experience was still a living (and unidealized) one for many of the elderly at whose funerals references to journeys and departures were related to the eternal destination of heaven. Or, early in their lives these people had traveled west, or exchanged farm life for urban. They did not, probably, have the photo collection Cardinal Bernardin enjoyed to accompany his parents' tales of northern Italy, but they could draw on a range of anecdotes, personal experiences, and published stories of what it was like to travel somewhere else far away.

Such cultural and experiential background helps to explain how images of travel, geography, and adventure could so thoroughly fill in where the Bible is silent or disinclined to elaborate anything. And no more popular poem for funerals, right up until the 1940s, could ever be imagined than Alfred Lord Tennyson's "Crossing the Bar." It appears in whole or part in every older sermon anthology. (Christensen, 121; Hallock, 180; Wallis, 27; among many others)

> Sunset and Evening star
> And one clear call for me!

And may there be no moaning at the bar
When I put out to sea.

Twilight and evening bells
And after that the dark!
And may there be no sadness of farewell
When I embark.

For though from out our bourne of time and Place
The flood may bear me far,
I hope to see my Pilot face to face,
When I have crost the bar.

This poem was used so often—recited by the preacher in the midst of the sermon, or at its finale—that Blackwood of the 1942 funeral manual actually complained, and put in a word of caution. Wordsworth, Browning, and Tennyson may be a pastor's favorites, yet perhaps not all congregations were composed of persons who could appreciate this caliber of literature. But, if they went to funerals with any regularity, they must have heard "Crossing the Bar" often enough to memorize it. It was clearly the funeral poem par excellence, and yet I confess that it was totally unfamiliar to me before I read these sermons. This alone suggests the vast abyss that separates "us" today, post–silence and denial, from "them" who lived before it.

Death is the subject of "Crossing the Bar." It is about death as departure, making for much less torturous funeral application than biblical passages about restored Jerusalem. The "bar" is the sandbar that shelters a harbor, from whence ships depart into the open ocean. Here there is no "domestic" image, just the opposite dominates the poem. The poem is steeped in a sense of mystery, of spaciousness. There is not even an image of a specific destination, another shore for arrival. Instead—and this is among the best features for those who wanted to stress its Christian meaning—is the hope for another kind of goal: to see Jesus, "my Pilot" no longer through a mirror darkly but "face to face" (1 Cor 13:13). Echo of Paul, the poet knows, and it is this image of trustful presence that outweighs any idea of an additional destination needed. Of course the sailing is at twilight, of course the image of day turned to night fits in with the wider image of natural closure and ending to life. Peaceful, yet intended, and filled with hope. Note the repeated injunction not to mourn, "no moaning at the bar," and "no sadness of farewell." For Tennyson, for Blackwood, and for all those who received this poem as a portrait of what lay beyond this life, the somber transition was not intrinsically sad, and it was the duty of the dying and the funeral preacher to remind the living of that fact. This stands out as another feature that would make this poem hard to resurrect for current usage at any funeral or memorial service. It is a fine poem, but it definitely belongs with "things that aren't there anymore," a piece of a past that cannot automatically become a "resource" for persons today.

Lesser poems, many of them much lesser, repeat these ideas endlessly. Hallock's *Cyclopedia* contains over 70 examples of "Quotable Poems," and Wallis' similar volume 114 in its poetry sections. Poems sprinkle most of the early twentieth-century sermons, integrated into their doctrinal messages. Clearly, something happened to poetry along with Christian messages about death and afterlife; we will return to this question later, especially since post–1970s sermons that do include poems are so radically different for what the poems intend, and in their authorship. But poems such as "Crossing the Bar" reveal the giant need of those who preached "doctrinal" sermons to use emotions and imagination, to evoke vivid and personal pictures in the souls of their hearers. "Doctrinal" did not mean dry and abstract, even when the sermons lacked the "personalized" focus on the biography of the deceased that most older preachers condemned. Poetry, along with music (the same anthologies also include extensive selections of hymns, whose verses repeat exactly the same themes we discuss here) made funerals as much of a "multimedia" experience as traditional mainline Protestantism could handle. One cannot imagine Blackwood or any of his pastor cohort accepting slide shows, photographs, or any such visual media into worship (although the technology was already there early in the century). But through vividly imagistic poems, the congregation had something to visualize internally if they did not want to just stare at the casket, the pastor, or the others in the pews.

Not all poems of travel and departure share exactly Tennyson's mood of somber mystery combined with hope. Take another poem, one written early in the twentieth century, that also relies on movement through space for its central meaning. "The Rose Still Grows Beyond the Wall" is another allegory of death as transition to a new location, and once a staple for the "appropriate poetry" section of funeral manuals.

Near shady wall a rose once grew
Budded and blossomed in God's free light
Watered and fed by morning dew
Shedding its sweetness day and night.

As it grew and blossomed, fair and tall,
Slowly rising to loftier height,
It came to a crevice in the wall,
Through which there shone a beam of light.

Onward it crept with added strength
With never a thought of fear or pride,
It followed the light through the crevice's length
And unfolded itself on the other side . . .

Shall claim of death cause us to grieve,
And make our courage faint or fall?
Nay, let us faith and hope receive;
The rose still grows beyond the wall.

Scattering fragrance far and wide,
Just as it did in days of yore,
Just as it did on the other side,
Just as it will for evermore. (Hallock, 213; no author is given,
although elsewhere it is attributed to A. L. Frink)

While this has been anthologized as one of *America's 100 Favorite Poems*, and appears endlessly even today on the web, it has dropped out of funeral sermons. It uses the image of "natural growth" to stand for immortality, in a manner rather different from Paul's back in 1 Corinthians 15. Shade into sun, with no loss or regret: this is the message about death it rather simplistically conveys. "Just as it did on the other side," suggests minimal difference; put bluntly, it denies Paul's promise that "[w]e shall all be changed." In spite of the reference to "God's free light," it is not truly theistic, although "faith and hope" dimly echo exactly the Paul passage Tennyson drew upon, 1 Corinthians 13. As with Tennyson, there is the direct injunction that grief and mourning are inappropriate responses to death, for life continues without disruption and with more sunlight "beyond the wall."

Based on the number of current Internet appearances of this poem (I found seventy-five easily), it is still loved and used for memorial websites by individuals and families, so the message itself retains appeal at some level. The website for Latter-day Saints police includes it, although the only other organizational use is by the Marin Rose Society of Marin County, California. But as a text recited during funerals, its time is past. "The Rose Still Grows" drops from more recent anthologies of funeral sermons, along with the entire section of other "recitable poems." One obvious reason is that its direct injunction not to mourn—"Shall claim of death cause us to grieve. . . . Nay"—goes directly against the principle messages of contemporary funerals: that death for the survivors is indeed disruption and loss. Perhaps the "crack in the wall" through which the rose grew is just not enough of a gap, a disjunction and departure. Even most of the same private memorial tribute websites that use the poem make it very, very clear that the bereaved family's experience is of intense loss and separation. To the extent that a memorial website is itself an expression of mourning, then such a cultural product violates both Tennyson's and Frink's "let there be no sadness of farewell." But these observations anticipate the shifts we will trace in parts II and III.

Remember that at the funeral before the era of silence and denial, those who were present were not "mourners," but "the future dead." What these two poems were really suited for was to offer imagery for the "journey" out of this life and into something else. The two poems, and the other examples gleaned from older anthologies of funeral sermons, suggest and perhaps compete with each other for imaginative space. The transition of death to what follows may be something like a night journey into the endless ocean, or perhaps more like a plant's growth from shade to sunlight. Both images are far more suitable than the "domestic heaven" of Phelps' *The Gates Ajar*, which was cluttered up with pianos and the other stuff of middle-class home life; neither so literalistically and laughably resembles western Massachusetts.

Still a third image of "journey" is expressed in an oft-repeated allegorical anecdote. Instead of the natural growth of the rose, this story is about human-caused movement. A gardener tends a rose in a greenhouse. Day by day, he water and prunes it. One morning, it is missing.

What happened to it? "The master came in the night and carried it off" (Hallock, 25). There can be no higher destiny for a cultivated rose than this. Transplantation, from the plant's point of view, is like the journey from the harbor to a new space. Moreover, here too the transition is positive and productive, only seemingly a loss for the gardener. The other striking feature of this allegory is that it is, unlike the other two, directly theistic. A rose by itself does not jump out of the greenhouse and into the ground, nor onto the master's own table. And yet, there is an assurance that this is the most "natural" destiny, or destination, for a rose. The greenhouse is preparation.

As we shall see, by some contemporary Christian theological criterion, all of these images are "sub-Christian," unworthy in their assurances and elaborations. But no one really thought so or could have called them that until past the middle decades of the past century. Persons who sat through Tennyson's poem may have privately rejected its ideas, and may have scoffed at the rose who "followed the light through the crevice's length." They may, in short, have personally disbelieved these, and wished for alternatives that settled for death as ending rather than transition. But they never would have questioned the link with Christian faith assumed by those who preached on death and recited the poems to emphasize the "doctrinal" point that "the world to come" was real. Skeptics, just as did believers, took this link for granted. Christian faith is based on the belief that "heaven is our HOME and death a homegoing."

These poems and stories raise the question of how far any imagery drawn from nature, from the realm of ordinary lived experience here in the world, can work when facing death, an ultimate transition that is *not* like any normal journey or growth. Paul's imagery of seeds into plants seems to rely on normal growth—and yet, the transition he imagines in 1 Corinthians 15 is so miraculous and extraordinary—"in the twinkling of an eye"—that the normal growth of the rose hardly accounts for it. Maybe "transplantation" will work better, but the very "normalcy" of the process inhibits any sense that it is a miraculous act, however surprising it may seem at first to the greenhouse gardener.

Moreover, spatial imagery is partial and flawed. Paul clearly does not use it. All the funeral sermons of the era before silence and denial feel comfortable with space and place as primary images. This suspicion of their adequacy, of the fittingness of once-popular ideas, arises not because I am more literal minded than those long-ago fans of Tennyson or more recent fans of climbing rose bushes. But my Christian imagination, and that of many twenty-first-century persons, works differently. To put this question at all is to look at one of the pervasive assumptions of the early twentieth century and before shared by American Christians, both leaders and persons in the pews. The two strands of imagery for heaven—as home and as journey—both worked because they depended not only on spaces and places as imagery, but also on what we will call "natural immortality." To this philosophical, theological doctrine, we now turn.

6

Natural Immortality

For I know that my redeemer lives . . . and after my skin has been destroyed, yet in my flesh I will see God.

—Job 19:25-26

This chapter confronts Christian "otherworldliness" head-on. Its philosophical plausibility and coherence are not the subject of our investigation: its emotional and spiritual power in dealing with death is what matters here.

Although most of us assume we know the meaning of "other-worldly," a close examination of the imagery of funeral sermons shows that "otherworldly" depended upon very close and accessible analogies with "this-worldly" phenomena. In other words, to make the Christian doctrine of "immortality" work, as it was understood in the age before silence and denial, immortality had to appear utterly "natural." An existence beyond or outside death could be presented as within the realm of possible expectations, nor was it miraculous in the commonplace sense of "violating natural laws." Just the opposite: immortality had to be made to seem obvious and expected.

Although we have separated images of heaven as home, and those of a journey to someplace new, both are part of the larger class of images:

of transitions in the natural world. Some of these resemble the rose that grew through the crack in the wall:

> As it grew and blossomed, fair and tall,
> Slowly rising to loftier height,
> It came to a crevice in the wall,
> Through which there shone a beam of light. . . .
> And it followed the light through the crevice length,
> And unfolded itself on the other side. (Hallock, 213)

Everyday, spontaneous observable events are here employed to signify change. Or, recall the story of the rose "carried off" from the greenhouse during the night. Some poetic examples of this popular image also reinforce its normalcy:

> *Gathered Lillies*
>
> And he asked, Who gathered this
> Flower? And the gardener answered,
> "the Master!" and his fellow
> Servant held his peace. (Hallock, 64)

> *Transplanted*
>
> Ere sin could blight or sorrow fade
> Death came with friendly care;
> The opening bud to heaven conveyed,
> And bade it blossom there. (Hallock, 66)

Here are journeys from the plants' point of view, but appropriate and not destructive transitions. That is how this image was used in the funeral sermons of the first part of the twentieth century. Even what might appear as sudden disruption is actually but a smooth and positive movement to the "next stage." The imagery blends hopes for a life after death into natural transformations, such as the caterpillar's metamorphosis into butterfly.

> A person unfamiliar with the workings of nature would be hard put to find much beauty in a caterpillar. Yet, that caterpillar ultimately lays aside its cocoon and turns into a gorgeous, multicolored butterfly. This is a part of God's marvelous design and the God-given forces of

> nature. . . . Just so, our earthly bodies are useful for a while, and then they are replaced by "spiritual" or "glorified" bodies. (Christensen, 84–85)

All of these images illustrate that what we think of as "death" is not ending, but a new phase of life.

> Let us not think of our departed dead
> As caught and cumbered in their graves of earth;
> But think of death as of another birth,
> As a new freedom for the wings outspread. (Wallis, anonymous poem, 60)

Death may in some sense be departure, but it is never a loss. That idea, central to the later death awareness movement's insight and imagery, would have been labeled "pagan" by those clergy whose sermons were anthologized earlier in the past century.

Such images of transitions as these from nature intermingled with those of home, and "Crossing the Bar." So many of the poems recited in sermons relied upon them to make death and what follows both seem "natural." Notice that the meaning of "natural" here differs radically from what the death awareness movement assumes. For them, and for us, "nature" is our connection with the realm of biological, ecological systems. Instead, what is really being offered by the transplanted or growing roses can be called "natural immortality." According to this view, from embodied life to an eternal spiritual state is the "natural" life cycle of the soul, everywhere and for all persons. Not "nature" only as organic, biological life, but soul as a universal, lawful, and yet unique-to-humans reality is what makes us who we are. "Souls" are not ghostly, spooky, or "otherworldly," they are what you and I consist of, our own true identities.

> Death is not the end but the beginning of genuine living. Man's soul is immortal but while he lives on earth his life is cumbered with many burdens. . . . But at death these are removed and the soul goes free, to live the genuine life God ordained it to live. (Shepfer, 30)

Or, "One universal law of God manifest: for material creations: beginning, growth, fruitage, death. One universal law for spiritual creations:

Life. . . . God's purpose is growth in life. The plant, the tiny egg, the grub, the chrysalis, the butterfly" (Ketcham, 295). While material existence includes death, spiritual or soulish existence is "life." Therefore, souls may have a beginning—although this is sometimes left open by the language of "eternity"—but they have no end.

When these beliefs are taken as the core of the Christian teaching about human beings, a certain understanding of the Bible and revelation follows. As we saw in the case of the Zechariah passage, here too: a vision of the soul and its immortality controls the way whole themes and sections are interpreted, and related to one another. Preachers rarely asked whether the Bible teaches "natural immortality." In their understanding, the Bible assumes and depends upon it, rather than introduces the idea to us. For this idea is too obvious to need an introduction via revelation. What the Bible does is illustrate and document in a specific manner the more general, intuitively accepted truth. Even the most doctrinally specific sermon anthologies included numerous statements to this effect. A conservative Lutheran sermon in a 1912 anthology claimed that "[i]f nature allows us to hope for immortality, revelation assures us that we will realize it" (Neumann, 70). In another sermon from forty years later, the same relation between natural immortality and the proof offered by Scripture is laid down: "In Christ, we have more than intuition, we have positive assurancy" (Wallis, 132). Natural immortality is a universal, basically accurate intuition, now proved and supported by specific Christian teaching on resurrection (Wallis, 86–87, 140). The historical fact of Jesus' resurrection confirms what "nature" already demonstrates. While later Christian theologies of the twentieth century choked on such assertions, they are the mainstay of earlier Christian death preaching.

Let us return to the popular funeral text that heads this chapter: "After my skin has been destroyed, yet in my flesh I will see God" (Job 19:25-26). In spite of the explicit reference to "flesh" and "skin," when pastors started from "natural immortality" as a given, they read the passage from Job as confirming Christian expectations for immortality of the soul. They may have had to explain how Job knew that Christ, his Redeemer, lived, but they did not probe that immortality of the sort we have described is what the passage taught (see Schuh, 1918, part IV, 18). The important idea, for those who assumed natural immortality, was that it will still be "me" who will, immediately after death, see God. Pastors could rely on it to express a universal hope for continuity between the person who was alive last week, and the one who lives and perceives in heaven. Moreover, persons who had known one another in life would recognize each other in heaven (Hallock, 39; Shepfer, 94ff.). The issue was not "with or without flesh," because "flesh" was not the core of the person anyway. The question was how to portray a nondestructive, orderly, and appropriate transition to a new state. Whatever the original meaning of the Job text in the ancient Near East, and whatever its importance now (e.g., as a support for some of the views that challenge "natural immortality"!) this is how it was used in the early twentieth century as a funeral sermon text.

Natural immortality in this sense is so pervasive in the texts of early twentieth-century funeral sermons that all Christians must have assumed the Bible taught and supported this belief unambiguously. The death of saints was precious in the eyes of God, not just because "human personality" was "sacred," but because "death" was universally and always a stage toward something better and other, not an ending. It was, perhaps, "the final stage of growth," but not in the sense Kübler-Ross and her contributors meant when she edited a book with this title early in the death awareness movement (more correctly, they wrote about "dying" not "death" anyway). The operative image was "growth," not "final," and for this the Job passage fit much better than, say, "There is a time to be born and a time to die" (Eccl 3:2) ever would have. Natural birth will not suggest this kind of transition, not as much as natural "second birth," as in caterpillar into butterfly, or even the "transplantation" of gardening. We will, in Part III, look at how these images are now used, but considered to lie outside of Christian teaching, if not in downright contradiction to it.

What strikes the contemporary reader of these sermons and poems where "transplanted" is the synonym for "dead" is how unquestionably and confidently everyone assumed "immortality" as the theme of Christian faith, the object of Christian hope, and the universal and *obvious* quality of it all. Yes, the New Testament witness to the resurrection of Jesus added "historical proof," but of something that barely needed to be "proved." Natural immortality was a fact of "nature," philosophically sound, yet imperfectly demonstrated until the clear historical example of

Jesus Christ. The belief did not rest on foundations as narrow and specific as church authority; it rested on what was knowable by anyone and everyone. It was clearly apparent that humans were "naturally" immortal, so that the world of gardens, birds, and bugs just confirmed what everyone intuitively knew already. When British sociologist Tony Walter contrasts today's *Eclipse of Eternity* with what came before it, what he refers to is not a decrease in private belief, but the loss of just this public obviousness of the whole thing. When "eternity" was so obvious and taken for granted, sermons could reinforce what was already common conventional knowledge; no one had to introduce new and startling ideas at funerals when it came to confronting death. Natural immortality was just as obviously Christian as was the need for salvation, or the moral example of Jesus.

By "everyone," I do not mean just the preacher, the professional public voice of the Christian church. It means his listeners too; everyone at the funeral, whatever their privately held views. There appears to have been no dissent that this was indeed the message the Bible taught and the Church proclaimed. That is not to say that everyone accepted it, as personal belief. Quite possibly, in the 1920s, and in decades beyond that, silent skeptics sat in the congregation, hearing it all but dismissing this belief as hogwash. Perhaps what they truly accepted was the other message: "Dust you are, and to dust you shall return." But they would not have spoken up to voice this doubt within the church, and their rejection of natural immortality would have been viewed by all, including themselves, as a rejection of the core of the gospel.

But by the early twentieth century there were surely plenty of voices outside the church who disputed this view of human beings, of "nature" and the soul. Take Freud's critique of the belief in an afterlife. Put very simply, Freud labeled such beliefs as natural immortality an "illusion," wishful thinking not based on empirical evidence, or on reasoned deduction, but on unconscious yearnings and desires. We would all like death to be transition not ending, we would all like to be inwardly exempt from the realm of decay and mortality. A belief that everyone would *like* to be true will of course be affected by that motivation. Maybe the "universal hope" for a positive afterlife for the soul is a reason in itself to suspect such a belief. This is Freud's argument in *The Future of an Illusion*, written in 1927 but relying on what by then were conventional skeptics' arguments. Wanting something to be true does not in any way make it more likely to be true. It only makes us more likely to skew the evidence, and be unable to examine the case for or against dispassionately (Freud, chap. 6, 47ff.). We may think of claims that dark chocolate is "good for you" because of the antioxidants in it as a trivial contemporary parallel.

Note that Freud too spoke of "proof," and assumed that an eternal existence of the soul is or tries to be an empirical fact. It claims to be the kind of fact for which seeking proof is a reasonable strategy. The resurrection of Jesus, however, would not qualify, since it might have happened long ago, and its supporters were credulous and depended on the authority of tradition rather than their own empirical investigations. Here Freud and funeral preachers obviously part company, even though both would agree that Jesus' resurrection potentially claims to be a "fact" to support a more general belief. But Freud wanted more up-to-date examples. This too was hardly original. Indeed, by the late nineteenth century the quest for scientific proof of life after death had been inaugurated, and generations of investigations by the Society for Psychical Research on the topic testify to this urge to settle the question once and for all, through empirical means (Moreman). Freud himself was a member of SPR, as were many other distinguished persons; like them, he felt that a belief so important to humans as the survival of the soul after death ought to be open to scrupulous and unbiased investigation. If "natural immortality" was a universal intuition, that did not make it accurate, but these researchers thought that made it the kind of belief claim that could be tested, supported, or invalidated. Neither Freud nor the early twentieth-century preachers who assumed and advocated natural immortality dealt with complicated theological arguments about "faith" versus "historicity," which came much later (if at all) into American awareness. No one in early-century funeral sermons touched upon such ideas, nor was faith contrasted with reason, empirical experience, or science when it came to natural immortality. You do not need such specialized religious epistemology when it comes to rose bushes and butterflies, nor does an adequate reading of the Bible require them.

If there is a "pre-Freudian" quality to these sermons, it is not in any difference over what kind of belief is being discussed. The conflict is over the suspicious versus tolerant emotional stance toward a hope that was believed by both parties to be universal. For the Christian pastors of the early twentieth century, a belief that was universal and consoling was quite likely, on these grounds alone, worthy of consideration, and very probably truthful in its intuitions about death. For Freud, the "consoling" quality was itself a red flag. Nothing that good could possibly also be true. He accused those who accepted immortality of being like the woman who happily told me, "It doesn't matter what you eat, so long as you stay healthy."

The Christians who assumed natural immortality had not just church tradition on their side. They shared in a distinguished philosophical heritage, one that Christians down through the ages had almost universally embraced. If we trace its philosophical roots back to Plato, its religious roots include most of the major theologies in the Christian tradition. Augustine, Aquinas, and Calvin did not contradict natural immortality, nor did they see it at odds with what revelation taught us. The latter supplemented, but did not contradict the immortality of the soul. By the late eighteenth century, Immanuel Kant included this belief as one of the cores for *Religion within the Limits of Reason Alone*. "Rational religion" included the belief in a cosmic moral order, and a Divine Orderer, but tied to these was the claim that the soul never really dies. It will be changed, it will be moved—or move itself—but there is nothing disruptive or "unnatural" about this process. That may be the key: the whole sequence is utterly normal and guided by rules or laws. There is a time to be born, a time to die, and a time to move into eternity. Reason supplemented by intuition meant that transitions and transformations in the natural world intimate this destiny of the soul after physical death. The "other" in "otherworldly" was once again, never a gash or an abyss or even anything uncanny; it lay within the limits of reason if not of this physical world.

For Christians, the resurrection of Jesus played an important role within this vision of reality. "Natural immortality" is a universal fact, it was stated over and over by Protestant preachers. Yes, God gives life, and gives everlasting life, but "revelation" proves a fact that was already established in a more general way in our minds. By "revelation" was meant the resurrection of Jesus, and his teaching about "eternal life." "Jesus never argued about life being eternal. He knew that He was eternal" (Shepfer, 22). "So Jesus saw beyond the death of the body. He knew the power of death was over the body one, and not over the soul" (21). Therefore, by rising from the dead, Jesus does not reverse a natural order, or disrupt it. He makes visible, tangible, and empirical an already acceptable truth. He becomes a historical example, in a way similar to that sought by the researchers from SPR who looked for documented cases of the soul's survival in the words of spiritualist mediums. Every single statement of Jesus about "eternal life" is understood within this view. It is no surprise that passages such as that from Job, which seem on the surface to support a different, more "fleshly" understanding, were automatically enlisted into support for "soulish" natural immortality.

However, when the relation between universal truth and particular historical revelation is put this way—and this is exactly how it *was* put—a door was left open for belief in natural immortality without need of the additional historical example of Jesus Christ. Suppose one simply set this to one side, as an instance of an already-known general truth, and concentrated solely on the general rather than the particular. A few of the older funeral resources and collections, particularly those by Protestant clergy Shepfer and Christensen, skirt close to this in their enthusiasm for intimations of "natural immortality," and the immense consolation this can offer those who listen *When Death Speaks* (Shepfer's title). Such ideas in themselves were not seen as "sub-Christian," as they probably would be now by most pastors and preachers. But they were decidedly non-christological, non–Christ centered. Christ became the proof text of a message that could be made to stand independently. From the perspective of theologies that made their impact later on, this is already a warning sign: watch out that what is being preached is not some smooth variant of deism, or Platonic philosophy! We will see how this criticism aimed to pull the rug out from under natural immortality, and how, for a variety of reasons, it succeeded within the church if not in the culture at large.

But back before that happens, we find natural immortality approaching a center-stage status in sermons where Jesus and particular doctrines concerning him are intellectually and rhetorically subordinated. This was most likely to happen at some less than ideal funerals, and not necessarily when the preacher was more "liberal" in his outlook. In contrast to what many of us might expect, reliance on belief in natural immortality seems to have cut right across the spectrum of liberal and conservative;

it was so widely accepted that people would not have judged the whole topic using these categories at all. But there may have been other circumstances and situations where it became politic to overstress the general truth of the soul's undyingness, and minimize the specifics of Jesus, his death and resurrection.

Remember the question of "problem funerals," where one of the standard dilemmas was when the faith of the deceased was not firmly established, or remained unknown to the preacher (or to anyone but God). At such a gathering, a clergyman was asked to give a funeral sermon preached in the funeral home, not in the church, and the family wanted something "religious" for their loved one who was not a member of any organized religion—all the circumstances where a Presbyterian pastor Blackwood (writing his manual in 1942) would have been reluctant to participate at all. However, for him as for others of an earlier era, the basic purpose of the funeral remained worship of God, with consolation as a by-product not the main aim. Yet the more the churchless situation became the norm, the more easy it must have become to keep attention on natural immortality, rather than the specifics of Jesus and salvation.

By the midst of the era of silence and denial, an uncompromising and really thoughtful analyst of American funerals, pastoral theologian Paul Irion, could see this connection. We will return to his landmark 1966 book, *The Funeral: Vestige or Value?* later in our study. Irion, like other clergy before and after who have written manuals and guidebooks on funerals, spots that the demand for "religious" funerals outstrips the actual demonstrable faith of many of the funeralized.

> One of the problems that is deeply involved in the American funeral is that the funeral is seen as "religious" even by those who are not religious themselves. . . . There is no viable relationship between the deceased or his family and a community of faith. . . . For the people involved, this is a pseudo-religious ceremony. (Irion, 127, 129)

The unfortunate compromise solution, Irion observes, is

> modifying the funeral service normally used for professing Christians . . . the focus is much more general than specific. The emphasis on the resurrection is not given the same stress as it is in the traditional church service. (Irion, 131)

Irion labels this the "pseudo-religious funeral." He detested this compromise, and tried to offer alternatives.

Irion's account makes it clearer why under these conditions, natural immortality imagery, however faded and overused, was still available in 1966 even when the recitations of "Crossing the Bar" were a thing of the past. Caterpillar into butterfly, the stock image of natural immortality, is certainly not the same thing as absolute silence, but it is a message whose Christian focus under these conditions is so blurred, so vague, so inoffensive that all of those present can feel "uplifted" without being challenged to confess faith in anything or anyone. Irion thought "pseudo-religious" the right word here. A funeral for a person without church affiliation would be one of the "difficult cases," but it could still be in some sense a Christian funeral, according to Blackwood in 1942. The difference is that Blackwood never, ever let go of the primary aim of the funeral as the worship of God. Nor did he let his guard drop against the encroachment of "pagan" elements and practices into Christian faith, even if his boundaries were drawn in ways we today cannot always trace. The difference is not just that Irion is less tolerant about "difficult" or "problem" funerals, or that "natural immortality" had become less securely tethered to central Christian doctrines about salvation, judgment, and "the world to come." What has happened between Blackwood in 1942 and Irion a generation later, is the triumph of silence and denial, so that the older messages fade and become dimmer, eventually just about impossible to hear at all. Yet nothing really new and vibrant has replaced them. That is the situation Irion so unhappily and cynically depicts.

For Irion paints a portrait here of a mid-century mainline Christianity already steeped in silence and denial about death. Ultimately, this is his criticism of the "pseudo-religious" funeral, and of the society that wanted to hear nothing real about death (see Irion, chaps. 2 and 3). "Natural immortality" is not the same as saying nothing, but the sermons that stress it read as "denial," as a way *not* to have death speak and tell us anything we don't want to hear. When other themes have faded out and this one persists, we do have the situation decried by Irion, and a few years later by the death awareness movement. A "pseudo-religious funeral" includes a "sub-Christian" message that boils down to "death is unreal." Irion, writing just on the brink of what will become a brand-new development, of imagery and ideas for death, knew that something was wrong.

He even tried to reform it by proposing a "humanistic funeral service" as an alternative (134, 189). This, he believed, could free up a Christian funeral to be authentically Christian, while preserve the ideal of human dignity—that is, that everyone deserves the honor of a funeral.

Irion's portrait of the "pseudo-religious" funeral represents a negative, albeit prophetic stance toward the spiritual ethos of American Protestantism that had grown imperceptibly more silent and denying about death. But another way to state this situation is that by mid-century, American religion generally had become less doctrinally specific and more generically theistic. This was the era of Will Herberg's *Protestant, Catholic, Jew*, which described this amalgam as a kind of faith in "faith," while backing off from any objective content. Another link would be to the "civil religion" made famous in the next decade of the 1960s by Robert Bellah, when it was already being challenged. "Civil religion" was the public religiousness of events such as presidential inaugurations. It invoked God but never Jesus, it assumed America to be a place God had blessed and would continue to bless. It was not—as Bellah saw it—entirely self-congratulatory, but it was surely aimed to avoid explicit doctrinal and creedal differences and to raise few hackles. A major difference between "civil religion" and the Protestant funerals we study here is that the only deaths of interest to the former are those of the war dead. Memorial Day, the Gettysburg Address, national cemeteries: Bellah found these excellent sites of the civil religiousness he identified. Such deaths were honored as "sacrifices," they held a special sacred meaning. The average Protestant funeral, however "pseudo-religious" and theologically empty, could not be classified this way.

All of these associations, I should stress, are negative. Irion, Herberg, and Bellah did not want to celebrate and congratulate Americans for having moved beyond specificity and doctrines. They did not see this "faith in faith" as an improvement. Even though none wanted to return to the bad old days of religious warfare and intolerance, they were highly critical of what seemed, by the 1950s, to have replaced them. It has been easy to lump faith in "natural immortality" together with their portrait of mainstream religion of this period, to yield an equally negative vision of Christianity sinking down into "pseudo-religious" inspirational messages about rose bushes and butterflies. We may ask if this is really a fair assessment.

Such a critique does not do justice to the evocative power and continuing appeal of natural immortality imagery. I look at plants, birds, and bugs, and do not find allegories of the soul's eternal destiny—but that does not make such speculations nonsense, or make me wiser than Plato. To state the case for natural immortality is to open oneself not just to death denial and wish fulfillment, but to a long philosophical and metaphysical tradition that Christians almost to a person enthusiastically embraced. The real source of natural immortality is not, therefore, the piety of the relatively recent past, or the empirical behavior of caterpillars, but the tradition of Plato and his followers. Christians have long pondered how this might support, coincide with, and render systematic the message of Jesus Christ in regard to death. If there is no one Christian "shape of death," then different answers to this question are possible. For some twentieth-century thinkers, the long-standing alliance between Plato and Christian faith amounts to a betrayal, a giant mistake from which the authentic Christian meaning of death and afterlife needs to be saved. When we begin to move beyond the era before silence and denial, theological challenges such as this play a role in what came next. A belief so central, so taken as obvious and natural and universal that it must be true, became the focus of a bitter attack in the name of the Christian gospel itself.

7

THE LORD'S WILL

The Lord struck the child that Uriah's wife had borne to David, and he became ill. David pleaded with God for the child. He fasted and went into his house and spent nights lying on the ground . . . and he would not eat any food with them. On the seventh day the child died. David's servants were afraid to tell him that the child was dead, for they thought, "While the child was still living, we spoke to David but he would not listen to us. How can we tell him the child is dead? He may do something desperate." David noticed that his servants were whispering among themselves and he realized the child was dead. "Is the child dead?" he asked. "Yes," they replied, "he is dead." Then David got up from the ground. After he had washed . . . he went into the house of the Lord and worshiped. Then he went to his own house, and at his request they served him food and he ate. His servants asked him, "Why are you acting this way? While the child was alive, you fasted and wept, but now that the child is dead, you get up and you eat!" He answered, "While the child was still alive, I fasted and wept. I thought, 'Who knows? The Lord may be gracious to me and let the child live.' But now that he is dead why should I fast? Can I bring him back again? I will go to him, but he will not return to me."

—2 Samuel 12:15-23 (NIV)

In the age before silence and denial, this passage was a frequent one for funeral sermons. Its quiet and complete disappearance is an even more dramatic sign of changed beliefs than is the equally total disappearance of "Crossing the Bar" and the children playing in the streets of heavenly Jerusalem. It clearly dovetailed with both of the latter, and with the message that "mourning" was needless and in some sense disobedient or at least an ignorant response to death. But the stark message of the story is that mourning before the death may yet persuade God, but once the death has occurred, to mourn is to go against the clear will of God. In this passage, the death of David and Bathsheba's child, in its timing, manner, and particularity, was "the Lord's will." Let us see how early twentieth-century preachers expressed these ideas, supplemented by "natural immortality" and the focus on heaven.

The 2 Samuel text was among those listed by anthologist Hallock as a "Suggestive Text for Sermons at Funeral of Infants or Little Children" (Hallock, 23). Its message, in a sample sermon outline, is threefold:

1. Persistent grief is always wrong, because it is useless. "Can I bring him back?"
2. Think how happy and safe the child is in heaven.
3. "I shall go to him." We shall go to the children. (Hallock, 29)

Another example divided David's behavior into two aspects: "suffering as a sinner" and "reasoning as a saint." The ideas here are "the unreturnableness of the dead," "the certainty of his own dissolution," and "the reunion after death," which "he believed was happy. There would be no consolation in the idea of an unhappy union. . . . Infants go to heaven" (Ketcham, 100–102). Note that heaven and natural immortality are not directly part of the original text, but interpreted by pastors into the final, seemingly stoic expression of finality. "Another great comfort, when a child is taken away, is the truth of immortal life" (Hallock, 36).

But the major message is that what has happened is God's will.

> One comfort is that it is God's will. . . . We cannot understand the strange providence which has brought such deep gloom; there really seems no possible explanation; clouds and darkness are about, but we know that in our Father's heart there is an explanation, that he has

> made no mistake, and that this very darkness is part of his great plan of love for us. (Hallock, 36)

> The sun goes down by the appointment of God. . . . To God belong the issues of even death. He never visits without the divine appointment. . . . God . . . does all things well, and whether the sun of our loved ones depart in the morning, at midday or in the evening, it will have a glorious rising in that perfect day in which there shall be no night. (Hallock, 86–87)

So, in the first decades of the past century, congregations were told that all deaths, however "untimely" they seemed, were the Lord's will. David's refusal to mourn after the death had happened was a sign of "Christian resignation," to be commended as an example of faith. Even when all mourning was not explicitly condemned, it was perceived as the lesser response, the weaker vision, a "sub-Christian" and vaguely "pagan" way to deal with death. We find this idea repeated and emphasized in a very wide range of circumstances, for a remarkable range of deaths. By mid-century, both this idea and the story of David's bereavement vanished, and at least for mainline Protestants, it never returned. The last example in the anthologies of a sermon preached in this text reveals the fading of its credibility, for the preacher's focus is on "[f]ew parents indeed are able to look on the loss of their little one as David did" (Wallis, 166–67), rather than on commanding parents that they should follow his example. When pastors influenced by the more recent death awareness movement use its language of "acceptance" and stress this as a Christian value (as we shall see in part III), they do not mean to resurrect this earlier attitude, either toward mourning or toward "God's will."

Let us challenge the interpretations offered so confidently by preachers who chose the story of David's dead infant to preach at funerals early in the twentieth century. What they found, as we saw already, were several ideas that more recent biblical interpreters dispute are truly there in the text, or that could have been there in the minds of ancient Near Eastern people. While "persistent grief is always wrong" will be challenged on psychological grounds in the 1970s, biblical scholars would particularly come down hard on the motifs of heaven and family reunions as truly the ideals of the ancient Hebrews. "Most of the scholarly world agrees that there is no concept of immortality or life after death in the

Old Testament" (Mendenhall, 68). The happiness of the dead child now in heaven and the anticipated future reunion of father and baby there are anachronisms for persons of ancient Israel in 1000 B.C.E. Sheol, the realm of the dead, is not a place of joyous reunions, and the ancient Hebrews did not accept "natural immortality"—a point about which we will say a great deal more later. The phrase "gathered to his ancestors" referred to entombment in a family gravesite (Mendenhall, 68–69), nothing more. But just as important is that biblical scholars today will not draw from the story of David's bereavement the generalization that such deaths as that of his infant always and everywhere are directly "God's will." No such universal view of death as purposefully intended by God, no matter what the circumstances, appears to control the biblical worldview—or, to be more historically based, the beliefs of ancient Near Easterners.

Yet here, the Bible appears on the side of the older theology represented in the sermons, in its insistence that at least some deaths are due directly to particular acts of the Lord. There is no denying that such deaths in both the Old and New Testaments are brought about by direct and unique actions of God, in response to some specific, particular sins of those who died or of their parents. David's infant dies to punish the parents for their adultery. David and Bathsheba could not be allowed to get away with a sinful relationship indefinitely, so David does indeed "suffer as a sinner" here. Nevertheless, the author of Samuel and Kings has the royal couple both live long and more or less happy lives as husband and wife. Bathsheba's next child, Solomon, becomes the next king of united Israel, so the punishment stopped with this one unnamed infant's death. But "punishment" it surely was; the Lord could not be persuaded or deterred by David's self-abasement and pleas.

More contemporary interpretations, however, follow the suggestion of Lloyd Bailey Sr. He distinguished between "death in general" and particular "bad deaths" when it comes to the many stories of punitive or retributive deaths attributed to God (48–52). These "bad deaths" were the subject of special interest for the biblical authors. While normal deaths just seem part of the landscape, the "bad deaths" are memorable and sometimes spectacular. For example, the deaths of Korah and his family are the direct result of an earthquake's sinkhole opening under their feet. This was caused by God in punishment for their disobedience to Moses. "They went down alive into the grave with everything they owned" (Num 16:31ff.). Fascination with "bad deaths" continues; in the early Christian community, Ananias and Sapphira try to cheat the church, and Peter rebukes them. They fall down dead, struck by God for their sin. "Great fear filled the whole church, and all who heard about these events" (Acts 5:1-11). Even more telling than the drama of these examples is the narrator's tone in all three cases—and in many others. These deaths are unequivocally the acts of the Lord, they are intended to punish wrongdoers, inspire fear and reverence in others, and serve as later allegories and examples (as in 1 Cor 10:1-11). But for Bailey, and other contemporary scholars, they are exceptions, from which it is impossible to generalize that all deaths are either as bad or as directly intended by God.

For if we look at the peaceful deaths of the patriarchs, who die "naturally" surrounded by their families, in old age, the story appears different. We might call these "good deaths," and at minimum the biblical accounts consider these "timely" and appropriate. Abraham lived until he was "full of years," and then "he was gathered to his people" (Gen 25:8)—which destiny is no longer equated with an afterlife.

True, if one could have asked a biblical author, he would probably have affirmed that it is God who sets dates and times, for the old and righteous as well as for sinners. In the historical books there is little doubt that deaths worth recording are worth attributing directly to the Lord. This is why a search for a view of "natural death" or even "good deaths" in the Bible is trickier than some religious thinkers of our era after silence and denial hoped. Nevertheless, there is no rigorous attempt to demonstrate that all of these "non-bad" deaths were, in their details and particulars, willed directly by God. But that, as we have seen, is exactly what the funeral preachers in the era before silence and denial wanted to claim. The passage from 2 Samuel was intended, they thought, to teach us about all deaths. Not just "bad deaths," but all deaths were "the Lord's will," however arbitrary, shocking, and "untimely" particular deaths might appear to us.

> What God does ever well is done!
> His will is just and holy;
> As he directs my sands to run,
> My spirit shall keep lowly. (anonymous poem, Schuh, 1918, 91)

And so, at the funeral of a child, “While we extend to this family our sympathy, we are forced to say: ‘How wonderful are the ways of God!’” (Schuh, 1918, 51). The special punitive aspect of David’s child’s death was overlooked, and (no surprise) there was never a reference to this at the funeral of any child. By mid-century, this attitude faded, even as traces of the basic idea remained.

The two features of particular deaths related to “the Lord’s will” most frequently were their timing and their manner. So for example, there will be some reference to “it was the Lord’s will” that the deceased lived long enough for family members to visit her one last time. Prayer may have extended the person’s life for a time, but ultimately the Lord’s own timing prevails. In one example, of a woman who died “at the wash-tub in another person’s house,” the pastor commended both the manner and the timing:

> Let us never forget that we are serving God when we are doing our work in the right way and spirit. Nor do I know of a more beautiful dying day that this one was . . . Ascension Day. (Schuh, 1918, 47–48)

Thus, even a potentially grotesque situation could be turned into a demonstration of “the Lord’s will” in regard to timing.

We should admit that even today, there is a sense of appropriateness when someone dies in the midst of doing what he or she liked best: wrapping Christmas presents for grandchildren, fishing on the beach, or running for public office (as the ex-Mayor Frank Rizzo making a comeback run, died suddenly before the election). In this, the preachers who exclaimed “How wonderful are the ways of God!” seem to grasp at some basic yearning for meaningful connection between death and life. Yet they relentlessly would have insisted that all deaths reveal these wonderful ways. Really bizarre or freakish deaths continue to puzzle and dismay us; the death of contemplative mystic Thomas Merton in an accident with an electric fan is a classic example. While many Christians now are reticent about which of any of these deaths are truly “the Lord’s will,” the earlier understanding was that all of them, regardless of appearances, were definitely to be considered so. Not one of these deaths, nor any others, could offer real challenges to what was accepted as the biblical view that individual deaths are directly the will of God.

As we have already seen, the deaths of children did not challenge this view either. Typically, the preacher could tell the parents as a message for everyone from the funeral sermon:

> All too soon, it seems to you, she has been taken away. But you are resigned, as Christian parents should be, to the will of God. (Schuh, 1918, part I, 14)

At least from the perspective of many preachers, the death of a child was an "easy funeral," which fit within a theology focused on heaven. Here and there, however, one does find a sense of struggle, although not over the issues directly relevant to the passage about David. Take, for example, the fourteen-year-old pastor's son who drowned while fishing. He died because the Lord willed it so.

> What has God done? . . . When this child was born, I am sure you recognized the fact that God gave him to you. . . . Now let me add a few more things God did: He took this son from you. . . . God's plans are too great to be comprehended by us. (Neumann, 27–28)

Yet this clearly raised doubts and despair in some minds, and so the sermon at the funeral directly explains that God mysteriously wills even deaths that to us make no sense at all.

Other traumatic deaths produced the same theological response. One of the anthologies includes the funeral sermon preached at the memorial for a group of over two hundred miners killed in a coal mine collapse (Hallock, 207–12). Their deaths were sudden and horrible. The text here was "Thy judgments are a great deep" (Ps 36:6), and the underlying theme was that this disaster was indeed "the Lord's will," unequivocally. No implication in these cases that the individuals who died were particularly sinful (210), or that their parents sinned in special ways; that dimension of the David story is *not* there. The sermon to memorialize the miners also steers entirely clear of any wider circle of human responsibility, so that moral and legal issues of mine safety lie completely outside its vision. This disaster was, however mysterious and destructive, the Lord's will. "We are sure that there is a God who ruleth and governeth whatever the mysteries that surround his operations" (210).

In the days before the transition into silence and denial, this claim was pervasive, and seemingly accepted as the rationale for Christian "resignation." Anger against the Lord's will would have been a sin, in and of itself. Had these events been far-away disasters, such as the sinking of the Titanic, there might have been a note of prophetic warning: "The rich and their luxurious decadent lives brought down God's just punishment, and the sinking of an ocean liner filled with such sinners was the Lord's will." But the two examples of drowned adolescent and buried miners were local, and the funerals were community events. The congregation personally knew the dead. What they heard was that the boy and the miners died because God directly intended their deaths. There was no glee, no sense of rejoicing, and no glow around "resignation" in their preacher's message.

The true and only exception to this understanding of death as "the Lord's will," in this era, is a telling one. It was possible to invoke "the Lord's will" to cover any death whatsoever, except suicide. This was the exception that proved the rule, and in all the volumes of exemplary sermons from that era, I have found just two for suicides (Neumann, 131–33 and Schuh, 1918, 128–33). Here, the focus was indeed on human responsibility, the terrible fate of those who, like the deceased, make wrong choices. And yet, God was not absent from the sequence of events.

> What a shock this community received when the sad news of the untimely death of ___ became known. We were dumbfounded . . . we have not recovered from the effects of the deplorable act that has culminated in the death of this highly respected man. . . . There are many problems that children of God cannot solve. . . . That God watches over the affairs of the world, and that nothing transpires without his permission, is very plain. (Schuh, 1918, 129)

The sermon continues to assure the shocked community that human nature is not only very weak, but very sinful. "Someday we will understand" is the final message. There was also an attempt to balance this, a reminder of our duty not to judge, but leave human fates in the hands of God. "Friends, hereafter let us have greater fear of sin, and of that sin especially to which our brother has fallen a victim" (Neumann, 132). Nevertheless, what separates suicide from all other deaths is that it alone could not have been God's choice, nor was the despair that must have precipitated suicide the will of God either. The shocked, dumbfounded, and grieving community was faced with a case of deep cognitive dissonance, not only a tragic loss. Because there are so few examples, it is difficult to say what proportion of pastors would have refused to funeralize and bury a suicide under any conditions. (Nor, of course, how many of the deaths attributed publicly to other causes were in fact suicides.)

Typically, while suicide deaths continue to be given space among the "problem funerals," the focus of more recent decades is on the sense of guilt of those left behind and the lasting pain they will feel. This is part of the shift from preaching to the future dead, to preaching to mourners. Alas, the fading out of "the Lord's will" as the direct explanation of all other deaths has not made suicide easier for anyone to bear, and suicide continues to rank at the top of the list of "difficult funerals" in pastors' manuals. But this change diminishes the *theological* problem of suicide for the minister, for it no longer stands as a horrible counter-example to the theology of individual deaths as "God's will." It is now a pastoral problem, as perhaps it always was for the family and friends of the suicide. Or, "Why didn't God prevent this death?" may be the current question, but this same can be voiced about many, many other deaths, too.

But all other deaths, those of infants, those of "accident victims," those of what we would consider preventable disasters, were ultimately the result of the Lord's will. That message was proclaimed directly, unambiguously, and frequently at Christian funerals. It was—but then it was heard no longer. For many of us today, this message in its stark and direct form is intolerable. I venture to guess that today, even the most conservative and stodgy congregation would rise up and throttle the preacher who offered this kind of message at a funeral whose aim was "consolation."

To experience firsthand this contemporary repugnance toward the older vision of "God's will" at work in every death, we turn to the eloquent outcry of Christian philosopher Nicholas Wolterstorff. His son Eric died in a mountain climbing accident in 1983. In an earlier era, the manner of his death—while engaged in a favorite activity—would have been seen as divinely intended, and its timing too "just and holy," although mysterious to us. But Wolterstorff the grieving father refuses to believe "*God* has shaken the mountain. God had decided it was time for him to come home." He cries out, "I find this pious attitude deaf to the message of the Christian gospel."

> The Bible speaks instead of God's *overcoming* death. . . . God is appalled by death. My pain over my son's death is shared by *his* pain over my son's death. And yes, I share in his pain over *his* son's death. (66–67)

Not only does God *not* "will" particular deaths, but God suffers with us, and God himself has been a bereaved parent. These ideas, so powerfully and plaintively expressed by Wolterstorff, are now the primary themes of many sermons, pastors' manuals, and books on grief. They are the direct replacement for the older view that particular deaths are God's will. And, although I looked hard, I found no trace of these thoughts in any of the older funeral sermons. Whatever the true message of the Christian gospel on this point, the two eras read it completely differently, and both would have accused the other of deafness. On this point alone, the past is what is gone and nonrecoverable. It is not a "resource," at least not for Christian public statements about how to understand and respond to death.

"God is appalled by death." While we will look directly at some of the more recent theologies that support this theme, it is worthwhile to repeat that such an idea is completely absent from any of the funeral materials from the era before silence and denial. The congregation gathered at the suicide's funeral may be shocked and dumbfounded, but God could never be. We humans, in our ignorance and sinfulness, may be "appalled," and may, with "pagan" fear, consider death "the King of Terrors." But Christians should acknowledge that even the most seemingly dreadful death is the Lord's will, and our response to it should be nothing less than "Christian resignation."

"Resignation" and "submission" were the synonymous terms to use here, and unlike Kübler-Ross' "acceptance" they did not seem "glow words." No one claimed that resignation was a spontaneous intrapsychic natural stage in coming to terms with loss. It was an act of will, and here the self-control of King David was exemplary. He refused to indulge himself in grief, he resumed his regular routine, and above all, he worshipped God. This kind of intentional realignment of one's emotions and actions was the human mirror, so to speak, for God's own intentions in causing the death. These people would have viewed today's psychologies of grief, whether of "stages" or "tasks," as encouraging slackness and self-indulgence and passivity in the face of circumstances.

Part of this heavy emphasis on resignation as Christian in the early twentieth century was almost certainly a reaction against the Victorian era's sentimental exaltation of exorbitant emotionalism and limitless mourning. Remember the moral drawn by the David story in a 1926 anthology: "Persistent grief is always wrong, because it is useless" (Hallock, 29). The change in customs had come quickly, right around World War I. Out went the long black clothing, "mourning garb," or "widow's weeds." Out went many of the social restrictions for mourners. Out went the well-defined social role of mourner. Along with this, out went the attitude that "perpetual mourning" showed one's true devotion to the lost beloved person. For pastors of the post–World War I generation, the memories of that kind of Victorian mourning would still have been available. Yet there is no sign of nostalgia for the vanished customs, just the opposite. To mainline Protestant clergy, that kind of exorbitant mourning would have been "pagan," unseemly and out of alignment with the whole message of the gospel. "Pagan" because ultimately, Christian funerals were to be hopeful, not dismal. Unseemly because the display of emotion, which for some mourners must have been evidence that they truly loved the deceased, looked to mainline Protestant clergy like signs of weakness. Not just weak faith, but a weak will. David who mastered his private grief and went back to his duties became the ideal. Although it was human to be sad, the value of self-control and the ability to manage one's emotions rather than give way to them were assumed to join with Christian faith and resignation to the Lord's will. There was probably a class factor in this too; the impoverished "backward" population of central Appalachia continued to weep, wail, and carry on during funerals, unlike middle-class persons addressed by most of the anthologies' sermons (Chrissman, 94).

Even with awareness of this background and history, the ideal of "resignation" has become repugnant, to put it mildly, in more recent thinking about how to respond to death. We must realize how resignation included not only an inward disposition toward God, but a demeanor of "stiff upper lip" such as that of King David after he knows for certain of his baby's death. Today this has come under bitter attack. The death awareness movement assumes that feelings and their expression go together, and that although tears and sighs may make everyone uncomfortable, at times of death there is something "natural" and appropriate to sorrow and its visible, audible expression. "Acceptance" may come later, but is not to be immediately commanded or even commended. This cluster of contemporary assumptions and psychological ideas permeates the past forty years of funeral sermons and advice manuals. But it leaves unaddressed the basic question about the ultimate cause of a death, the question that preachers of an earlier era believed it their task to answer so directly.

According to that view which extolled and idealized Christian resignation, grief is not wrong. But it is human, and the point of view taken by Christian clergy at funerals was theocentric, focused away from us and toward God. Grief as a human emotion, they believed, tells us nothing about God. The underlying theology of death as "the Lord's will" reduces human grief to something of no religious significance, and most frequently it will distract us from focus on the divine power of the world to come.

This irrelevance of grief is what Wolterstorff, along with many other recent theologians, disputes. He saw the "message of the Christian Gospel" as God's enmity toward death, a point we will take up in detail. For him, God does not will or want death, and God grieves even more deeply than we do. In refusing to accept that God "shook the mountain" to cause his son's fall, Wolterstorff invokes divine suffering and pain. God is a bereaved father, whose pain makes Wolterstorff's suffering . . . not "good" or even "acceptable," but sufferable. The suffering of a loss is not good in itself, nor the springboard to "Christian resignation," but it links a particular, seemingly arbitrary death with the death narrative of central meaning for Christians, the Passion Narrative of Christ's dying. In this, Wolterstorff's example reveals a current turn toward christological thinking vividly unlike the theocentric vision of the earlier American Protestant religious framework. When we turn to theological opposition to the views so solidly assumed in the early twentieth century, we find the door left open for this claim, that grief *can* indeed tell us something about God.

Here we may note what is almost an irony of quietly accomplished shifts in religious meanings. While Protestant pastor Irion complained about "pseudo-religious" funerals and Herberg lamented the mushy contentlessness of American "faith in faith," elsewhere we can find evidence that Christian thought on death was becoming more *Christian*, or at least more particularistically focused on Christ. Moreover, the displacement of an earlier theocentric approach with one focused intensely on the specifics of Christ's suffering and death depended on a change that happened as quietly and uncontroversially as any in the world of religion, with even less regret than the passing of Victorian mourning customs.

For grieving father Wolterstorff, writing in the 1980s, it seems unexceptional to use the phrase "God's pain," and even to imagine God as a mourner. For the clergy of the early twentieth century, such a wording would have been unheard of, possibly blasphemous, and certainly at odds with their traditional theological training. While there are clearly references to Jesus and his passion and death in all the older anthologies of sermons, there is no mention of "divine suffering" in the sense Wolterstorff and so many others now use this idea. Yes, Jesus suffered when he fulfilled his Father's will; but of course the main principle at stake was that his death was clearly *willed* by God. Therefore, Christians use that as the model, but then, as we have seen, even seemingly accidental or senseless deaths can be attributed to God's will. Christ's death is not unique in this respect at all. It is God who wills, the human Jesus assents, as should we. Wolterstorff will not say this, and in fact turns this theme on its head. God now suffers with him; God does not impose, ordain, or will the suffering of others. Moreover, Wolterstorff is convinced that his view is indeed "biblical," in spite of stories such as 2 Samuel 12 and all the rest of the dramatic and punitive examples.

Interpreters, theologians, and preachers who challenge the traditional view of death as "God's will" show that there was another intervening factor at work in that tradition. This they identify as the pervasive Hellenistic and Platonic understanding of divine "impassibility." This word, hardly in anyone's day-to-day vocabulary, meant that Whatever/Whoever was truly divine was beyond being harmed or destroyed, nor was It/He vulnerable to decay or any other trace of mortality, pain, or loss. Impassibility also included the idea of *apatheia*, beyond emotional impulsivity and the domination by passions. Divine freedom from suffering was a sign of transcendence and permanence, it was one of God's attributes, just like omniscience. This was the traditional meaning of "impassibility," and while it came from Plato and the philosophical thought of the ancient Mediterranean world, the idea was firmly included in the Christian theological and spiritual tradition until the early twentieth century. Christian "resignation" in some sense mirrored divine "impassibility," even though for us the former was a duty to achieve, while for God immunity from suffering was intrinsic to his nature. While there is no direct defense of "impassibility" in any of the funeral sermons themselves, the portrait of God relied upon by the preachers of these depends in part on this long-standing motif.

But sometime still during our era of preaching death, this idea of "impassibility" starts to be questioned in systematic theology, and is quietly abandoned. According to Warren McWilliams, this theological shift happens so softly, smoothly, and without any direct conflict, that impassibility is just dropped from the list of divine attributes. There were no defenders of divine impassibility, no outcry over its abandonment. It became more important to say other things about God, and an ideal of "freedom from change and decay" no longer was worth upholding. With that shift, and perhaps fueling it, came the freeing up of biblical interpretation, and increased ability to come to grips with much biblical material. Read Hosea's plea to Israel, the faithless wife, to return to her husband Yahweh; one cannot impose an ideal of divine dispassion and detachment and immunity from pain, without entirely ignoring the text. God now appears extraordinarily passionate, suffering along with the people in exile, and rejoicing with shouts of joy at their return. Once we have allowed this dimension of the biblical texts to be recognized, it is a relatively short step to Wolterstorff's identification with God the Father as fellow bereaved parent. Considering the very long history of "impassibility" as a divine attribute, it is astonishing how quickly and uncontroversially it was dropped from the theological lexicon.

Once this has occurred, it impacts "the Lord's will" as the category to apply in the face of particular deaths. We will look at theologians' condemnation of this idea, their utter revulsion at the portrait of God upheld as "just and holy" earlier. Remembering those dead coal miners, whose deaths were "God's will," and even the death of the fourteen-year-old who drowned while fishing, we find ourselves on one side or the other of an immense gap. Not that the phrase "the Lord's will" has disappeared entirely from religious consciousness, or that it will never be used by Christians in interpreting particular deaths. But the confident doctrine that all deaths in their timing and manner were the Lord's will is no longer to be found in mainline Christian funeral sermons. Not in those that are anthologized, not in those I have listened to, and not in those referred to by authors of pastors' funeral manuals.

While it is difficult for me not to side with Wolterstorff, to see things from his side of the gap, there are some consequences to this changed religious consciousness and set of ideas that need a more nuanced treatment. When both the timing and manner of death were clearly "the Lord's will," this meant that preparation for death was our constant duty. We were to be vigilant because while we were ignorant, the Lord definitely knew the day and the hour when each of us would die. What's more, we *knew* that he knew. The preacher's task was to remind us of this, and to reawaken our consciousness that the Lord would, one day, will our own deaths. Remember the funeral for the man who the week before had been at his office; "Today we bury him. So you too may die. Are you living under the power of the world to come?" (Ketcham, 18). When the theology of individual death as the Lord's will was an undisputed belief, personal "readiness" to die made obvious, intuitive sense. Preparations for this event made equal sense. Without this certainty of God's direct intentions for me, it may not help if I ponder and prepare for my own death. The era of silence and denial is also the era when such preparation would have been considered morbid, not prudent or spiritually mature. To that period, when all thoughts, practices, and emotions related to death seemed taboo, we now turn.

PART II

The Age of Silence and Denial

8

"Please Omit Funeral"

I refuse to go to his funeral. Funerals are barbaric anyhow. When I first went to Hollywood, a director I'd known in the old days on Broadway died, and they buried him in Forest Lawn. They hauled all of us out to that ghastly place. . . . I was so revolted I've never gone to a funeral since.

Nobody's asking you. I feel the same way. When I die, I want an announcement in all the papers: "Please Omit Funeral."

—Dolson, 123

If the previous chapters revealed a solid and relatively uniform rationale for Christian funerals, and messages about death that seemed convincing to those who preached them, this is only part of the story. While the stated meanings of Christian funerals persist unaltered onward from the start of the twentieth century until its middle, funerals were never so undisputed as the sermons might indicate. There was a degree of discomfort and discontent with some aspects of the American way of death. It is hard to tell how much, or among how many. Not all of it, as we have seen, came from outside the church. Complaints about "pagan" practices that focused attention on the body (rather than the soul) appear in sermons, even when all the manuals for pastors stress the very good relations that normally prevailed between clergy and funeral directors.

Complaints about the expense of funerals lavished by the poor upon their dead are also part of this discontent, although there is no evidence that clergy actively intervened or protested at the time of any particular funeral at which they officiated. (Nor do any of the advice manuals suggest that this would be appropriate.) While minister and funeral director were "fellow professionals" all during the period examined here, there was uneasiness at how thoroughly some aspects of death had escaped from the control of clergy, and perhaps how business interests were entangled at this juncture in the sequence of events at the time of death (Laderman, 2003, chap. 1).

It is not fair to set up the protest against "traditional" funerals as a case of purely antireligious interests versus Christian faith. And yet, there is a certain degree of truth to this, as if funerals for at least some persons became part of the perceived struggle between science (progressive, rational) versus religion (backward, superstitious). The story is quite a bit more complicated than this, but since our focus is on the religious ideas and images about death, that is how we will begin. We will later move on to the challenges posed by new religious ideas in and of themselves to the views of death and heaven that prevailed in the older preaching on death.

We will not start directly with the consumerist critique, as voiced by authors such as Jessica Mitford in *The American Way of Death* nor by satirist Evelyn Waugh in his classic, hilarious *The Loved One*. These are both important texts, since Mitford required a direct response from the funeral industry, and Waugh tried to make the entire euphemizing and sanitizing of death absurd for us. Instead, I find the clearest statement of the philosophical and antitraditional stance toward funerals in a slight yet entertaining murder mystery by Hildegarde Dolson, titled (appropriately enough) *Please Omit Funeral*. Dolson's mystery novel from which the above dialogue was taken accurately captures exactly the secular-rationalist critique of funerals that had been building up all the while the pastors such as Blackwood and his successors preached. To better understand the challenge to funerals, and the set of attitudes and beliefs we have labeled "the age of silence and denial," Dolson's sly comedy of manners is a wonderfully revealing key. Even as it was written, however, the stance it represents was already under a new attack. Perhaps because Ms. Dolson, the author, was in her late sixties when she wrote this antifuneral piece, she could express the rationalist/secularist sensibilities of a generation who had once sat miserably through Blackwood's funeral sermons.

In *Please Omit Funeral*, both the amateur detective and the murderess agree that funerals are "barbaric." They agree that neither one of them can abide others' funerals, nor do they want one for themselves. Funerals are as absurd as the opinions of a third character, who campaigns to ban books from the school library, and against abortion. In the story, both these activities are indications of an irrational, bigoted, and superstitious stance to a rational, practical choice, unworthy of consideration as moral dilemmas at all. It is simply obvious, to the author and her heroine, that high school students should be allowed to read anything that they want, and it is just as obvious that only the bigoted and weak minded would feel the need to worry about death, either the death of a fetus or the ceremony that traditionally marks the death of a full human being. To go on record against abortion is also a breach of good taste, since it involved showing a dead fetus in a jar. Murder of one adult by another, of course is still wrong, but it is a kind of social *gaffe* in this story. Fittingly, the murderess avoids arrest by suiciding, a gesture that is approved under the circumstances because it is neater, cleaner, and once again more rational than other options. As one character says in admiration, "She gave her greatest performance—and retired" (Dolson, 233). The heroine—and the author herself—could not agree more. Presumably, any formal mourning would also have been "barbaric" and a waste of time.

Dolson was able, within this amusing piece of genre literature, to express without inhibitions the attitudes many persons wished to hold about anything connected with death. To be educated, enlightened, and progressive about social issues such as book censorship meant to pooh-pooh traditions when it came to death. Abortion and suicide are not worth arguing over, because only a complete idiot or bigot would find these problematic. We are all rational beings, in charge of our own lives and deaths, and to place any inhibitions on our own choices for ourselves is restrictive, a remnant of traditional oppressive authority. Nor should we ever do anything to restrict others' choices for themselves either. It is wrong to murder, although the heroine and the murderess come close to agreement that some folks just about ask to be done in. But that is because murder of another violates the principles of free choice and fair play, not because of some claim that "life is sacred," or that God forbids our playing God for others. Most of all, too much dwelling on death is in bad taste, it is unhealthy ("barbaric") and inhibits our enjoyment of life. Anything that enhances our fear of or interest in death ought to be rejected as a kind of moral duty. Although given the context and light tone of *Please Omit Funeral*, such language may seem odd, there is an aura of seriousness in Dolson's outlook; at some level, she is not joking but making a genuine moral argument. The core is this: there is nothing meaningful anyone could or should say about death. We find here, in stark form, our welcome to the era of silence and denial, and to the rationale that sustained and justified it. It does not lie in advancements in high-tech medicine, nor in the consumer education movement, but in a distinct philosophy of life—of life minus death as the ideal. Paul Irion, whose complex analysis of funerals from the same era we already touched on, called this "vitalism," and found it a pervasive belief in contemporary culture (1966, 28ff.).

Of course, a "murder mystery" is, ironically, a book all about death. The genre itself flourishes to contain death, to repackage it as part of a comedy of manners, to sever death from grief, horror, or loss. No one's death, in this genre, ever provokes such emotions, and the entertainment value of such books always depends upon this separation of deaths within the story from any of the emotions we would normally feel if someone close to us were killed. It is intriguing to trace the rise of this genre—and of authors such as Agatha Christie and Dorothy Sayers—as part of the era of emergent silence and denial. But our primary purpose is to isolate the arguments in Dolson's specimen as a real set of beliefs and attitudes, against which in turn those who believe that funerals have value and purpose must argue.

Dolson's "no funerals" approach is not based primarily on the consumerist critique against them. Wisely, she does not rely on the idea that funerals are a waste of money spent on the dead, or that funeral directors are rip-off artists waiting to prey on vulnerable customers. Such arguments often mask the ones she brings forth, but the Dolson approach shows their secondary nature. For one thing, we do not object to wasting money on other ceremonies, such as weddings and graduations, even though these are just as "impractical" as funerals. Indeed, more so, because the young marrying couple and the new graduate need all the resources they can gather in order to start a new phase of their lives. In the case of the dead, their funeral is truly the last expense they incur on earth. The difference is that the realities behind marriage and education are still meaningful to us. Those who still "believe in marriage" want to make a statement by doing it right, with all the trimmings, so to speak. Graduations and the parties that go with them matter because education makes a difference in the lives of those who receive it, and because getting out of school via graduation is believed to be a genuine accomplishment. The rest of us want to celebrate these events, and celebrate along with those whose lives are changed by them. Yes, they are happy and not "barbaric," but the enthusiastic celebrations are sometimes meant to overcome the ambiguity with which all changes in life are faced. This is also the case for baby showers, although these have a practical purpose, to supply the mother-to-be with all the gear she and the baby will need. All these transitions are meaningful to us as clues about the human condition. They mark off something of value, proclaim that something important is happening here, now, to these people. Death, in the eyes of Dolson and those who accept her views, can tell us nothing. It is even worse than mourning was for the Christian pastors whose sermons extolled "resignation" to the Lord's will. Focus on it will bring nothing but pointless discomfort and social embarrassment, for it makes no sense, and has no wider deeper significance. Like the obnoxious woman who shows a dead fetus to campaign against abortion, it is ridiculous, intrusive, and unworthy of any consideration.

Death tells us nothing. It no longer speaks. But perhaps, it tells us something too frightening, too horrific to be spoken of at all. It is hard to make a serious case for vitalism, or that mortality is so utterly disregardable. It is, instead, the elephant in the middle of the room that no one wants to acknowledge. It has grown larger, elephant-size indeed, by our refusal to encounter it. When we decide that death can tell us nothing, and therefore we will have nothing to say in facing it, we have not truly banished death. It returns, like Freud's "return of the repressed," on every page of Dolson's book about murder, suicide, and abortion, but in a form unmournable and unassimilable by us.

Dolson's is a genteel and funny example of what sociologist Geoffrey Gorer called "the pornography of death," fascination with death and violence that marks our era's entertainment. Just as with sexual pornography, sex and love are entirely severed from one another, so an analogous rule holds for death pornography. This "pornographic" response to death was the flip side of our denial and silence when facing it for real, for ourselves. When Gorer wrote, in 1965, the era of silence and denial was in full swing, and he wrote in England where the attitudes expressed by Dolson had gained far more social space and popularity than they did here. Nevertheless, his thesis remains relevant. We never completely banished death. But pornographic death is death severed from grief, death in a form so alien that we can learn from it nothing about ourselves. We cannot learn the two really useful and important things, how to die and how to mourn.

In 1966, when Protestant pastor Paul Irion published his exceptionally thoughtful book, *The Funeral: Vestige or Value?* the complaint that funerals were "barbaric" had to be confronted calmly and nondefensively. Irion is writing to the Dolson faction, those whose plea for "please omit funeral" might be mistaken for the voice of the future, the secular rational and progressive approach to death. The title alone is significant: a "vestige" is a remnant of a faded and failing tradition, of no more value to anyone in a rational, scientific modern age. Funerals of any kind, let alone Christian funerals, might be "vestiges" in this sense. By 1966 we are in the midst of the age of silence and denial, and also in the midst of the sixties counterculture when lots of traditions were challenged as "vestiges." To at least one very articulate group of persons, for whom Dolson acts as our spokeswoman, and whose ideology Irion wanted to take seriously, the answer was clear. Funerals were a sign not just of a dead person, but of a dead past. Like opposition to abortion seemed to Dolson in 1975 and religion seemed to Freud in 1927, these all rested on tradition and weak mindedness; they were on the way out and good riddance.

Irion makes the case that psychological denial and fear of death are the real source of such ideas (Irion, 59). Those who wish, like Dolson, to banish death and all reminders of it as "barbaric" are engaged in full-scale denial. If the arguments against funerals remained on purely practical grounds, they could be met when evidence is produced that by and large people are not ripped off by funeral homes, and are satisfied with the services these provide. Periodically repeated studies have shown exactly this. But Dolson reveals how the underlying power of the "vestige" argument has little to do with economics. It rests instead on an existential stance of denial and terror in the face of death, masked by an attempt to pass this off as "rational" and "liberating." Irion stresses this psychological and philosophical argument; to him there is nothing "rational" at all in denial of death. Nor is it cleaner and more reasonable to eliminate the body, and only celebrate "body-free" memorials for the dead (215). Indeed, the whole "please omit funeral" approach strikes Irion as an expression of "neurotic flight from reality" (59). In short, as a lie that hides both life and death, and a recipe for human self-deception and deep pain. This psychological-existential view is not that of earlier generations of clergy worried about "pagan" practices, for Irion does not rest this part of his argument on Christian or even theistic assumptions. What matters to him is that the claims of Dolson, to have achieved a nonmorbid, enlightened, and scientific stance toward death, are shown to be utterly flimsy, as flimsy, we may say, as is the plot of *Please Omit Funeral*. He proposes that a valid function for the funeral, in contrast, is possible. It can provide

> [t]he support that is necessary for the individual to confront death and loss realistically. It can undergird acceptance and defiance of death rather than the denying of death. It can resist the radical separation of death from life and deepen life's meaning by acknowledging the dramatic encounter with the reality of death. (Irion, 59)

Irion's book comes during the era of silence and denial, but in this analysis he is already a precursor of the death awareness movement. These same ideas—that American society "denies" and "represses" death—became conventional and clichés, but one simply does not find them voiced in this way by any of the pastors and clergy working only a very few years before. Instead, they seem to have become participants in that ethos, saying less and less and using faded-out imagery well into the era when Irion and Dolson wrote.

Indeed, saying nothing about death, avoiding funerals and everything that reminds one of death, turns out to be as morbid a defense strategy as anything "traditional" could have been. That is one of the ironies Irion would appreciate. The "no funerals" approach extended, in some cases both real and fictional, into the fanatical attempt to banish death altogether. The twentieth century produced several cases of this kind of death denial so extreme that they became twentieth-century legends, our versions of the rich fool in the Bible (Luke 12:16-21) who imagines he can accumulate life's goods indefinitely. The central character of Aldous Huxley's *After Many a Summer Dies the Swan* was based on the real-life example of newspaper publisher William Randolph Hearst, who tried to defeat and exclude death from his personal realm, living in grandiose seclusion within his own castle. Similarly, Walt Disney and Pablo Picasso were so death avoidant that they refused to hear the word "death" spoken in their presence. They continued to postpone even minimal rational planning, in spite of the sure and certain knowledge that this would cause problems when it came time to distribute their huge estates. These notorious examples fascinate not just because of the personal pathologies of famous and wealthy persons, but because these cases take the Dolson argument to its logical extreme. Even to mention death is a faux pas, a failure of a social contract to ignore the elephant in the room. The very rich could try a practice of consistent "vitalism." Yet the result is not a fulfilled life, but a fearful and restricted one.

Irion therefore argues that to avoid funerals as "barbaric" is itself a denial of life's fullness, for life includes death. To deny this is to deny ourselves. It is not a religious argument as such; Irion makes that very clear. We may call it humanistic or existential. It grounds the need for funerals in the human need to say something in the face of death, not on the truth of what in particular gets spoken. This is, needless to say, a very different view than what any of the earlier era's Christian clergy would have expressed. It meets head-on a criticism that must have been building up all during the decades before silence and denial, during those years when "Crossing the Bar" was a regular text at funerals. To Irion, the destructive power of denial is at work when we wish to banish death and treat funerals as "vestiges." He did not examine the specific imagery of the Tennyson poem, nor of "The Rose Still Grows Beyond the Wall" for signs of denial, because by 1966 these had faded out from sermons. But even more, because the move was on to replace them with . . . nothing. It is not that earlier Christian views of death had been ultrarealistic in facing it. Indeed, Irion joins with the newer theologies in challenging the traditional Christian dualist anthropology (144ff.), and it is unlikely that he would have any patience with the rose growing toward the sunny side of the wall as a metaphor for death. But those views and images had at least been there, and spoken. The new spirit of silence and denial had nothing to offer at all. It therefore failed at a deep and basic level.

The next thesis on behalf of funerals is that their function, among those who credit them with a function, is now unclear because there are several possible, simultaneous, and not always compatible "functions," each relevant to a particular constituency. Irion charts these, diagramming how various participants hold very different hopes and expectations about the purpose of a funeral (124, fig. 2). For clergy, the funeral continues to be primarily an occasion of worship. A funeral that fails to worship God fails, even when other needs are met. A funeral from the family's perspective, however, must fulfill certain psychological needs. These, which are often barely articulated and sometimes overlaid by long-term intrafamilial conflicts and communication issues, are increasingly paramount in public thinking about funerals. The seller's language of the funeral industry is aimed at the family, and uses the language of psychological consolation and familial duties to the dead.

Irion shows that there are other constituencies, points of view. We lose something when we overlook these. There is the sociological function; funerals are expected to do something for the wider community as a whole, not just for the family. By 1966 this is more problematic than it had been at the start of the century. The community, once clearly present not only physically in the church but imaginatively in the mind of the preacher as he prepared to remind them we are all future dead, has receded, its reality has become blurred. If you did not know the person who died, and care about him or her personally, there is no reason to come to the funeral. (If you are Dolson, you might not show even if you did care about the deceased, especially if you knew he or she had felt the way you do about funerals!) Finally, there is the funeral director who himself has both a business interest, and wishes to be perceived by all parties as a "service professional," alongside the clergy. Irion charts these divergent aims and ideas, and it seems clear to him that one of the problems Americans now—by 1966—experience with funerals is that expectations from one point of view do not necessarily match the ideals and aims of another.

On the surface, this seems a different kind of criticism and analysis than that coming from Dolson, who would deny funerals any true function. However, the very strategy of thinking in terms of different interest groups or constituencies shows how clergy control over funerals and their meanings had slipped away. The church is now one perspective among several, an idea never ever entertained by any of the earlier generations of pastors. The family as an interested party was not ignored by their sermons, but when all of the congregation are addressed as the future dead, the family was rarely singled out, isolated from all the rest. Once that has happened, their outlook, their concerns, and their power to dictate the nature of the funeral itself become critical. Because the funeral director deals with families as his customers, he is more aware of what they desire, and more willing to articulate it (or put words in their mouths, perhaps) than is the minister. Irion claims pervasive discontent with funerals may be due to this difference in interests and needs.

As for the wider community, represented by what Irion would call the sociological or anthropological perspective, its status as a "constituency" was never articulated directly in the earlier understanding of clergy, but Irion finds that it was presupposed all along (Irion, 18). While "community" was never a separate constituency directly, it did not have to be in earlier Christian views of funerals. For, remember, those present at the funeral are understood to be the future dead—all of them, regardless of their relationship or lack thereof to the deceased. This does not make them a "community" in the Durkheimian sense, but rather a collection of individual souls. Still, one way or another, they are usually present.

Evidence for this is found in one feature of Blackwood's and other earlier pastors' manuals: the important role played by Protestant clergy in civic and public occasions. The minister must know the protocol for these, and public expectations about his deportment and activities. For instance, earlier advice manuals assume every preacher must be prepared to officiate at military funerals, even if these are rare in his community (Blackwood, 162ff.). Such discussions recede and sometimes vanish in more recent manuals, as if "pastoral" became restricted in practice to the church congregation and its relatives. The sense of an inclusive society within which the clergy take on distinct and necessary roles is just no longer there in such writings, even though the actual public presence and participation of clergy at collective occasions (such as commemorations of disaster victims) is still a fact of American life.

There are times when they are not. A telling example of this is the case—always among the "difficult funerals"—of the homeless vagrant's death. When such an individual was discovered dead, his anonymous body frozen in an alley, perhaps, clergy were called up to provide some sort of ritual or ceremony, even when the only humans present are the city workers who must bury the dead man in the paupers' graveyard. A pastor should agree to such a request. Yes, say all of the earlier authors of funeral manuals, each and every human has a relationship with God, and the funeral reminds us of this. It may as a side effect bring even the grave diggers closer to God. What made this situation sad and difficult is that nothing could be known for certain by any human being about the dead person's own salvation, or relation with God. That was known to God, but for us even a guess was impossible. When a funeral was clearly "worship," this rationale sufficed. The lack of human mourners—family, friends—was very sad, but did not affect the most important purpose of a Christian funeral.

When the family's psychological perspective is given priority, this purpose no longer makes sense. If a funeral is to offer comfort and closure for those with close personal ties to the deceased, it makes no sense to hold one for a person who has no such ties. Dolson might have been willing to grant that those who truly wanted a funeral still had a right to it, yet she would surely have joined with those who believe a funeral for a friendless person, a funeral with no mourners, would be a ridiculous waste of time. Why bother? What could possibly be the point? (At least some of my students voice this argument in exactly these words.) There is no doubt that Irion disagrees with this, but he must frame his disagreement without reference to God or worship. For him, even without family present, every human being has a "right" to a funeral, to be honored as a human being who once lived (189ff.). A community—present in the mind of the preacher, and perhaps represented by the casual attendance of the municipal grave diggers on the scene—has an obligation to mark the death of its members. Humans qua humans are valuable, when we die someone is lost. It does not matter that no other humans feel this loss as personal grief. We are of value, apart from and beyond our impact upon the emotions and memories of others.

Irion's argument here brings us back to Dolson's "please omit funeral." Here, in the sad case of the friendless vagrant's death, he would say that we have our test case of what the real "value" not just of funerals but of people may be. Our lives' endings matter, because we ourselves matter, intrinsically, as ends in ourselves. We can imagine Irion offering a formal reply not just to the Dolson "omit funeral" view, but to the overall treatment of death in her novel. He would find Dolson's dismissal of funerals of a piece with her flimsy and wishful vision of suicide as the solution to life's difficulties. When life becomes difficult, embarrassing, or even just boring—go ahead and end it. It may be "neater" and less hassle for oneself as well as others to do so. So the heroine approves the murderess' rationale for suicide, and just as directly, anyone's rationale for abortion. For Dolson, no one should have the right to prevent or punish any of these decisions. For Irion, the dignity and value of all human beings need to be protected and affirmed. The real role of "community" is to guard this, to keep reminding all of us of it. The vagrant qua human is worthy of a funeral, and no one's suicide should be commended when her life becomes too inconvenient for herself or others. The denial of death, he would say, feeds into the erosion of this sense of the intrinsic worth of all humans, and it is Dolson whose "please omit funeral" furthers both.

Irion's perceptive defense of funerals shows how far Americans had come by the 1960s. We had left the world where funerals were automatically understood as religious occasions and were ordered and presided over by clergy in their churches, and where the religious ideas about death were coherent and articulated. The irony is that what replaced this was not a world where "please omit funeral" was the actual practice, where most people did nothing to commemorate the dead, and consequently lived less "barbaric" lives than before. Most continued to do exactly what Dolson (and Jessica Mitford) thought pointless, and sat through funerals filled with the faded-out remnants of earlier religious ideas and images. But it was a world where they were unhappy and confused over what they did, and where the idea that death was itself too "barbaric" to mention flourished. Welcome to the age of silence and denial.

9

The Challenge of New Theologies

If you really reject natural theology you do not stare at the serpent, with the result that it stares back at you, hypnotises you, and is ultimately certain to bite you, but you hit it and kill it as soon as you see it!

—Emil Brunner and Karl Barth, *Natural Theology*, 76

Halfway across the world, and a million miles away spiritually, the early twentieth century was a time of theological ferment and challenge. European religious thought struggled to encounter biblical scholarship, socialism, scientism, trade unions, and a wide range of explicitly antireligious ideologies. While at least during Protestant funerals, American Christians continued to hear Victorian poems, allegories about rose bushes, "heaven as home," and so forth, a whole new world of religious thought was taking shape in Europe. These new theologies were, like so many other movements within Christianity, touted by their advocates as "rediscoveries" and "recoveries" of the Bible and the Reformation. But in other ways, they were new, intentionally disrupting thought patterns and habits from the past. These newer theologies were written in Europe, with the earliest just as World War I got under way, so they are not chronologically later than many American anthologies of sermons we have examined. But they are a blast from another era and another part of the world. It may have taken several decades, but by the 1950s thinkers such as Barth, Brunner, and Tillich were already familiar to students and graduates of divinity schools, which in turn trained the next generation of Christian pastors.

There is an irony in their reception and their impact here. The irony is that whatever the high and serious intentions of such very important theologies, one decided result was a de-emphasis on personal death in the overall understanding of Christianity. And so, perhaps, however wildly unfair this claim may sound, their effect in America was to converge with other factors to hasten the trend toward silence and denial. These theologies turned away from the existing, older language about death, in the interest of expanding Christians' horizons. Yet such a redefinition of Christianity that avoided traditional focus on personal death and afterlife, coming when it did, contributed to a religious rationale for silence and denial. This occurred even as it opened up many possibilities for Christians to say something relevant and important on other topics.

On the other hand, it nevertheless makes sense to claim that these newer theologians were "better," and that their efforts to replace the conventional otherworldliness of heaven as home and of "natural immortality" were a step forward. Advocates of newer theologies argued that "better" here meant more authentically "biblical," and it is true that they drew on the ideas of critical biblical scholarship, albeit selectively. By midcentury if not much earlier, no one who paid attention to biblical scholarship would have been happy with the conventional funeral use of that Zechariah passage about playing children, for instance. For the representatives of the new theologies, this passage—and many others like it—belonged within the framework of "salvation history," although theologians argued intensely about the relation of this history to "history" as this is conventionally defined. But gone, altogether gone, was the automatic otherworldly allegorization of "Jerusalem" into a personal heavenly afterlife, so prevalent and undisputed in the American sermons. While the goals and methods of "biblical theology" have been questioned, criticisms of its premises and methods do not include regret or nostalgia for what immediately preceded it (see Kelsey).

But "better" has an additional meaning for us. Just as important as their intent to recover the Bible's full meaning was the newer theologians' effort to respond to the large-scale events of their own century, and to the challenges of their own contemporary history. The Christian preacher should hold the Bible in one hand, and the newspaper in his other—and read both. This was not unprecedented. Although funeral sermons were not the place to display such concerns, nineteenth- and early twentieth-century social gospel movements had also worked to connect the gospel to social and political concerns here on earth. In this effort, it was possible to show that the kingdom of God could refer to better lives for the poor here on earth. But it is striking how seldom such concerns enter the world of early twentieth-century funerals, and how the taste for Victorian poetry and echoes of domestic piety remain the norm there.

In contrast, the newer voices spoke with a tremendous sense of urgency and crisis. They tried to answer how Christians should respond to various secular political ideologies, especially totalitarian systems. They wondered if the Marxist vision of a "classless society" corresponded to, or falsely imitated, the true Christian hope for the future. Underlying these questions, these theologians raised the possibility that Christian faith does not deal exclusively with individual and personal history and identity, but speaks to the destiny of nations and collectivities. If so, then it is urgent to know how to talk about large-scale events and issues without conflating the gospel with nationalism or European imperialism. When we move into the world where these questions are the ones theologians address, we are very far away from the piety of "before silence and denial." And, by the way, this is not because one set of authors were "head tripping" academic theologians uninterested in the church, while the others were truly hands-on pastors. No, the reform of the church, and an intense interest in preaching as encounter with the living word of God, was central to the newer vision.

These theologians referred to themselves (or were labeled) as Neo-Orthodox, just as Roman Catholic equivalent thinkers were Neo-Thomists. The "neo" meant that there really was something *new* about them, but in both cases they wished to stress a fundamental link to the past, "Orthodoxy." In the case of all Protestants, that past is going to center on the Bible, but it also included Luther and Calvin and the original depth of theological reflection attributed to the Reformation. So, thinking "Neo-Reformation" might be even more helpful as a label, were we interested in how Barth, Brunner, and others restored a sense of "the Church" rather than of many different churches and denominations. But in regard to our topic, the specific tie with the Reformation may not be so important, and antagonism to other long-standing assumptions and teachings (including those of Calvin, for example) was probably more noticeable. When thinkers influenced by existentialism and Marxism wrote about "the Christian view of man," or "the biblical sense of history," they said something new and disruptive, very, very different from Neumann's *When Death Speaks* or *Sowing with Tears, Reaping with Joy*. Curiously, the title of a much later, post–death-awareness-movement pastors' manual for funerals, *A Trumpet in Darkness* (Hughes, 1985), much better describes their intention. The gospel message was like a trumpet, sounding powerfully and surprisingly in the darkness of the human condition and contemporary history. In this chapter, we do not dwell on the differences and particular positions of theologians, but present a composite portrait of their agenda, their attempt to hear and respond to the divine trumpet blown in darkness.

For no longer did "Death speak," nor was generic human intuition a safe ground from which to build a vision of human hopes for an afterlife. "Revelation" or "the word of God" spoke, and human beings were supposed to listen and respond. (For a good presentation of this issue, see Linwood Urban's *A Short History of Christian Thought* chaps. 7 and 8.) The starting point was God, and God is "other," discontinuous with what we or any group of humans might create. The "what" of what God says is overwhelmed by the presence and self-revelation of God as God; this, and not information about God, is what the Bible opens for us. One of Barth's titles, "The Strange New World within the Bible" (in *Word of God, Word of Man*, 1957) puts this marvelously. The Bible is really "strange" when it is heard aright. It does not sound like our most treasured natural yearnings, it cuts through them, or decisively tells them, and us, "No." It has no automatic link with Victorian poems, or with any human creative efforts. "Revelation" comes in from beyond or outside or above wherever we are, and this includes our "religious" places and emotions. Our religion, our images of God: these are *ours*, and bear all the marks of our twisted, distorted, and rebellious imaginations. Interestingly, this division between "revelation" (God's) and "religion" (ours) could freely be applied to the text of the Bible itself. The New Testament churches were in their day as much into "religion" as were those of Germany in the early 1900s. For example, it made sense to Karl Barth not just to ask "Did the first Christians baptize infants?" (a historical question for biblical scholars to answer) but *should* they have, in light of the deepest implications of Christian faith based on revelation. His answer: no, they should not have. Maybe even Paul, let alone his readers, did not get the full meanings of what was really going on. As this example shows, those who mistook such theologians for "biblical literalists" or "fundamentalists" (two terms of dubious usefulness, in this and many other contexts) really did not understand how these newer theologies worked. Intensely aware of history, they were the last people to fantasize that anyone could time warp back to the first century of the common era, or to imagine that any merely historical era was the gold standard for all others. Yet "revelation" as they understood it did concern history, and large-scale history at that.

From this stance, the story of the Bible is the story of "salvation history." God's transcendent otherness engages in the lives and destinies of a particular people, and Jesus Christ is the divine mediator, the central linking point where all earthly histories find meaning. He is never merely the individual "proof" of a more general truth such as natural immortality. Nor did God stop being interested in "peoples" at the end of the Old Testament; God extends "salvation history" so as to make clear how it encompasses universal, cosmic ultimate reality. Within that framework, "salvation" points toward a completion of creation, and indeed the whole action of God might be described as one giant ACT rather than divisible into first creation, then salvation, then consummation. Even such a scheme was still "salvation history" rather than focused on an entirely atemporal Platonic realm of divine reality. The God of Abraham, Isaac, and Jacob was not the same as the God of the philosophers, and not the same as the God whose dealings with humans on earth were restricted to their eternal, disembodied, and isolated souls. "Platonism" became a kind of insult, while "Hebraic" faith and categories were its opposite, the positive pole versus such falsely etherialized and dehistoricized visions of the self and of God.

We will have much to say about some specific applications of this dichotomy to the question of death. Note, however, the value judgments given to both poles. "Hebraic" thought is dynamic, revelatory, concerned (as these theologians were) with change and history. "Greek" or "Platonic" thought is static, metaphysical, indifferent to real historical existence. An earlier era of Christian thought sometimes found the worst aspects of the Bible, its most "primitive" features, to be tied to its "Hebraic" legacy, while its more enlightened and universal qualities could be linked to its "Greek" influences. Now, the plus-minus values of these two choices were reversed. Perhaps this reassessment of Christianity's "Hebraic" legacy was tied to a new sensitivity to Christian anti-Semitism. But the Hebraic versus Greek dichotomy continues as a theological strategy even into the second half of the twentieth century. When Moltmann criticized an earlier generation of Christian Neo-Orthodox thinkers such as Brunner, "Platonists" was about the worst thing he could think to call them (1965)! Existentialism, the philosophy that provided some of the underpinnings for their systematic thought, looked too contaminated by Platonism, to him and others of this ilk. Its philosophy seemed to continue the long-standing Western tradition of an isolated inward individual whose salvation lies in ignoring any of the material conditions and societal processes around him or her in favor of a dehistoricized inward self. Edith Wyschogrod's powerful critique of the Western "authenticity paradigm" for the self is an even more recent version of this idea (see *Spirit in Ashes*).

For our purposes, it is not entirely relevant to question how literally historically accurate this "Hebraic" versus "Greek" division was, within the world of Hellenized Judaism at the start of the common era (Nickelsburg and Cooper both review this question). Here, the many contributions of this era of "new theologies" can be focused upon two themes: the sense of the "otherness" of revelation, contrasted to the indigenous possibility of humans, and the thorough redefinition of "eschatology," or "last things." To summarize a whole era's theological contributions with the respect these deserve is impossible here, and if what follows sounds like a caricature, it is aimed to reveal some basic, pervading negations of the versions of Christianity where the Bible and "Crossing the Bar" intermingled. Because we look at Protestant theology here, it is not intrinsic to our treatment to include seemingly parallel efforts by Roman Catholics to invigorate and rediscover Thomism, or to engage with modern philosophical thought, as Maritain, Rahner, or Lonergan did.

Books by Protestant theologians speaking for the newer, Neo-Orthodox movement, regularly begin with a contrast between the "theological anthropology of the Bible" and all alternatives from various modern secular movements. "Theological anthropology" or "doctrine of man" was an abstract but vividly relevant category. Here I keep the original gendered language, not because I believe the views we discuss apply only to males (although this has been suggested) but to keep a sense of the historical distance between the Neo-Orthodox and the present, a distance that now extends to almost one hundred years. When they wrote of "the Christian doctrine of man" some favorite contrasts were to the naturalist/scientific view of man that reduces him to organic processes within nature, or to instinct and biological drives. The other modern opponent was the Marxist view that sees man at the mercy of historical/economic forces; these operate as inevitably and inflexibly as "laws." This view claimed to take "history" seriously, yet paradoxically absolutized and departicularized it, eliminating human freedom in the process.

The "Christian view of man" was of a being paradoxically "in God's image," and yet sinful through and through. He is sinful not because of personal misdeeds, but because of basic existential anxieties, envy, and hatred of God. Beneath these is the hidden and disguised desire to replace God as the center of the universe. So deep was "sin" in this sense, that even the claim to be "in God's image" might no longer hold without qualification. The issue for the early twentieth century had become, were we as humans still in any real way "in God's image," or was this image now shattered beyond recognition? Could we achieve any "natural" knowledge of God on our own? This was not a question that the literal text of the Bible answered, and none of those who asked it were at all committed to Adam and Eve as "historical" persons. This is a philosophical/theological question, and an urgent one. A famous debate on just this point between Barth and Brunner (published in English as *Natural Theology*) illustrates just how far their shared language was from the world of Andrew Blackwood and his "problem funerals" for known sinners. The issue was never over bad individual behavior, or over any of the pathetic sleazy sins pastors had in mind when they funeralized dead drunkards, prostitutes, or even suicides. The historical context for the debate over the "divine image" was how thoroughly any human community qua human community could claim to know and represent the divine will, or unequivocally be the bearer of divine destiny. The claim of the Nazis that German history participated in something "sacred" and ultimate should be rejected. Yes, but if one allowed that some "divine image" remained, then perhaps some national or ideological movement could ride its coattails, so to speak. Something humans could create "in history" was directly "divine." Brunner had not advocated anything like this, but Barth was sure that once the snake was allowed to hypnotize, it would surely bite. The door to "natural theology" was opened a crack, in would troop all the worst, most idolatrous claims of their era's evil possibilities. Hence, his answer to the question of "natural" knowledge of God, was a resounding "No!" "Human nature" must be shown to be utterly contaminated by sin, our original created tie to God unbridgeable by us. Nothing in us could truly unsinfully reach out to God; the saving movement came entirely from the Other.

And yet, paradoxically, this view of human nature certainly has a definite grandeur about it. Brunner and Barth both participated in it, even when they disagreed bitterly. Sinful, yet not in sleazy, sordid backstreet ways. Sinful in our intellectual and moral accomplishments and heights, sinful even in our humanitarian efforts and our highest cultural pursuits. Sin in this vision, this theological anthropology, is *hubris*, pride in overstepping our own creatureliness. It is not cheating on one's income tax or one's spouse. Thus, "the Christian view of man" was actually more heroic than that of scientists who insist that man is merely a natural organism, with no claims to transcend nature and no capacity to go beyond its possibilities. Freud was a target here, of course. But so were many earlier views attributed to science, or rather to "scientism," the philosophy that turns the legitimate empirical inquiry of scientists into a pretentious all-encompassing worldview. ("Scientism" in this sense has made a comeback in the works of some evolutionary psychologists and cognitive neuroscientists. Barth and Brunner would be as hostile to this as they were to earlier editions of these ideas, while remaining entirely supportive to the factual claims of biology about evolution, or of astronomy to questions of the age of the solar system.)

Much more vigorous and immediately dangerous opponents than scientism, however, were those ideologies that fueled nationalism and totalitarian politics. Both Nazis and Communists claimed that "human nature" had all its reality within the sphere of this worldly collectivities, and both laughed at the Christian focus on the individual. This, theologian Thielicke was to note, made it so easy for these ideologies to glorify death (xxiv–xxvi) . But these political movements rested on visions of history—such as the one-thousand-year Reich promised by Hitler—which were themselves idolatrous false religions, with false hopes for "last things." Such religions promised triumph over finitude and death, and so became themselves evidence of sin rampant, albeit decked out as inevitable historical "progress" (Brunner, 1954, 15ff.). These ideologies were more evil than liberal Enlightenment democracy, but it too placed idolatrous hopes in the capacities of humans to go beyond our own inherent limits, and effect progress.

For all theologies of this era, the notion of "progress" received special contempt. By the end of World War I any shred of hope that European Christian civilization could produce "progress" in transforming human nature had been smashed, and looked as illusory as a promise to teach a pig to fly. For what was so wrong with "progress" as an ideal and a hope was its underlying hubris.

> Belief in the progress of humanity has therefore had a short life. . . . In the ecstasy of its enthusiasm about the stupendous success of science and technics, and its emancipation from the fetters of feudal authoritarianism, Western humanity has deified formal freedom based on man's natural reason and has confidently expected this combination of freedom and reason to usher in the millennium. (Brunner, 1954, 24)

The promise of even the most democratic vision of progress was not just better housing or health care, or universal suffrage; behind these specifics (which theologians accepted as helpful) was the dream to establish the kingdom of heaven here on earth, by our own efforts, and according to our own design. In their rebuttal of these hopes, the Neo-Orthodox insisted that there never was a truly "divine" nation or political system. In the Old Testament, kingship was always balanced by prophecy, and the message of the prophets was antithetical to any version of ancient Near Eastern "divine kingship." We must remember that this is the Bible read through early twentieth-century lenses, by persons already ultrasuspicious of nationalisms. (The German example was the most relevant by the 1930s, but there were already parallel attempts to conflate "Christian" values and the spread of the kingdom with the expansion of the British and French colonial empires.)

Much of this goes very far afield from our focus on death; that is in fact our precise point. These theologies redrew the map, redefined what mattered. Whether it was in dealing with political ideologies, or the doctrine of the church as more than an aggregate of saved individuals, or almost any other topic, the result was a sense of "over-againstness" between the Revelation of God and anything humans did or said. This alone might not have killed off poetry in funerals. But it does eliminate "natural immortality" as a trustworthy bridge between what humans intuitively know, and what the Bible "proves." That was exactly the kind of relationship Barth, Brunner, and others spent a lot of effort to demolish. They would have found such ideas completely at odds with the fundamental claim that Jesus Christ alone is *The Mediator* (Brunner's title). If we had such "natural bridges" we would not need a crucified messiah or divine savior to leap over the abyss on our behalf. Plants grow, birds migrate, and caterpillars become butterflies: but all these events are so profoundly irrelevant to the true core of Christian faith that they are beneath mention, not even worthy of refutation as allegories for us.

As for the elimination of Victorian poetry at funerals, Neo-Orthodoxy provided, inadvertently, another rationale for this. We see how a deep mistrust of reliance on human creative efforts to use for sermons would be the stance of Neo-Orthodox preachers. The word of God—Jesus and then also the Bible—should stand as a voice from beyond ours, the trumpet in darkness. We must listen to it as "the strange new world within the Bible" (Barth's fine title) for this is what preaching is all about. This word comes as a trumpet in darkness, unexpected and powerful, and different from ordinary nightly noises. To convey this strangeness the poetry would have to be jarring and unfamiliar, precisely what the Victorian poems heard at funerals were not. I am uncertain if the problem was that any poems at all would have been viewed negatively, as somehow in competition with the Bible rather than augmenting its impact. But when "natural immortality" and other "natural" capacities are no longer smooth entry points leading into Christian faith, then most of the poetry favored by editors of funeral resources would have been entirely unsuitable. Maybe Wallace Stevens, Rainer Maria Rilke, or T. S. Eliot wrote poetry suited to this message—but such poems just are not recitable by an American mainline Protestant preacher at a funeral. One might more suitably quote Kierkegaard, Dostoyevsky, or Camus, whose philosophical existentialism somehow captured the jarring and unfamiliar and meaning-challenged world of modern persons. Given this theological attack on "natural" continuities of all kinds, one can imagine Barth or Brunner forced to sit out a funeral where "The Rose Still Grows Beyond the Wall" was integrated into the sermon. Both would grind their teeth in angry frustration at the effrontery of its message.

The second major disjunction between what had come earlier and what Neo-Orthodox theologies offered was the redefinition of "eschatology" and its role in biblical faith. The term itself means "the doctrine of last things," and traditionally it had been a minor topic in the range of those covered by a systematic theologian. Eschatology had not been a high priority for Schleiermacher when he wrote the first "liberal" systematic theology in 1831 (*The Christian Faith*). Nor had most of the early twentieth-century American Protestant pastors thought very much about how "last things" could be revisioned so as to go beyond the set of ideas we have already examined; at least, there is no direct evidence of such reflection in the text of their anthologized funeral sermons. Mainline Protestants were not "premillenialists," not tolerant of or interested in the details of various "dispensations," or disputes over how to calculate the texts of the biblical book of Revelation with modern events. This is the version of "last things" that seems to have been elaborated in the nineteenth century by various nonmainline groups such as Millerites and Seventh-day Adventists. Later, by the end of that century, the scheme of serial "dispensations" continued this fascination, and ironically it is this which today has received a major revival and lots of publicity. Details of "the Rapture" and the future fate of *The Late, Great Planet Earth* and of those *Left Behind* are really interesting to many contemporary Christians. But these approaches were of no interest to Barth or Brunner or any of their cohort. They did not want to place "the end times" as a set of events within chronological ordinary history. Brunner explicitly mentioned possible future ice ages, for example—only to reject any such ideas as entirely irrelevant to the *Eternal Hope* he wrote about (1954, 120ff.).

Instead, "last things" did point toward "salvation history," God's ultimate intention beyond time yet linked to it. Sometimes "existential ultimacy" replaced all references to temporality, so that "eschatology" lost the implicit meaning of "last" and simply began to mean "deepest," or "most foundational." This was the direction that Paul Tillich's theology took, which once again made him vulnerable to the charges of the next generation that "Platonism" secretly infected his theology. Even when complete detemporalizing did not happen, the category expanded so that "eschatology" became an umbrella for a whole cluster of theological concerns, no longer one topic out of many. Books such as Hans Schwartz's *On the Way to the Future* imperialistically take this approach. Moltmann's *Theology of Hope*, a far better and much more original work, essentially does the same thing. Hope and future are the foundation for what theology struggles to express, versus a false and static vision of God as "timeless" and the past as a kind of golden norm.

In this new focus on eschatology as the central core of theological reflection, what got decentered was a concern with personal death, my own or that of another. Brunner's *Eternal Hope* was written, he tells us, to respond as a theologian to the tragic death of his son in a train accident (219). But one would never guess this from the text itself, which remains within the style of Protestant systematic theology (unlike Wolterstorff's *Lament for a Son*, from which we have already quoted).

Eschatology visions the future, so that questions of what future or whose become central. God's future, basically. Not "the Rapture," and not ice ages or global warming (to update Brunner's example). But this theologically well-grounded response could be taken to paradoxically ill-grounded conclusions. *In the End God* by John A. T. Robinson takes this theme of theocentricity to a conclusion neither Barth nor Brunner, let alone any of the earlier preachers, would have accepted.

Namely, that because the only true focus of Christian eschatological hope is God's universal reign, no message regarding personal death is necessary. Focusing on this, or even inclusion of any messages about it, is a distraction from a focus on God's future and therefore becomes selfish idolatry. Robinson notes how an earlier generation held that without belief in a future life, humans would live without ethics or hope.

> This strikes the contemporary humanist, whether Christian or not, as not only incredible but immoral. If this is all that keeps a man responsible, then he is less than responsible. Morality must be self-authenticating or nothing; it must validate itself because it is true, whatever the consequences for the individual. . . . I believe this is a healthy

> perspective, and that in this matter we are truer to the Biblical outlook than many of our forefathers. (Robinson, 24–25)

We are interested in ourselves when we seek "eternal life," not God. Our personal deaths and any—improbable—afterlives are simply not what the authentic gospel is about.

> The doctrine of the resurrection of the body is misunderstood if it is regarded as a preview of what the future holds in store for the individual. Information about this no more forms part of the Christian revelation than prognostication about the end of history. Of course, something must actually happen to the individual, just as the world must end in one way and not in another. But it is not the function of Christian theology in either case to assert what this will be. (Robinson, 101)

Therefore, individual death is no longer a worthy theological topic, and concern with an afterlife is submoral because it is self-interested. These remarkable conclusions led to many complaints when this mid-1960s book first appeared. This English bishop trashed all traditional Christian hopes for an afterlife!

But when many decades later we look back on this, the reason for a sense of outrage may be different. Not how Robinson could destroy traditional conventional piety, in this oversimplified version of some Neo-Orthodox preoccupations. But how cleverly he managed to put Christianity in the service of his own era's silence and denial of death. He made that silence and denial seem not just more "healthy" in regard to the gospel message, but more in step with what contemporary persons would find relevant and credible. Robinson read the newspaper as well as the Bible, and the newspaper was very likely to report "please omit funeral." Robinson's message was not typical of Neo-Orthodoxy or theological existentialism. But this extreme instance does reveal one consequence of a Christian commitment to expanded "transhistorical" eschatology. It excused and condoned the silence and denial by then surrounding personal death. It erased the legitimacy of any concern with personal mortality, as a "sub-Christian" selfish preoccupation. So Christians could join the crowd who found funerals "barbaric" and all thought about death (one's own or anyone else's) too depressing and "unhopeful." How totally ironic!

This was not the Neo-Orthodox intention. It was not the intention of any existentialist thinkers, religious or otherwise, who may have served as sources for Neo-Orthodoxy. But it shows how denial of death can take many odd forms, can be justified even using theological frameworks. This example tragically adds support to the very doctrine of sin that Neo-Orthodoxy promoted. We want to escape our mortality and creaturehood, we want to be ourselves divine and at the center of things. Our own deaths, "last things" on earth for us, can be avoided by magnificent "religious" reasoning. Denial becomes masked as God-centered altruism, a higher, self-authenticating morality. This was a new kind of denial, too. Not that of "heaven our Home" and "natural immortality," which certainly had given space to death, but a new kind that intentionally said *nothing*. Ironically, this was made to seem more "authentically Christian" than any attention to personal death and dying.

Given this as one admittedly extreme and oversimplified result, it remains true that Neo-Orthodoxy had more to say on Marxism, scientism, and the hubris of "progress" than on the topic of death. It is not surprising that when an attempt to overcome silence and denial in regard to death began, it did not come directly from theologians. It came from those who worked with the dying and the bereaved. It included chaplains, right from the beginning, but they wisely left Barth—let alone Robinson—at the door to the hospital room. Neo-Orthodoxy had not offered a full replacement for the older language and images, whatever its original intentions. Selfish or not by theological criteria such as Robinson's, people were still interested in their own deaths, and those of others near to them. Natural immortality might have faded, and been theologically discredited, but saying nothing—or "please omit funeral"—was never truly a Christian option.

10

Death as Enemy

Where, O death, is your victory?
Where, O death is your sting?

—1 Corinthians 15:55 (quoting Hosea 13:14)

Recall one of the titles for a sermon collection early in the twentieth century: *When Death Speaks*. When Death spoke, the message was one of "natural immortality," and of the link between the living and the recently dead. What went unnoticed at the time was that Death was a personification, who could "speak." It went unnoticed because this was a long-standing convention in Western culture, and particularly present in much of the poetry that the preacher included in his sermons. There is no sign that anyone, in the early 1900s or before, would have objected to this, or felt it was strange or fanciful. Within and beyond the sermons, Death was conventionally referred to as "the King of Terrors" and "the Grim Reaper," depicted with a scythe. Today, one rarely finds this imagery outside of Halloween. It is no longer in sermons, it is certainly not in greeting cards or Internet memorials, and the poetry that kept it alive has also disappeared. Curiously, while these images vanished from sermons, a new use of "personified death" appeared, right along with the theological challenges we looked at in the previous chapter.

Let us be clear: even when Christian pastors continued to use this image of personified Death, their message of heaven as home and of "natural immortality" completely outweighed what they said about Death as evil, threatening old man. There was no evocation of the skeletal figure with the scythe, no picturing of "Death" at all. No questioning why Death should so consistently be male, either. The whole motif of personified Death was a conventional legacy, but no longer one that seemed to genuinely capture Christian imagination. Even when "Death spoke," there were no "dialogues with Death" in any of the sermons, little rhetorical mileage gained out of the personification. A Christian pastor of the early twentieth century such as Blackwood would have considered most of the traditional Death imagery morbid, insufficiently hopeful. Even the most somber, doctrinal warning sermons ("Are you living under the power of the world to come?") did not try to evoke pictures of Death the macabre, leading his Dance of Death that included all classes and kinds of persons.

Suppose someone had asked any of these preachers to justify their continued use of this rhetorical device of personification. There is no sign anyone did, but the answer to this unasked question would have been to cite the above verses from Paul, along with his earlier "[t]he last enemy to be destroyed is death" (1 Cor 15:26). But no one in the early twentieth century raised questions about the appropriateness of this imagery, and its diminution was already under way by the time immediately "before silence and denial." Significantly, the Pauline verses become much more common and central as a sermon text after cultural silence and denial had set in. This is the story we examine in this chapter.

The personification of death did not just fade away gently. It—or something potentially resembling it—received a new burst of life, from the writing of a theologian whose influence outweighs that of Barth or Brunner, in his challenge to earlier theologies of death. He disrupted the earlier imagery we have already examined, and unequivocally attacked many of the assumptions that had dominated and guided it. What burst onto the scene, mid-century, was a blast against "natural immortality," and against the ethos where personal death and the afterlife destiny of the soul was the central theme of Christian preaching.

This blast came from Swiss biblical scholar and theologian Oscar Cullmann, who lambasted Christians for their substitution of popular Platonism for the message of the New Testament about death. For Cullmann, that authentic Christian message is that death is the enemy of God, and Jesus' resurrection is a "victory" over an enemy. For Christians postresurrection, death still exists, but as a "defeated enemy." Moreover, Christianity may have made use of body/soul dualism, but was at its core holistic, committed to the resurrection of the body, and so of the entire person. A radically negative view of death went together with a radically different theological anthropology.

Cullmann was particularly harsh in his critique of "natural immortality."

> For the first Christians the soul is not intrinsically immortal, but rather became so only through the resurrection of Jesus Christ, and through faith in him. (11)

Moreover, death was never a gentle, upward transition from caterpillar to butterfly; it was a horrifying terrible annihilation. Until Jesus' defeat of death, and in and of itself even today, death was the enemy of God and the enemy of all of us, naturally and appropriately to be feared. We will examine and unpack this radically unsettling view, which directly attacked the mainstays of previous Christian ideas and images.

However startling and powerful Cullmann's theology was, he never actually took full advantage of death's personification as an enemy. Death was not "Death," there was no dialogue between Jesus as victor and Death as defeated foe. Cullmann could have written such, he could have exaggerated his portrait of a cosmic battle by dramatizing Death's defeat. Another early to mid-twentieth-century theologian, Gustav Aulén, had accomplished this, by his depiction of classic ancient atonement theology as *Christus Victor*. According to Aulén the ancient church fathers had proposed a vision of cosmic battle and defeat of Satan in order to explain how God effected salvation through Jesus Christ. Cullmann, like Aulén, reveled in the imagery of military victory. But although he freely relies on "enemy" language, Cullmann avoided exploiting its full implications. Perhaps the device of personification was already too archaic, too remote from daily use, to help him convey his more basic point. A truly medieval-style confrontation and encounter with Death would have been almost (but not entirely—as we'll shortly see) unimaginable, especially as death's terror, horror, and exclusion grew stronger amid the fading of older imagery.

Cullmann's specific ideas and arguments did not arise in a cultural or theological vacuum. These came from the same milieu of European rethinking that led to a focus on "salvation history," on God's utter transcendence, on the need for Christ as the one mediator, and on the expansion and redefinition of "eschatology." Cullmann took these themes, and applied them directly to the view of death in the New Testament, hoping to smash past conventions and religious assumptions about what was truly "biblical." The original Cullmann lecture, "Immortality of the Soul or Resurrection of the Dead?" may have been stated as early as 1943 in French, but it appeared in *Harvard Divinity School Bulletin* (vol. 21, 1955–1956), and was then reprinted in the 1965 edited volume *Immortality and Resurrection.* Cullmann's presentation was delivered as an Ingersoll Lecture, an endowed series established in 1894 on the topic of "The Immortality of Man." (Somewhat ironically, given what he says about this idea!) Clearly the time was ripe for something new to be said, something to replace older, worn-out "natural immortality" imagery. Yet whether Cullmann's contribution was ultimately a help (for pastors? for mourners?) or a hindrance to a better theology of death is not to be decided easily. In light of our concerns, it is possible that Cullmann's "death as God's enemy" approach played right into heroic militaristic imagery in medicine, and an overall cultural suppression of death, the era of silence and denial.

While personification remains implicit, the militarism of Cullmann's model is unquestionable. By the time the lecture was delivered in English Cullmann could use the analogy that Christ's defeat of death was like "the decisive battle," yet "V-day is yet to come" (33). D-day and V-day; in short, World War II had become part of the theologian's imaginative storehouse. How far from imagery of heaven as home, or the peaceful sea voyage of "Crossing the Bar"! Along with this went the radically different sense of biblical eschatology we discussed in the previous chapter, where personal death no longer took center stage. It was swallowed up in victory, Christ's victory at the end of time, and therefore put into the wider context of a universal consummation of history and creation. After the large-scale events of two world wars, it seemed that Christianity too should proclaim a large-scale vision, including the defeat of death the last enemy. Unlike Robinson, however, Cullmann believed that personal death could be fit somehow within this picture, rather than just ignored altogether. But Cullmann's direct target was the older imagery that now appeared too cozy and domestic, too small scale for a world of mass death and destruction. This was an important part of Cullmann's appeal.

Cullmann eloquently made the case against "immortality of the soul," the belief that had for so long been considered the core of Christian faith. His lecture begins with a vivid and dramatic contrast between the deaths of Socrates and of Jesus (12–18). Socrates, confident in his soul's immortality, calmly drank the poison, and met death peacefully as "a friend." He knows it will liberate his soul from the body, an encumbrance to existence in the realm of ideal forms.

> Socrates goes to his death in complete peace and composure. The death of Socrates is a beautiful death. Nothing is seen here of death's terror. . . . Death is the soul's great friend. (14)

In contrast, Jesus is afraid of death and begs his Father to be spared from it. Jesus knew the true horror and terror of death. "This is not 'death as a friend.' This is death in all its frightful horror. This is really '*the last enemy of God*'" (17, emphasis in original). Yes, and Jesus was afraid of death, says Cullmann.

> Jesus is afraid, though not as a coward would be of the men who will kill him, still less of the pain and grief which precede death. He is afraid in the face of death itself. Death for him is not something divine; it is something dreadful. (15)

This is the heart of Cullmann's message. He speaks the unspeakable: death is not a homecoming, it is not "growing through the crack in the wall," and there is no Christian assurance of natural immortality. The words "horror" and "terror" and "dreadful" are repeated over and over, as Cullmann drives home a contrast not just with Plato, but with the vast majority of conventional Christian words on death and afterlife. The hundreds of sermons that had conflated Socrates and Jesus, whose message was of "natural immortality" as a universal intuitive truth, were just plain wrong.

What defeats death is Jesus' resurrection by God. This is a totally "unnatural" miraculous event, establishing a new situation. This is our situation, and ours is an "interim" time (between D-day and V-day); it is this that Paul proclaims in 1 Corinthians 15. Jesus' resurrection is the promise for our own, but the latter has not yet happened. Moreover, Cullmann intentionally uses the Pauline language of "those who sleep" (36) and therefore who remain "on hold" until the day of Christ, yet to come. This "intermediate state" is what he believes to be the most authentic New Testament teaching on what follows death. It is not the same as "immortality of the soul," for our hope will include eventual whole personhood, transformed embodiment. Moreover, as the "sleep" image retained by Cullmann implies, the amount of consciousness and capacity for experience among the dead is not very high, and speculation about this goes directly against what a Christian's proper focus should be (45). Gone, therefore, will be all scenes of "reunions" (family or otherwise) in heaven, along with children playing in the streets of Jerusalem. Cullmann allows that perhaps the traditional belief in "the immortality of the soul" might approximate what Christians hope for (44)—but then contrasts the two beliefs, resurrection versus immortality, and declares that the New Testament's advocacy of one and rejection of the other is "unequivocal" (47).

As if this were not enough, Cullmann in the "Afterword" to his original lecture notes and responds to his critics. This section, published in 1956, shows that French and German Christians of the day were just as horrified by his attack on their piety as their American counterparts. They accused him of serving up stones instead of bread (47) and of causing "astonishment, sorrow and deep distress" (48). "This remarkable agreement seems to show how widespread is the mistake of attributing to primitive Christianity the Greek belief in the immortality of the soul" (48), he concludes. Such outraged letters from pastors and laypeople do not impress Cullmann because they are not based on objective exegetical findings, but on desires to hold onto beliefs we find consoling.

> Does it not belong to the greatness of our Christian faith . . . that we do not begin from our personal desires but place our resurrection within

> the framework of a cosmic redemption and of a new creation of the universe? (51)

Thus, traditional popular Platonism is not only bad biblical interpretation, but based on wish fulfillment—and small-scale wish fulfillment at that. Here, Cullmann sounds something like Robinson, or even something like Freud. At least he sounds utterly different from the authors of volumes such as *When Death Speaks*. Their argument for "natural immortality" was that it intuitively suited us, it was a universal built-in instinctual hope. For Cullmann, this cuts no ice at all. If anything, this is the kind of argument he can demolish via his Socrates versus Jesus contrast. Revelation does not fulfill preexisting universal hopes, it is truly and radically "other" than these. Maybe we cannot share the faith of the primitive church, Cullmann concedes, but this is different from distorting it to suit our desires.

In previous writings, I argued against Cullmann and his baleful influence on subsequent Christian theological engagement and dialogue with the death awareness movement (Bregman, 1992, 124ff.). But here, having looked at the era before silence and denial, I find Cullmann's voice comes as a breath of fresh air. Read through countless sermons that rely exclusively on "natural immortality," or on images of heaven as home, and one might ask, "Oscar Cullmann, where were you when we needed you? Wouldn't it have been a relief to hear that the Lord hated, rather than 'willed' death? That death is something *bad*?" By the 1950s, it seems, the Protestant Christian community was still not quite ready to hear his message, hence the need for his rebuttal to their protests on behalf of traditional "immortality of the soul" piety.

But by this time, American society as a whole was committed to the view of death as bad, of the defeat of death through medicine, and to the view we have labeled "please omit funeral": that death and all connected to it was too morbid and meaningless to allow space for at all. In this climate, leftover Platonism no longer cut any ice, and at least some people were indeed prepared to listen to Cullmann. More than those of any of the other European theologians who challenged traditional religious sensibilities, his ideas became part of American Protestant imagery about death. Theologically trained pastors accepted the centrality of "death as God's enemy," and soon one finds this theme of

"Christian victory over death" as one of the newer cluster of ideas. The text from Paul serving as the motto for this chapter replaces Zechariah's playing children and King David's refusal to mourn to guide funeral sermons (see, e.g., Joyce's *The Pastor and Grief*). Even when the liturgical emphasis was on resurrection "victory" the underlying assumption was that death in and of itself was a terror, and we Americans were correct in our heightened anxiety over it.

From hindsight, we may ask what Cullmann did accomplish. And what did he distort, ignore, or deny in the process. We can ask if his portrait of the New Testament's view of death is "accurate," based on actual exegesis as he claims. This has been extensively debated, and the arguments summarized in John Cooper's *Body, Soul and the Life Everlasting*. The huge amount of scholarship on this topic shows how influential Cullmann's thesis has been. Moreover, it helps to remember that the key texts for this discussion—the four canonical Gospels and Plato's dialogues—were available to everyone, and have been continuously so. No new discoveries, such as the Dead Sea Scrolls or the gnostic gospels, really affected the basic terms of the debate. So, even the question of how different or how alike were the deaths of Socrates and Jesus is not based on historical-critical scholarship alone, but on prior assumptions about what death is *really* like. So, while Jesus meets his death in agony and abandonment in Mark's and Matthew's Gospels, the same is not true for Luke's and John's. In other words, the four canonical accounts that we have—and the only accounts Cullmann or anyone could use—are divided on the exact emotional state of Jesus at the time of his dying. Preference for one set of texts over the other is just that: a preference based on our sensibilities, which favor "agony and abandonment" as more realistic. The ancient church wisely kept all four accounts, side by side, rather than editing out these and other inconsistencies.

Even more important, I believe, is the fact that Cullmann himself supplies the words "horror," "terror," and "dreadful" to his vivid narrative. These words are not in the Gospels, they are not in Paul, they are not in the New Testament at all in the passages Cullmann cites. Yes, "enemy" is there in Paul's 1 Corinthians 15, although its second appearance is a quote from Hosea, and no modern interpreter wants to incorporate Hosea's original context (God's anger against the north Kingdom of Israel) into Christian theology directly. It is revealing that Cullmann's critics did not point this out, nor did they apparently suggest that his—and others'—contemporary sensibilities made death into something more "dreadful" than it had been before. Yet the emotional and rhetorical power of his presentation seems to rely on this reality, as a background factor in how he reads the New Testament. Hence, Mark's and Matthew's passion scenes strike modern persons, including obviously Cullmann, as "more realistic"; Jesus' dying is worse in these.

To continue with our scrutiny of the historical accuracy of Cullmann, if one were to read through the New Testament, the Gospels particularly, and ask the question "Does God have a personified enemy?" the answer would be "yes." It is Satan, whom Jesus sees "fall like lightning from heaven" (Luke 10:18). God's enemies are also the many demons who know the secret of Jesus' Messiahship, and whom he defeats repeatedly in the stories of exorcisms (e.g., Mark 5:6ff.). These are real, personified enemies. They speak, they try to make bargains, they are loathsome, degraded, and corrupt beings, and they degrade and corrupt those whom they control. They appear as well in Acts, and as "powers and principalities" in Paul. The book of Revelation also elaborates this, as the dragon, "that ancient serpent called the devil, or Satan, who leads the whole world astray" (Rev 12:9). There is no lack of enemy language, and dramatic contest and battle scenes here. Military images are central to all of this. This was the imagery Aulén rediscovered in the ancient church thinkers' understanding of atonement. But the personified enemy(ies) is not "death."

So, to take up Cullmann's own striking image, Christ's D-day is over Satan, but the promise of the gospel is that eventually, there will be a V-day, a complete victory. Those Christians who in the 1970s and after brought back this Christian imagery of evil would say that this is "authentically New Testament," and they would be right. It is really there, as Cullmann's "death personified" is not. I do not want to imply that every contemporary use of "demonic" imagery is valid or helpful, or that the New Testament itself does not set limits on the presence and activity of spiritual evil. There is no indication, for instance, that all of the illnesses Jesus healed were caused by demons, or attributed to them by the people of his time. Satan tempts Jesus in the desert, but does not make a direct appearance in the Gethsemane scene, or at the crucifixion (although in the 2004 movie *The Passion of the Christ* he/she does! Hollywood fascination with "supernatural horror" triumphs over the text here). Yet anyone who seeks an enemy for God in the Bible really is not being "objective" in ignoring all this material, and instead fixating on death.

To have asked Cullmann why he ignored demons, and "dreadfulized" death, is to ask a question as foreign to his mid-century era and worldview as his whole approach appeared to the earlier advocates of "natural immortality." Demons represent the "mythological" content of the New Testament, they were part of the ancient Hellenistic world (which, if the Gospels and Acts are any indication, must have suffered from an epidemic of them), but they were not elements of Cullmann's theology; their comeback is a later development, for better and worse. However, if one bases one's case against Platonistic popular Christianity on "authentic New Testament views," as Cullmann claims to have done, then he can easily be criticized for misinterpreting, for overlooking exactly what he finds least believable, credible, and appropriate for post–world wars Christians.

At another level, it is important to turn from the text of the Gospels to the immediate historical context in which Cullmann wrote. For Cullmann, a European, the wartime experience meant a huge amount of ghastly and violent deaths, so different from the deaths of individuals funeralized in more normal times. Moreover, the European war experience meant exposure to an ideology that glorified the death of individuals who sacrificed themselves for the sake of the state. For soldiers anywhere, there may be a certain amount of this, but the ideology of Nazi Germany made this far more explicit. Death was the springboard to glory, the individual was worth nothing in himself until he merged his being into that greater whole of the (undying) Reich. Helmut Thielicke, another theologian of this era, explicitly confronted this ideology, and like Cullmann believed the authentic Christian view of death to be more negative, inglorious, something it was appropriate to fear. Cullmann uses military language of "warfare" versus death, because he was all too familiar with military language used against human enemies, where death was turned into an apotheosis. No wonder he stresses "terror" and "horror." These words are not in the New Testament, they are in a response to the recent past. He, and lots of others who had survived the war, and by 1955 were still coming to terms with its meaning, could not avoid how easily death had been glorified for the worst purposes. Yet unfortunately, when this language traveled into America in the 1950s, it converged with other shifts in sensibility and apprehensions. It could become a kind of justification for our own exaggerated horror and avoidance of death, as neither Cullmann nor any of the other theological challengers ever intended. Of course, Cullmann would not have supported the "please omit funeral" movement; instead, he might have wished a marching band and victorious heroic songs about resurrection at every Christian funeral. This raises the question of how deeply Cullmann really undermined his own era's beliefs about death, or was his underlying message secretly congruent with the era of silence and denial? Perhaps he attacked the recent conventional Christian past, but a past that was already secretly a "vestige" even for Christian believers. For the more official Christian responses to Cullmann took the form of appreciation, and resulted in liturgical reforms that tried to make funerals into occasions of victory and joy over the defeat of death, focused intensely on Jesus' resurrection. This was Cullmann's own intention, and here he would have joined with Blackwood's much earlier claim: Christian funerals are to be hopeful occasions. So, for instance, white and not black was the appropriate color for vestments and church décor. However, Blackwood's somber and restrained idea of "hope" would have been replaced by a much more blatant triumphal spirit, so that at least on the surface, no one could have accused Christian funerals of remaining morbid. But it was not a message that could capture the other side of Cullmann's message: "horror" and "terror" of death were as unthematized as in the days before silence and denial. Besides, pastoral concern for the needs of mourners soon tempered this emphasis on "resurrection triumph," as we shall see.

Cullmann's theme of military victory over death dovetailed exactly with the contemporary hope that medicine's goal was to defeat death. The era of Cullmann's American influence was the era of high-tech medicine's expansion, of its success, and of doctors as heroic figures in the never-ending battle against not just particular causes of death but mortality itself. (See William May's *The Physician's Covenant* for a fine discussion of this imagery's impact on medical ethics.) Death became more ultimately "dreadful," always a negative force, and never "acceptable" under any circumstances. Instead of "Christian resignation" and preparation for one's own inevitable end, one was to opt for death's defeat. While this version of Christian "prolife" thought cannot be attributed solely to Cullmann, echoes of his language and military images survive in argument made for life-prolonging technologies by Christians. If Cullmann is right that death is "something dreadful," then we are morally obligated to oppose it, always and everywhere. No appeal to the "immortality of the soul" will be admitted, since this represents an alien and almost anti-Christian point of view.

Cullmann may not have wanted this. His ideas were not formed by immersion in the problems of life support in the ICU. But during the era of silence and denial, many views of death could be interpreted into making denial seem normal and reasonable. Robert Lifton notes how Freud's very complex views on death and the death instinct were misappropriated by American psychoanalysis to justify ignoring all death imagery and reducing it to sexual concerns (48–50). What triumphs in this co-option of Freud, and Cullmann's vision of the New Testament is actually close to "please omit funeral," a kind of "vitalism." That was Irion's name for the worldview where death cannot tell us anything about ourselves, and is best omitted from our picture of human existence.

On this note, we can turn to a more radical, "foreign," and disrupting alternative from the same era. By contrast to Cullmann, this took religious ideas and imagery and used them in service of a message "barbaric" and horrific by any American standard. The personified figure of Death, no longer in sermons and as a "defeated enemy" for Cullmann, remained among the resources of Western persons' imaginative storehouse, and could be used successfully even in the age of silence and denial. The 1957 movie *The Seventh Seal* by Swedish director Ingmar Bergman was the oddest and yet most successful use of exactly this traditional idea. Here Death spoke, although what he said had no similarity to the lines Protestant funeral preaching had earlier supplied. Nor did it match Cullmann's message of "victory." Far from it.

The movie is set in the fourteenth century in Sweden during the time of the Black Plague. It appears to have been filmed in the fourteenth century as well, an extreme example of non-Hollywood moviemaking. In this film, a knight returned from the Crusades plays a chess game with Death, amid a landscape of violence, chaos, and pain. Death is a spooky white-faced, middle-aged man wrapped in a long black cloak. In one scene he even wields a scythe or saw with which he saws off a tree limb on which one of his victims perches. Bergman had half expected people to laugh at this personification, but the opposite happened. "This is Death," everyone agreed, and accepted it with complete suspension of disbelief.

In the movie's plot, the knight searches for meaning, for knowledge. "What do you know?" he asks Death, delaying the next chess move. "Nothing," Death replies. God is apparently absent, although perhaps the young family who escape from Death—Joseph, Maria, and their baby—symbolize God's lurking invisible presence. Only they escape. Everyone else dies, and a previously mute character pronounces the last words of the film: "It is finished." But it is the final scene we remember. We see all the characters lead by Death, silhouetted against a mountain ridge in the classic "Dance of Death" of that long-ago era. Death, who knew nothing and offers neither hope nor meaning, has triumphed over them all. This is not a military victory, but it is a defeat for the heroic knight and all of the other human characters.

Bergman's knight, and the movie's overall message, seems existentialist, a mid-twentieth-century expression of chaos and anxiety. The loss of meaning, paradoxically conveyed with Christian symbols laden with pain and catastrophe, marks this as something utterly different from anything conventional American religion offered, just as the movie itself was a direct alternative to Hollywood (it was shown only in "art theaters" when first released in America). Within the movie's medieval setting, Death made perfect sense, and that's why the "Dance of Death" scene was so totally appropriate as a way to end the film.

But when *The Seventh Seal*'s Death spoke, he said that he knew nothing, held no great secrets, could not reveal God. He did not uphold silence and denial, but undermined these. Yet neither he nor the movie as a whole could truly convey anything that could be understood or integrated into ordinary American consciousness. Out of this movie came no new message about death's meaning as part of human experience. Of course, such a film was just so "foreign" it could never have played this role. Cullmann, on the other hand, denied that death was meaningful in another way. "Horror," "terror," "dreadful" made sure that our society's increased denial of death seemed normal and reasonable, even when

Cullmann taught that an authentic Christian should rejoice in Christ's "victory" over it.

Contrast this to the death awareness movement's new words and images, yet to come in the 1950s. When the new language for death and dying began, with Kübler-Ross and the death awareness movement, it too drew in selected ways on the legacy of existentialism. However, one could never jump from *The Seventh Seal*'s Death into "death is natural," and indeed the death awareness movement eliminated any vestiges of personification altogether. Death is no longer an "encounter," a humanized "other," and indeed such imagery, especially when linked to military fantasies of "conquering death," is exactly what the movement sought to correct (see Kübler-Ross, chaps. 1 and 2). The human experience of dying, as the death awareness movement portrays it, includes no "dialogues with Death." What it may have substituted are dialogues with the therapist, who helps the dying person reassess his or her life, and prepare to say good-bye, or the conversations recorded in *Tuesdays with Morrie*.

Attentive readers will notice something odd in the names of those featured in this chapter. Oscar Cullmann, Ingmar Bergman, and finally Kübler-Ross: we have a trio of Europeans who said something new and different about death. These names join the others of Neo-Orthodox theology, whose ideas we discussed in the previous chapter. Two of these figures, Cullmann and Kübler-Ross, eventually made an impact on mainstream American Protestantism. Bergman may not have influenced American ideas about death, but he stretched what movies could do, and the kind of questions that could be raised in films. Even with the limited distribution of *The Seventh Seal* the film allowed American viewers to hear Death reply "Nothing" to the knight's question, "What do you know?"

These three were European outsiders to America—to conventional Christian eschatologies, to Hollywood, and to the high-tech hospital scene. Being "European," with presumably the closer personal experiences of war and disaster, made them less satisfied to say nothing about death, or to be patient with the remnants of "natural immortality" and domestic piety. Their "Europeanness" could have functioned as a plus, rather than a drawback, to their reception here. A recent, fascinating analysis of existentialism's role in redefining "European-ism" (George

Pattison's *Anxious Angels*) sees it as a response to cultural losses. Extend this idea, and the role of Europeans in America in the 1950s and 1960s could be a way to draw attention to what had been lost here as well, in the realm of intangible cultural resources if not in destroyed buildings and lost civilian lives.

To draw attention to Death, with his "nothing" message, was a specific task for which mainline Protestantism in America seemed thoroughly unsuited. Pastors who preached at funerals remained too nostalgically locked into images and ideas lingering on from the era before silence and denial. Sermon anthologies from the 1950s persist in repeating the same messages as did those from the past, albeit toned down and faded. The rose that grew from shade to sun, heaven as home, and hopes based on "natural immortality" continued to inform funeral sermons, even when theological alternatives appeared. It would have been difficult to integrate Cullmann or Bergman into a 1950s-style funeral. If Dolson found normal funerals "barbaric," how much worse a funeral that emphasized Death's "nothing" would have been! Or that used words such as "horror" and "terror" freely—although this might have been closer to the bone of what the funeral congregation felt. By the 1950s, we had as a society entered well into the era of silence and denial. When that silence was broken, it was not by explicitly reexamining the images and ideas of the recent past. Instead, they were ignored, and without protest or tumult, discarded and forgotten.

PART III

What Came Next

11

New Words for Death, Dying, and Grief

Who shall separate us from the love of Christ? . . . For I am convinced that neither death nor life, neither angels nor demons, neither the present nor the future, nor any powers, neither height nor depth, nor anything else in all creation, will be able to separate us from the love of God that is in Christ Jesus our Lord.

—Romans 8:35-39

This chapter tells how suddenly, Paul's assurance in Romans 8 could become a relevant biblical text at the funeral, a popular one for sermons as it had not been earlier. The promise that "neither death nor life will be able to separate us from the love of God" is a response to the threat of loss, to the experience of human separations. It is not about "the world to come" or "natural immortality," it is about human experience now, in this life. Its promise is that God will never abandon us. While Zechariah's heavenly Jerusalem dropped out of funeral preaching, this Pauline text took center stage in the shift into the era after silence and denial.

> Separation—it's a mournful, frightening word. . . . We mourn Homer's loss, for now we must face life separated from him. . . . Nothing

> separated Homer from the love of his family and friends. Days in a hospital or bedridden at home are never easy, but Homer seemed to find great comfort in the steady procession of loved ones who came to visit and to add their strength to his. . . . If there is a sense of separation in Homer's death, it is in the loss that we feel. (*We Are the Lord's*, 25–26)

This quote from the start of a 1980s funeral sermon, which focuses primarily on "the loss that we feel" and says almost nothing about Homer's own situation now, captures the story of what came next, late in the twentieth century.

As we have seen, the ideas offered at Christian funerals did not keep pace with other shifts in sensibility, theological learning, or emergent attitudes about medicine. Neither did funeral practices change during the mid-century period; theirs is a tale of incredible stability. In short, the whole complex of ideas and customs became a stagnant backwater, while in other places Christian twentieth-century thought and practice flowed forward. Remember, "denial of death" need not equate to "saying nothing," especially at a funeral where *something* must be publicly said. The older language weakened but persisted. "Doctrinal" sermons still were preached, but the doctrines were expounded less forcefully, "natural immortality" was just as central to the message but the poetry lost its literary quality, its sense of awe and mystery. Funerals remained funerals, in spite of Hildegarde Dolson and the entire consumerist critique of *The American Way of Death*. For Christians they were not "barbaric" vestiges, and yet in light of newer theological insights, what was said at the funeral by the preacher became increasingly isolated from what he and other Christians said elsewhere. This captures what we mean by "silence"; applied to those many aspects of the human situation of dying, death and grief unthematized, ignored or disparaged. In this sense, "silence" and "denial" ruled, and the meanings of death were "vestigial," faded out shadows of a past era. When new words were spoken, they appeared dramatically discontinuous with what had gone before.

Elsewhere, outside of funerals, Christian pastoral practice changed noticeably. The pastoral counseling movement is one of the great success stories of American twentieth-century religion; its impact on mainline Protestantism is immense. Its focus on "this-worldly" human situations and conflicts helped clear the way for the fresh approaches of the death awareness movement, as well as undo the lingering view that the purpose of Christian life here was to live solely under the power of the world to come. Even as funeral sermons repeated earlier themes such as "natural immortality," the pastor as counselor dealt with family conflicts, depression, and existential anxiety among his congregation (it was still "his" at this time). The pastoral counseling movement and its practices would become the route by which the death awareness movement's new perspectives and images for death came to dominate American Protestantism. (In the following discussion, I am indebted to Brooks Holifield's *A History of Pastoral Care in America*. Holifield shows how this was a "movement" with its own articulated agenda and aims.)

The pastoral counseling movement originated in the interesting and provocative work of Anton Boisen and others; it wished to link the Christian message to care for the mentally ill, and to the insights of newly emergent secular psychotherapies. Boisen developed what became clinical pastoral education (CPE) and was himself the pioneer mental hospital chaplain (he was also, intermittently, a patient!). But the major impact of this movement was through its spread into ordinary parish settings. The minister needed to know something about mental illness, something about contemporary psychology, in order to counsel his "normal"—i.e., nonhospitalized and merely neurotic—parishioners. This was intrinsic to his role as pastor, as a "shepherd." The people in his care did not generally have "religious problems," in the sense of questions and difficulties over doctrines. They had human problems, such as family conflicts, guilt, and anger left over from childhood. These nonmedical "problems in living" could be treated by a secular psychotherapist. But the pastor *as pastor* was much more likely to be the first source of help, and he had better know how and when to help. Few ordinary persons in the 1950s would have gone immediately to a psychoanalyst unless they lived in an urban center. Church members with delinquent children, bad childhoods, or bouts of depression showed up in their minister's office. The outstanding work of Seward Hiltner and Howard Clinebell took up this challenge, and welcomed the perspective of psychological theory and practice (especially via the nondirective counseling method of Carl Rogers). In their own eyes, this was not to capitulate to the forces of secularism; such training was to make what pastors did anyway more helpful, better informed by in-depth awareness of the dynamics of the psyche.

So, while funerals used the same worn-out set of ideas and images as had been current at the beginning of the century, when it came to situations of life and living, the pastor as counselor was open to what really troubled the people he served, and committed to dealing with their daily problems with empathy and acceptance. Hiltner stressed this by contrasting his work with the counseling methods and aims of a nineteenth-century pastor, Ichabod Spencer, whose diaries he could use as a source (*Preface to Pastoral Theology*, 72ff.) in discussing his vision of pastoral care. Although Hiltner admired his predecessor's human skills as a pastor, he noted with dismay that the sole goal of earlier "counseling" was to achieve "a sincere and inward verdict for Jesus Christ." All of the actual pastoral wisdom was in service to a statement from the sufferer, "I accept Jesus as Lord and Savior." This aim struck Hiltner as "the compartmentalization of religion," a major flaw (83). Deathbed scenes were part of the old casebook, with of course an emphasis on the saved or unsaved state of the dying person, as the pastor paid one final visit. We can almost hear the voice of the preacher whose funeral sermon asked the future dead, "Are you living under the power of the world to come?" Hiltner found this repellant; he did not include any deathbed scenes in *his* book (Denial? Or a realistic portrait of the newer loci of death in hospitals and nursing homes?). The goals of his counseling were entirely different, although "shepherding" was a term that he used to cover both eras' aims.

Hiltner's books—and those of other leaders in the movement—show pastors in the midst of life, dedicated to helping persons with whatever methods were even partially compatible with Christian faith. Freud's atheism, or the hostility of Carl Rogers to traditional organized religion, could be set aside, and the method of psychotherapy adapted to the pastoral setting. Not until a few decades later did a serious backlash against this enthusiasm for secular psychotherapeutic models set in. Once that began, the distinctive "resources" and setting of the Christian tradition could be brought back into focus. (See Browning's *The Moral Context of Pastoral Care* for a clear statement of the need for this.) Backlashers insisted that what pastors did was not just Rogerian therapy in a church, it was something with its own values, visions, worldview. Hiltner had never doubted this, but at the time he wrote the agenda of the pastoral counseling movement was to awaken pastors to the need for the best psychological training possible.

The pastoral care movement, and not Christian funeral practice, provided the pathway to Christian acceptance of the death awareness movement. "Acceptance" is too weak a word: enthusiastic embrace is more accurate. Early efforts in "thanatology" were interdisciplinary, and a book such as Bowers' coauthored *Counseling the Dying*, which appeared in 1964, exemplified how specialists and professionals could collaborate in practicing care for the dying. When the similar work of Kübler-Ross burst upon the world a few years later, and the phrase "death and dying" became commonplace, among those who first endorsed the new approach were hospital chaplains and those who trained pastoral counselors. The psychological framing of "death and dying" with labels such as "denial" or "depression" was not a problem for pastoral counselors well accustomed to Carl Rogers.

Moreover, Kübler-Ross focused on dying as human experience, and grieving the death of another as a parallel experience. These were problems of the living, and not of "death" in itself. It was dying, and not death, which she felt we all fear (268). As a part of living, then, dying could become included in the pastor's care, although absent from Hiltner's examples. But then, there were also no old-style deathbed scenes in *On Death and Dying*; rather, every patient's interview was a kind of deathbed retrospective on his or her life. What we do not see is anyone expire on the book's pages, the very scenes that Ichabod Spencer (Hiltner's nineteenth-century precursor) could not have omitted. A book *On Death and Dying* without such final moments would have been greeted with incomprehension by those for whom "the power of the world to come" outweighed by far any temporary troubles of dying here in this world.

New words for dying were also new words for bereavement, because coming to terms with one's own impending death was a process of coming to terms with loss. One of the death awareness movement's central foci is grief as an appropriate and universal human response to loss and separation. At the start of the movement, the parallel between one's own anticipated death and the anticipated or after-death grief for another was more or less assumed, rather than argued. Just as the patients in *On Death and Dying* go through "five stages," so their families also experience these "stages," although perhaps not in sync or sympathy with their dying member (Kübler-Ross, 1968, chap. 9). In 1968, bereavement as well as death had been considered "vestigial" and "barbaric"; there had been a long period of almost total silence on the topic of grief and mourning, in psychiatry and other secular disciplines.

But all that changed, dramatically and quickly. Almost immediately after the publication of *On Death and Dying*, the pastoral care and counseling experts moved into the area of grief and loss. By the mid-1970s, works such as Donald Bane's edited *Death and Ministry: Pastoral Care for the Dying and Bereaved* and Wayne Oates' *Pastoral Care and Counseling in Grief and Separation* showed how smoothly the basic framework of Kübler-Ross could be adopted by clergy, just as the therapy of Rogers had been the mainstay of an earlier decade for pastoral counselors.

> Pastoral care to the grief sufferer begins the very first day you enter a parish to serve as pastor. . . . All that each member of your parish is and his/her total life experience will directly affect how he/she deals with dying, death and grieving. It is extremely important, therefore, that dying, death and grieving be considered a part of the total ministry which you give and the total ministry of the members of your congregation to one another. (Joyce, 9)

These words, from a manual titled *The Pastor and Grief*, continue Hiltner's rejection of "compartmentalized religion" in favor of an embrace of "the total life experience" of the parishioners. The framework of "dying, death and grieving" is new, however, and dominated by psychological categories such as "denial," "anger," and "depression." Indeed, by later "backlash" standards, pastors simply surrendered all theological content in their enthusiasm for a psychological model of "coming to terms with loss."

Note that with a title such as *Grief and Separation*, any experience of loss could be fit within the model. Divorce, unemployment, amputations, geographic moves: all of these were "losses." We are, in short, in the very same territory as Hiltner's books: in the midst of daily life, among living ordinary persons whose problems are rarely voiced in "religious" language. What is different from Hiltner is the explicit focus on dying and bereavement, as experiences previously "denied."

Eventually, this perspective required a more sustained theological treatment, and the fine 1983 work by Kenneth Mitchell and Herbert Anderson, *All Our Losses, All Our Griefs*, tried to provide this. Mitchell and Anderson began from the recognition that loss and grief had not been Christian topics, had in fact been ignored or denied, in favor of a focus on death. Yet, for them, "[d]eath is only one form of loss" (10), and so following the lead of the death awareness movement and earlier pastoral care appropriations, they center upon loss, offering both psychological and theological perspectives.

> Society does not encourage awareness of powerful loss feelings. . . . This is a Stoic position; it represents in our view one of the most powerful anti-Christian stances in our society. It is apathy or indifference which breeds a callous disregard for the sacredness of all life. Loss is inescapably painful precisely because attachment is a human necessity. . . . To be human is to be a griever for all kinds of losses. (Mitchell and Anderson, 51–52)

To subsume death under "loss" in this way would have been unthinkable for Christians half a century earlier. Death was, and had always been, utterly special, absolute, and ultimate; it was not "only one form" of anything!

Meanwhile, Mitchell and Anderson also looked anew at what space was given to grief at funerals. Alas, when it came to preaching a funeral sermon, pastors could find little or nothing that would truly help. Cullmann's military language of "defeat of death" had indeed, for some preachers, already replaced the more static and less christocentric vision of "natural immortality." The aspect of Cullmann most often highlighted was the sense of Christian triumph over death, not of Jesus' fear and horror of it. Christian "victory" over death might have narrowed down Cullmann into what could be palatable at a funeral, but it had a few very unintended consequences. Like "natural immortality," it kept attention on the status of the deceased, and away from the current situation of the bereaved. The tone of such Cullmannesque sermons was relentlessly and abstractly upbeat. Unlike "natural immortality," Cullmann's message of military victory could not be bolstered or fleshed out by allegories for natural transitions, sailing or returning home. Christian hopes were discontinuous with any "natural" views; God had reversed, not fulfilled normal human responses. Therefore, according to this theology, Christian funerals were occasions for affirming Christ's conquest of death, and the joyous shared certainty of resurrection. It was wrong to be sad, then, at an authentically Christian funeral. This was what Blackwood might also have agreed to, but the tone of his 1942 "hope" was utterly subdued when compared to that of Cullmann-dominated sermons. White and not black was now the color for vestments and church decoration, and a better symbol of relentless one-dimensional "joy" could hardly have been chosen.

Mitchell and Anderson, advocates of "loss" and grief, find this a new kind of denial. While Cullmann himself wanted to restore a sense of death's intrinsic "horror," this does not appear in funeral sermons that are obviously based on his ideas. Instead "victory" and "resurrection" became the norm, and this emphasis was surely a denial of the very human sadness felt by the mourners. Indeed, complaints about revised "resurrection-filled" funeral liturgies poured into the church bodies that had authorized them. As Mitchell and Anderson's comment on this resurrection focus put it, "The theological assertion is accurate, but from a pastoral perspective the theological priority has been misplaced" (142). By the time the death awareness movement percolated through chaplains and pastoral caregivers into the general sensibilities of the public (and this happened very, very rapidly, so powerful and persuasive was its message), to leave space for grief, rather than denying it, seemed honest and necessary.

> We have gathered as members of the Body of Christ . . . to share the heartache, the faith and the hope of the S__ family. The pain of grief is always heavy; so our acts of friendship can help to shoulder their sorrows. In these moments when they can feel bewildered, our faith bolsters theirs. And when the tragedy of it all clouds their way, our presence can brighten the horizons of their days. (*We Are the Lord's*, 57)

Here, the presence of other human beings serves as a sign of the continuing presence of God. What people in this situation need to hear was what Paul proclaimed: God will be with you in the midst of life and death, God will never abandon you, even when you are sure you are alone. In other examples of anthologized sermons, the pastor's own reactions and feelings model how important an honest expression of the full range of grieving should be:

> My first reaction was one of anger when I heard the news. When the hospital called to tell me that ___ had died of a massive heart attack, it seemed so unfair to me that I couldn't even begin to think about what I would say until my own angry feelings had eased. (Richmond, 68)

Without this acknowledgment of where we are now, as grievers, any assurance of resurrection "victory over death" will appear "misplaced."

Let us put things more bluntly: if Christians are forbidden to be sad at a funeral, the message will not be a joyous one of hope, but a repressive sense that our real emotions do not matter one bit to God. Whatever Cullmann and others with his message of resurrection versus immortality had intended, it was not this. "Victory over death" seemed to backfire as a motif for consolation, or a meaningful human response to a death. Mitchell and Anderson's point has been heeded. Indeed, a more recent author noted how by the 1990s omission of the resurrection altogether had become one liturgical pattern. Pastoral care author Gene Fowler, in his advice manual about funerals, warned against this, but noted how it was justified by a sincere desire to curb "avoidance" and denial of the reality of death (143–44). Although he disapproved, the arguments for and against this reveal the contemporary triumph of "pastoral" over strictly "theological" approaches, in discussion of this issue.

There was still another, less direct reason why "victory over death" did not work well in the setting of the 1970s and later. The death awareness movement drew attention to the plight of terminally ill hospital patients whose basic condition was of "acceptance." Yet they were pressured to "keep fighting," and the military model of medicine was so pervasive that patients, doctors, and everyone else had bought into it uncritically. It was assumed that doctors fight to win the war against death, and when the patient dies, that war is lost. (To this day, such a death is announced by "Today, he lost his battle against cancer. . . .") In fact, Kübler-Ross and her cohorts in the death awareness movement insisted, this military "battle against death" was itself born of denial, and for patients it could be a disaster. They were not "giving up," losing a war; they were truly "in a state of acceptance," and should not be forced to endure further treatments (Kübler-Ross, 1968, 112–14). Often the major reason for further interventions was not the betterment of the patient, who would die soon anyway, but to bolster the doctor's sense that *he* at least had "kept on fighting."

Kübler-Ross and the early death awareness movement hated militarism, and in what Southard called the "post-Vietnam ethos" of the new language for dying, death, and bereavement (xxx), he rejected any use of military imagery. An undercurrent of the movement's moral agenda was to advocate an alternative, peaceful mode of approaching one's own death and those of others. Although no one could reasonably blame Cullmann himself for advocating overtreatment of the dying, or any of the practices the death awareness movement condemned, it appeared that his heavy-handed vision of "death as enemy," D-day and V-day, and so on made his ideas look just like what the new death awareness movement protested. Cullmann could bolster the idea that the authentic Christian response to death was to fight and postpone it, at all costs, in all contexts, without limit. It was this relentless battle against death as enemy that made dying in a high-tech hospital a worse human experience for patients than old-fashioned traditional dying in one's home.

We may ask if this is indeed a valid conclusion to draw. It is not found directly in any of the American death and dying literature, in sermons with the explicit theology of "victory over death," or in the medical ethics literature that uses a theology of "life" and its value to oppose euthanasia and physician-assisted suicide. There is, most professionals and experts recognize, no absolute Christian mandate to extend the lives of the terminally ill by futile and uncomfortable treatments, just because "the defeat of death" is what the gospel message is about. Ordinary Christians certainly have drawn this conclusion, and insisted on medical interventions for a family member on this ground, even when informed by doctors that such treatments would do more harm than good. Many of my Christian students assume this connection, assume that their faith requires them to be so consistently "antideath" so that no withdrawal from treatment should be allowed. The language they use is not that of formal medical bioethics, Catholic or Protestant. It is streamlined Cullmann all the way.

I have found only a sole theologically trained voice to represent such a perspective. This comes from German Lutheran thinker Eberhard Jüngel. In *Death: The Riddle and the Mystery*, written and translated in the early 1970s, he flies in the face of both the older "pre-Cullmann" tradition and the emergent death awareness movement by stating, "In life, man can never resist death enough. Dying, he can do nothing at all against death" (136). Not only could death never be "the Lord's will," and therefore "acceptable," but the basic practical agenda of death awareness movement, hospice, and pastoral care for the dying is invalid since "we can do nothing," and therefore should not pretend to try. We must fight only against death, our enemy. As a stringent Lutheran, Jüngel based this doubly dismal conclusion on his suspicion that all *Ars Moriendi* activities (e.g., what hospice would provide) constitute "works righteousness," and therefore oppose true "faith." But Jüngel's theology also depends very heavily on Cullmann for his reading of the "authentic" Christian view of death as absolute enemy (53ff.). By the 1970s, this message mercifully never had a chance here, especially given the pervasive acceptance of the pastoral counseling approach to problems of living, and now of dying and grieving. American chaplains and pastors could not have credibly argued that compassionate care for the dying be dismissed as mere "works righteousness."

In the mid-1970s, the funeral sermons and handbooks for pastors were primarily guided by the newer death awareness movement approaches already intrinsic to pastoral care authors. Away from the hospital situation of the end-of-life patient, the focus was directly on mourners and their experience of loss, separation, and grief. The funeral message, following Paul in Romans, was to assure those present that while loss and separation were real, nothing could separate us from God's love. By 1985 pastoral care author Robert Hughes' excellent handbook, *A Trumpet in Darkness: Preaching to Mourners*, could assume that this is the purpose and audience for a funeral sermon.

> Of course, the mourners are the target of the sermon. In a real sense it is for them. Yet how can sensitive pastors prepare sermons that take into account the location of key mourners on the continuum of grief? . . . How is the pastor to use the sermon, one malleable element within the liturgy, to target the particular feelings and questions of mourners? (10)

No longer a collection of the future dead, the congregation was a community touched by grief, experiencing a natural and appropriate sorrow in response to loss. Whether white or black was the color for the funeral, it was to be an occasion to recognize God's presence in the midst of pain.

So, in light of this, an appropriate theological message must be given to comfort mourners. While not denying death, the sermon should not merely repeat the message of psychology. The biblical text from Romans displayed at the beginning of this chapter was one answer, and it is now among the most popular sermon texts. Nothing can separate us from the love of God, even at a time when the weight of separations and loss dominates our immediate feelings. Nothing can separate us even when God does not appear as present or in control. Note that in this passage, as it is now understood and used for sermons, there is no promise at all that nothing can separate us from the dead. The dead are gone, absent; the funeral does not promise eventual family reunions, or any sense of immediate intuitive spiritual presence or nearness. Nor is there any reference at all to their or our future state; nothing can separate us even now, when we hurt. But the one to whom this refers is only God, who is always present, even if hidden, in the midst of our sorrow.

> The essential promise of the gospel is that we are never separated from the love of God. . . . Much of the gospel hope is realistic and this-worldly. It has to do with the ability to live joyfully in this world despite irretrievable loss. (Mitchell and Anderson, 159)

Or, in the closing section of a funeral that used the Romans 8 passage as its text,

> But what was true for C__ is also true for us, nothing can separate us from the love of God. . . . We have experienced God's love in this place today as it has enveloped us and flowed through us, and it will accompany us as we leave to begin our daily routines. (*We Are the Lord's*, 44)

Sermons with this focus on grief and addressed to mourners rely heavily on psychological theories of grief. Not just because of the prestige of psychology, but because there essentially were no Christian theologies of grief. That was one of Mitchell and Anderson's complaints. Even if anyone in the 1970s, 1980s, and 1990s had tried to look back to Blackwood's era for resources, they would have discovered not one sustained theological reflection on mourning as loss. So, books from these recent decades utilize the current model of grief in vogue at their time: first the "stages" model, then William Worden's "four tasks," then Therese Rando's more complex "6 R-processes" serve as the pastor/preacher's resource for understanding grief as a human process. (See Bregman 1999, for a discussion of these psychological models.) But it does not seem to matter; even if some grief theories are now discarded by experts, a book of funeral advice could remain helpful, if well written and sensible. What matters is that the Christian funeral, when defined as "preaching to mourners," takes grief seriously as human experience and attempts to relate the gospel to the actual spiritual state of those in the pews who mourn. Even the status of the deceased, for whom the funeral is given, changes with this new focus. "Last week he was here, now we bury him." The older message was that "he is with Jesus," once again returned "home" or now set sail to encounter his Pilot face to face; so where will we soon be? It is we, the future dead, who must be made aware we will follow him. Today, a sudden death is the occasion for our intense shock and grief, our sense of a gap or hole right here in this world that seems impossible to fill.

But when the focus of the funeral is on the mourners, and they are promised that God will never be lost or separated from them, there may still be a role for the deceased. It is true that the funeral is for the living, not the dead. After all, the funeral home deals with the body, say authors of contemporary manuals, while the minister focuses on the needs of the living (*not* on the "souls" of either). And yet, there is more. Mansell, in *The Funeral: A Pastor's Guide*, puts it well: the pastor should ask himself, "Am I doing right by the departed?"

> The funeral sermon is a time when the faith community weaves fitting words of faith around the life of the departed. During the funeral sermon, the life of the departed is remembered in ways that authentically convey Christian caring and respect for the bereaved. (Mansell, 37)

The purpose of the funeral is now defined by this strong sense that the living owe the dead person something, as a primary obligation of our role as mourners. Nor is this a debt only for those who are "mourners" in the psychological sense. Perhaps the pastor represents the entire Christian community, or all of society and humanity, in fulfilling this duty to the dead. A funeral that "does right by" the deceased will leave everyone with a sense of completion if never happiness. The living owe the dead the honor, the recognition, that a good funeral provides. Mansell, writing in 1998, offers this repeat of Irion's 1966 justification for the "humanist" funeral. A person who lived deserves by virtue of his or her humanity to be honored as an individual, as one for whom we should say, "Someone was here." To "do right by" this person is to provide for the living an experience that will represent the dead, so as to commemorate that indeed, an individual unique person was once here and is now gone. This would be the case even if the deceased had left no mourners, or even left the family instructions for "please omit funeral." The rest of us owe him or her something, a duty that overrides the dead person's merely subjective preferences. Some theories of grief make "commemoration" an important "task," which helps to express what is going on at a good funeral. But this psychological justification may be superfluous. Once the funeral itself focuses on the mourners *as mourners* now, their obscure sense of duty toward the dead is made visible in and of itself, more than in the days when the funeral-goers were all the future dead. The practical advice offered by manual authors Hughes and Mansell may duplicate in many details Blackwood's of fifty years before, but the underlying reasons and assumptions are indeed very different.

It seems legitimate to wonder if this newer view is "Christian." Its advocates, unlike earlier generations of manual authors and anthologists, are not worried by "pagan" remnants and influences in the Christian funeral. Their worries are about denial, and about false and useless theologies that could make mourning worse. One of these was the belief that this particular death was directly "the Lord's will" in its manner and timing. No preacher should include this idea in his sermon, and it is pastorally inappropriate to encourage it privately—unless it is clear that this is the only means by which the family can make peace and sense of the death. Instead, Hughes states,

> Scripture tells us that God understands suffering and pain. God cares for the deceased and mourners. God is on the griever's side, supporting, strengthening, and healing. God suffers when God's people do. God reunites believers to divine fellowship. God recenters lives and reforms what has been shattered. All these and more are God's actions, the present work of a crucified and living Lord in particular loss situations. (76)

Other theological messages to avoid include exactly the focus on afterlife, heaven, and the happiness of the dead, which—now—appears to cruelly disregard the real sorrow of the bereaved. Absolutely no more children playing in the streets of Jerusalem, and for Hughes, Mansell, and all others in the contemporary era, the death of a child is automatically in the "problem" category for theological as well as pastoral reasons. Sermons with titles such as "My God, Why?" are a direct expression of this current atmosphere and understanding.

> We come together at this time for various reasons . . . to pay tribute, to take time to remember Tina . . . to express our feelings to those who most deeply mourn . . . and we come to share our faith. . . . But if we are honest, we have to admit we have also come to this place to ask, "Why?". . . But there are no easy answers to the question of why. We cannot give the reason for this turn of events. We can only join the very human question of the moment, "My God, my God, Why?" (*We Are the Lord's*, 77–78)

The funeral that works, however, not only "does right by" the deceased, but is a "celebration of life" in his or her memory. "We are here today to celebrate the life of Bill" (Mansell, 42) are the opening words of the ceremony. This for many funeral-goers and pastors may be the best purpose of the funeral. While Irion wished to distinguish between "Christian" and "humanistic" funerals, for the sake of eliminating "pseudo-religious" in-between ones, later guides intentionally avoid such a division, with such a basic grounding of "celebrating the life," for all funerals, including those clearly Christian. Someone, a human person, was here and is now gone. To this, the preacher must convey the presence of God in the midst of exactly this human sorrow. But it seems reasonable to ask what makes "celebration of the life of x" a Christian goal, even when this is presided over by a pastor in a church setting. Perhaps it could be fulfilled better by the family and friends themselves, in an intimate memorial service. Perhaps it belongs in the funeral home, as a theme for the viewing, but not at the funeral or burial. I am not suggesting that such a "celebrating the life" statement of the funeral's purpose is "pagan" or "secular." These pastors, following Seward Hiltner's lead from the mid-twentieth century, would criticize the restriction of "Christian" topics to those that looked explicitly "religious." This would be a new version of "compartmentalization." If the pastor can counsel a woman whose son is in trouble at home and at school, then surely he—and now, she—can honor the life of a dead member of the congregation by "celebrating" this person as an individual. Christian faith is no longer to be defined by otherworldly goals, ideas, and images; it is a living relation to God through Jesus Christ here in the midst of life, and in the midst of sorrow when someone loved has died. For those who write and preach funeral sermons today, to "do right by" the deceased, to celebrate his or her life, is fully compatible with a sense of God's presence and concern and love for all. It is compatible with a vision of God suffering along with us, rather than ordaining particular deaths at particular moments.

But if funerals that "celebrate a life" seem to fall short of an earlier era's main ideals theologically, there is also another perspective from which to evaluate these attempts to "celebrate." This revisioned purpose and message for funerals may not really express what the death awareness movement had as its goal, when it looked at the anguish and loneliness of dying hospital patients and grieving families. It is possible that the movement's original agenda could have been expressed and appropriated in a manner that led Christian pastors and preachers in alternative directions. We need to ask how "loss" became "celebration." And perhaps, just perhaps, *loss* is too narrow and too "normal" a category to appropriately mark off a death.

12

The Triumph of the Biographical

There is no epigraph at the head of this chapter. It is intentional, an omission that reflects the turn to "sermons" that are actually "celebrations of the life" of the deceased. In some contemporary anthologies, these sermons without biblical texts appear, lively, filled with anecdotes and memories. But I wonder if these truly qualify as "sermons." We will ask what theology of death is preached, when the funeral takes this form. In the previous chapter, we closed with contemporary focus on "celebration of the life of x" as the dominant pattern for *Preaching to Mourners*. In this chapter, we elaborate on this development, and look at one vigorous, controversial, and doomed protest against it.

In the era before silence and denial, Earl Daniels, a pastor who wrote a manual on funeral preaching, divided sermons into "doctrinal," "biographical," and "occasional." This last term refers to the special circumstances of the death (e.g., a mining accident) . In Daniels' mind, "doctrinal" was far preferable to the others, for clear theological reasons. Blackwood, writing his manual a few years later, agreed; the focus of the funeral was not to be on the person who died, nor on the pastor, but on God. That advice might still have made a certain amount of sense even for those committed to *Preaching to Mourners*. After all, their task was, in Hughes' image, to become the musician who could play that trumpet sounding in the darkness, a voice from the distance that reassures and encourages those frightened by the night. And even when the sermon title is "Why, God, Why?" it is still clearly focused on God, and voices the agonizing questions that those who have lost a child, for example, are often afraid or unable to ask directly.

But this is not what actually happened. The dominant pattern by far, in the framework of *Preaching to Mourners*, has been to focus the sermon on a biographical representation of the deceased, his or her life and its meaning to those present. This is the "celebration of a life" with which the last chapter ended. In anthologies of contemporary funeral sermons of this genre, we can find the following examples of "biographical" sermons:

> You all knew ___. He contracted diabetes very early in his life. Because of that disease, he lost his eyesight at a young age. Perhaps he despaired, but not for long. He went to a school for sightless people and learned to get along with[out] his eyes. You all knew ___. He was the man who, little by little, lost bits and pieces of his legs to diabetes until he completely lost both legs. He may have despaired, but not for long. He learned to get along without them. You all knew ___. He was a man who did not always live in such a way that everyone agreed with him. He was no saint; you know that. (Richmond, 68)

> For Beth, he was a husband. You shared your love over 44 years. There are many memories which you will hold. You will remember meeting at the Roller Skating Rink while he was stationed here in the army. (*We Are the Lord's*, 53)

> We have come together today: to say "Thanks be to God for the life of Mabel!" We have come together in her memory and we thank God for her life as we remember her years among us. To each of us those years and our memories will be different. As for me, I will remember her delightful sense of humor. . . . One who has this, as Mabel did, and shares it with other people, shares something deep and helpful . . . and that is worth remembering. (Joyce, 110)

Although typically, the definition of a funeral is when the body is present, and a "memorial service" is when there is no body, the actual content of both has become a "memorial" in the sense of a remembering and commemoration of the dead person's life. People want to hear about the person who was here, but is now gone. "Someone was here," and it is very important that it was not just an anonymous Anyone, but a unique individual with a life, loves, vocation, hobbies, and so on that can be lovingly recalled. "To do right by" this person requires evoking all of these, in a spirit of gratitude for the life he or she lived. Therefore the key phrases for opening the ritual become "We give thanks for the life of *x*" or "We celebrate the life of *x* as we gather here together." Note that neither "the body" nor "the soul" is really the subject of this event, it is "the person" and his or her life that matters.

Of course, it is the life as remembered, as represented, and not the fullness of the life in all its details, including those unknown or mercifully hidden from everyone in the congregation. In the above examples, the diabetic had an ambiguous public reputation, and Beth the widow must have told the story of how she and her future husband met at the roller rink many times. Although Daniels, Blackwood, and all the other ministers from whatever era insisted that any and all biographical details be checked carefully beforehand, when the preferred form of sermon was "doctrinal," one could minimize attention to the individual life poorly lived. Doctrinal sermons compensated for either the lack of biographical details (as in the sad case of the friendless vagrant) or a life of visible failure. This is less of an option today. How to "do right by" someone who did not, when alive, "do right by" others remains a problem. Today, it becomes a "problem funeral" for this biographical reason; it is a problem of how to represent a life without inundating the mourners in recriminations, guilt, and bad memories. That is why the funeral for Mabel is so easy to preside over, in today's climate. In contrast, one dismal example I experienced featured speeches by several of the dead woman's grown children. They rose up in turn to rehash how bad their relationships with their mother had been. This was a "difficult funeral" to sit through, although not primarily because the ultimate eschatological destiny of the dead person remained unknown to all but God, the traditional earlier reason. It was a funeral where there was no good answer to the demand that we the living "do right by" the dead.

This turn to the biographical has become the subject of controversy and media attention, although in actuality the amount of both is very small. What many people who remember old-style funerals will notice is that today's are less likely to be "standardized," and relatives, friends, and work colleagues will contribute by speeches (hopefully, short) or poems or even musical performances. Yes, this can backfire, but when the aim becomes "to do right by *x*" those who knew *x* have the upper hand. But some examples from anthologies show the deceased as well known to the preacher, who supplies his or her own anecdotes and memories. Contemporary "sermons" can then become meshed into other tributes. Even the pastor is free to forego traditional "preaching" from a biblical text, to share stories of the dead person's peculiarities, private dreams, or happiest times. When this happens, it may be odd to call the public talk a "sermon"; it is as much a biographical tribute as are the tales by younger family members of their uncle's generosity in funding their college education.

The pastor may even feel free to tell what others could not have known. One "sermon" in an anthology includes a long account of how, when Doug and Barbara learned of her cancer, they all met together in the pastor's office and cried. The original text includes many more medical details, and discussions of insurance and end-of-life care in which the preacher participated.

> Barbara's first hint of trouble came with coughing and pain in the chest. The X-rays and following biopsy confirmed the worst fears and marked the beginning of her long slide toward death. "Lung cancer" said the doctor. "We'll remove the lobe immediately and follow with radiation." But it was not to be that easy. . . . At forty-six the specter of death seemed doubly upsetting. Barbara had found real happiness for the first time in her life. In childhood she had been abused and had seen her mother mortally burned in a gas explosion in their home. After the failure of her first marriage, the second marriage was a dream come true. "Why?" became the incessant question over the next eighteen months. . . . [The pastor continues] Together we explored the heights of heaven and probed the depths of hell. No small part of the exploration was the uncovering of the deep childhood hurts which had so attacked her self-esteem and led to heavy cigarette smoking. (*We Are the Lord's*, 34–35)

While this plethora of painful medical and familial history details brings a level of reality to the "celebration" of Barbara's life, it also would have deeply offended an earlier generation of preachers. It draws attention squarely to both the pastor and the dead person and away from God, undercutting the very purpose of a Christian funeral as Blackwood saw it. Today, the preachers and editors of this and other anthologies ignore such a theological objection. Significantly, the questionable taste of this kind of anecdote, and whether this is appropriate coming from the pastor, is never directly debated either in any of the current manuals and anthologies. The pastor's good judgment is assumed, while that of the family members who may want to use the occasion for revenge, or who just may not know how to speak well in public, is a focus for concern.

Moreover, since the goal is now "to celebrate the life of *x*" the entire service now reflects this ethos of personal memorial tribute. So, for example, the music chosen reflects the personal tastes of the deceased, as perhaps it always did, but the limitation on this principle is minimal. Earlier funeral manuals usually included lists of "appropriate hymns," songs whose words and tone expressed both Christian hope and the somber tone of the occasion. The minister, not the family, determined the selection, and his criteria of "appropriate" were the only ones that counted. When the aim of the funeral is focused on the bereaved family and its need to "do right by" their dead member, the criteria shift. Of course, a hymn loved by the dead person is fine, but now so is a performance of a favorite piece of music by a family member. Here, the point is not excellence in execution, but to reinforce the sense that everyone "brings something" to offer in memorializing the dead. A brilliant performance by a stranger will not work, while a so-so one by a son or daughter will fit the purpose of the funeral.

Sometimes, music that is not "traditional church music," or which in some way jars, raises the same problem as other contributions from mourners. In one instance, the congregation sang Christmas carols, for these were the favorites of the dead person, even though his funeral was in July. In another case, a dead veteran's family asked to have the congregation sing both "America the Beautiful" and "The Star-Spangled Banner" at his funeral. Both songs were in the hymnal, but that alone did not make the choices a success. We the congregation really tried, but our national anthem is by now a performance song, and there are certain special settings for it. At the close of the valiant attempt by a small congregation of not-very-musical people, someone whispered loudly "Play ball!" And, of course, there are styles of music that most pastors, however liberal theologically, do not want played in *their* church. Outside the church, anywhere else, but not *in the church*. As baby boomers die, there will probably be more requests for Beatles, Rolling Stones, Doors, and Jefferson Airplane classics. Protestants have no denominational policies on this kind of issue, and even the best authors of funeral manuals today consider it a matter of pastoral negotiation, rather than theological principle. But remember that the aim of the funeral is now "to do right by" the departed, and so to represent the dead person that a biographically oriented service will succeed in this goal. If Lucy is the departed, she would rather be commemorated and celebrated by Janis Joplin's "Piece of My Heart" than by most of the selections in the hymnal, and those left to mourn her will surely be aware of that preference.

Just about the only popular and stereotyped news stories about funerals feature this emphasis on personal taste and choice, as the ultimate criterion for what the funeral includes. Media attention on the whole topic is so low, that the stock "weird funeral" story is about coffins that reflect the hobbies of the deceased (as in Nigeria) or about funerals advertised as the chance to "throw a party for yourself." When the Frank Sinatra song "My Way" was first selected as funeral music, this set the pattern for this repetitive and unimaginative media involvement. And yes, the "biographical" funeral can now be planned in advance, and by the person whose life will be "celebrated." Therefore, every funeral ought to be an expression of "my way," in planning and staging the event. Commercially, when a funeral can be reconceived as a party for oneself, and doing that in style, according to one's own tastes (however wacky), more specialized gear can be sold. Such specialized décor and paraphernalia to reflect the hobbies and lifestyles of the deceased are now part of a "celebration of life" package, available at funeral homes. So this trend is both a news story and a marketing strategy.

Sure enough, this trend in turn fits into the one way funerals have been discussed and criticized for almost the past one hundred years: the consumerist critique. According to this view, the "I did it my way" ethic is really just another way for the funeral industry to make a buck, when everyone knows it is pointless to waste money on the dead. Although Hildegarde Dolson lived before the "throw a party for yourself" redefinition of a funeral, she might have allowed that this was the least "barbaric" way to do things. Yet I suspect her own rationalism and wry sense of humor would still have led her to insist "please omit funeral." The party should better take place later, well away from the funeral home.

It is too easy to make fun of "freaky funerals," or to mock the mix of "expressive individualism" and commercial savvy that makes for them. But when the aims of a funeral are defined as "celebration of the life of *x*," a Christian funeral may become simply a less wacky or tacky instance of this. Doug and Barbara and the pastor crying over her cancer diagnosis is sadder and probably more emotionally powerful than much of the advertised gear for "celebrations of life," but it looks no different in kind. There is no qualitative gap between a "biographical" sermon without a biblical text and "I did it my way."

A vigorous theological protest was mounted against the unrestricted triumph of the biographical funeral sermon. This came from Roman Catholic Archbishop John Myers of Newark, and so lies outside the mainline Protestant sphere of this study. But in his direct attempt in 2002–2003 to curtail the practice of turning the Roman Catholic funeral into "a celebration of life" for the individual dead, Myers expressed the same frustration that Daniels and Blackwood would have shared. The difference in church polity meant that he had the power, at least in theory, to enforce his view. In the most heavy-handed manner imaginable, Myers laid down the rules: the sole focus of a Catholic funeral is to be "the saving mystery of Jesus' death and resurrection" (Myers). To safeguard this principle, no one but the priest may speak, and even the priest may not include personal anecdotes and memories of the deceased in his homily. Other settings and occasions, such as at the viewing, may permit some of this, but the formal funeral is not the place for them. The focus is so clearly christological because the primary teaching of Christianity about death is centered on Jesus' death and resurrection. Myers here offers an account of Christian faith that Barth, Brunner, Cullmann, and other Protestants would accept. This is not a Reformation issue, and gone is all reference to "natural immortality." These theological questions are no longer the issue at stake, as they were for Cullmann.

For Myers wished to impose this christological, theological focus as the sole content and meaning of the Christian funeral, in direct opposition to the contemporary "triumph of the biographical." The response was outrage and dismay, shared by parishioners and many of their priests. This outrage prompted Myers to offer a "clarification" of his policies, but to the best of my knowledge, he has not backed down in principle. (More recent, post–2003 postings on his website deal with topics such as stem-cell research.)

To better grasp what this conflict was about, we can retrieve the terms proposed in a fine contribution by Robert Krieg, a Catholic liturgical scholar. Krieg, writing for a Roman Catholic publication twenty years before Myers, believed the funeral homilist needs both the big and the little stories; these "interpret one another" (Krieg, 234). The "big story" is of course the narrative of Jesus' death and resurrection. The "little story" is that of the person whose funeral is celebrated. Both stories are needed. The dead person's faith may have been imperfect, the response of the mourners is also imperfect, but to squeeze these out of the story told at the funeral is a dubious strategy. The task of the funeral homilist was to balance and juxtapose these two stories, not to attempt to replace the one entirely by the other. This is a goal that Hughes and Mansell, the contemporary Protestant pastors who wrote funeral manuals, would share; it is not a distinctively Roman Catholic one. However, in a climate where anthologized sermons focus intensely on Doug and Barbara, the "balance" and mutual interpretation Krieg sought seems to have been relinquished. Hence, Myers' outright attack on anything that smacks of the biographical, the "little story" of the dead person's life, and the mourners' grief. Myers wanted to make sure the "big story" alone got told at Catholic funerals in his Archdiocese of Newark.

Outrage and dismay greeted Myers' attempt to return funerals to what he saw as their proper focus. Instead of "I did it my way," Catholic critics of this policy said privately, the funeral is now the place where the church hierarchy does it "*their way*." The giveaway is the "only the priest" policy. Even this does not capture all of the problems with Myers' agenda. For the priest too is forbidden to tell stories, or focus on the deceased as an individual. There is no room for a "eulogy" at a Christian funeral, Myers insisted. But his critics believed that to squeeze out the "biographical" entirely does not necessarily honor God. The hidden consequence may be to abstract faith from a living community of mourners, from the presence of God in their midst at a time of sorrow and confusion. Also, as one non-Catholic friend put it, "This is the one size fits all for funerals, right?" A "big story" that was universal can also become a means of ignoring individual differences, to deny what an earlier generation of preachers called "the sacredness of the human personality."

Nor did Myers seem to uphold the collective nature of the church as Christ's body, in his stance against "biographical" funeral preaching. He did not extol the communion of saints, as a critique of American (Protestant?) excessive individualism. The "little story" in all its forms is so totally excluded that even the communion of saints would be an unsuitable topic for the funeral homily in Newark. Nothing other than Jesus' death and resurrection should be preached. While an anthology of "sermons" without texts, filled with Doug and Barbara stories reflects the triumph of the biographical, a Myers-type corrective seems too extreme on the other end. There is a real difference between the focus by a Blackwood on individual salvation and relationship with God and the level of "biographical" sermon that keeps attention on Doug and Barbara in the pastor's office. The first fits within a vision of the funeral as primarily an occasion of worship. The latter turns it into a group commemoration. The "little story" once separated from the "big story," to use Krieg's terms, takes on a life of its own. In the end, such biographical sermons cannot help but make it harder for the congregation to hear the sound of that trumpet in darkness, the true source of Christian hope in the midst of death, loss, and sorrow.

Perhaps it is not only the sheer presence of God now, among the mourners, that ought to be the focus of Christians' hope. The triumph of the biographical is not without another level of theological implication, and it is remarkable that Myers did not point this out explicitly. A biography deals with "this life," the history of a particular individual embedded in a social history, a world and a time and a place. The diabetic who lost first his eyesight and then his legs, or Barbara who found happiness in her second marriage: these are the protagonists in the biographical sermons. A "biographical sermon" or a eulogy that "celebrates the life" is a retroactive reconstruction, a look back at a life "lived" and complete. This is still another reason why children's funerals are now so difficult: how difficult it is to make the child's short life seem "complete." Those who write full-scale memoirs about their dead children face the same problem. (Deford's memoir for his dead young daughter makes this clear.) Popular terms such as "life span" and "life cycle" suggest exactly this need on our part for a sense of "closure" and completion.

Our underlying assumption is that a "natural" life lasts into old age. When it has done so, the funeral sermon reinforces our assurance that, to use Kübler-Ross' own expression, "The circle of life is closed" (120). Yes, this model presupposes that "death is a natural event," and carries with it a vision of "natural cycles" normally taken as given rather than argued. In the psychological theories that use this imagery, "nature" is a system in itself, and organic processes of growth and decay are the underlying imagery. When a human being dies "full of years" as did the biblical patriarchs, we can fit his or her "little story" right into this pattern of imagery, whether or not the Christian "big story" is mentioned at all.

With this model, the role for resurrection or any kind of afterlife is difficult to fix. Any "post-life-cycle" existence may have a tacked-on quality to it, if it is introduced at all. We see here, when this imagery is brought into close scrutiny, a very different view of what "natural" means than in the once-pervasive idea of natural immortality. In that version of things, "nature" never "closed," but caterpillars "naturally" turn into butterflies, and plants grow through the crack in the wall into sun on the other side. The natural immortality view was once, pre-Cullmann, assumed to be "Christian," rather than "sub-Christian" or "Platonism." But now we must wonder how the "circle of life is closed" view is also to be considered Christian. A case can be made for it. The presence, love, and guidance of God through every stage of our lives is indeed the theme of many contemporary Christian songs. But what is missing is any direct reference to what lies beyond or after. Resurrection or immortality (and here it makes no difference which we choose) is not part of the "little story" of a biography that fills a biographical sermon.

Recall "Crossing the Bar," a poem where the personal past of the speaker is left behind as he sets out to sea beyond the safety of the harbor. So, too, Archbishop Myers might have pointed out that to "celebrate the life" of a dead Christian is to forget what lies ahead, omit the open ocean where he or she already sails to meet the Pilot face to face. Myers did not mention this explicitly. Nor do the many Protestant funeral sermons that focus on the needs of mourners qua mourners now, let alone the ones that are purely eulogies. (The strength of Thomas Long's recent *Accompany Them with Singing: The Christian Funeral* is precisely what he picks up on this point. A Christian funeral ought to assume a step beyond this life, into God. It is not memories and commemoration of the life on earth now complete.)

Here is a major shift, one that has affected not only sermons but also Christian songs. Contemporary songs (we mean Christian music, not "I did it my way"!) are much more likely to focus on God's continuous presence throughout our lives and our journey through them. Such songs as "Be Not Afraid" and "Borning Cry" take the individual through allegorical dangers, and through the life span. Deserts, floods, and foreign lands are all intended to be references to situations faced now. These songs lack, however, the traditional hymn-lyric pattern of departure-arrival, yearning-fulfillment found in earlier Protestant songs, including those in the "Appropriate Hymns" sections of the older funeral manuals. Those shared a distinctive beginning-middle-end structure. Take the most familiar of these: "Amazing Grace" traces a journey with an explicit destination.

> Through many dangers, toils and snares
> I have already come;
> 'Tis grace that brought me safe thus far,
> And grace will lead me home.
>
> Yea, when this flesh and heart may fail,
> And mortal life shall cease,
> I shall possess within the veil,
> A life of joy and peace.

It concludes,

> When we've been there ten thousand years
> Bright shining as the sun,
> We've no less days to sing God's praise
> Than when we've first begun.

In many contemporary renditions, the verse about "mortal life shall cease" is left out. Its reference to "within the veil" may be too obscure, or perhaps it is simply too direct in its reference to death. With or without this verse, the song, like Tennyson's poem and like the theology of death before silence and denial, does not rely on any image of life ending "full circle." A biographical sermon, a "celebration of the life of *x*" inevitably does.

The older pattern of "Amazing Grace" is not purely "otherworldly." No, for it covers "dangers, toils and snares" now. But it includes another life "within the veil," hidden and separating the living and the dead. That other life in the end supersedes the life celebrated and remembered by mourners now. A biographical sermon is "this worldly," and a model of "life span" or "life's circle" upon which contemporary biography is based revisions Christian life itself. The presence of God at every stage, rather than a hope for a final, anticipated opportunity to "see my Pilot face to face" is not godless, nor reducible to "my way." But if this is what Christians today stress, then it comes at the expense of other choices and commitments when framed as it is now. In the context of a funeral that "celebrates the life" of the departed, it is hard to avoid a one-sided stress on the "closing of life's circle," just as it is hard not to have the "little story" squeeze out the "big story" of Jesus' death and resurrection. Note that no belief in an afterlife is ever explicitly denied, nothing is ruled out by this model of a natural life span completed, a life lived, over and now "celebrated." But whatever the shape of what comes after, it is no longer the central and explicit focus of attention at the biographical funeral. Those at the funeral, preacher, mourners, and their friends, will think, "Are we doing right by the departed? Are we truly celebrating his/her life?" They will not be encouraged or urged to ponder each within themselves, "Are you living under the power of the world to come?"

It seems appropriate, in a chapter that starts without a biblical text, to end with an account of a funeral where the "biographical" was balanced by the "doctrinal," this world by the world to come, where individual and communal also interpreted each other. To the monks of St. John's Abbey, a Benedictine community in rural Minnesota, death is a familiar, yet very solemn occasion. There was no doubt that someone had died; the brothers held an all-night vigil in their giant dark church. Nor was the central theme of Christ's death and resurrection ever neglected during the funeral mass. Nevertheless, the Abbot's sermon included a biography of the dead monk, and expressly focused on what made his life unique. This particular man had worked for more than fifty years at the library, but his hobby had been fishing in the local lakes. As an elderly, already retired man, his greatest joy some years before had been to host an environmental survey team, and take them out fishing. This was part of his long life that those present wanted to remember.

After the actual church funeral ceremony was over, the entire congregation—monks, family, guests—walked slowly through the monastery garden, and then down the road and up the hill to the cemetery. This was early December; it was a cold walk over already snow-covered ground. (The elderly and disabled got to ride.) At the cemetery, atop a windy hill, everyone gathered round while a brief and very formal service was completed. The coffin was lowered into the ground, something that could not have happened in the old days (before mechanisms to heat the ground) since the temperature for the whole month had not risen above nine degrees Fahrenheit. At the close, I looked around, and took in a good view of the lake. The dead monk could rest among his brothers, await the resurrection; but he could also see how the fish were biting. Contra Myers, it seemed perfectly appropriate to join these hopes together. Contra Cullmann too, although I later realized that the latter part of this extra-biblical eschatology owed more to Thornton Wilder's *Our Town* than to Plato or any formal theology.

A monastic funeral is an event for a community that values a different model of personhood than Sinatra's "My Way." Yet a monastic funeral is not an abstraction from the lives, vows, and places of those who participate. Moreover, due to value placed on hospitality, outsiders such as myself were drawn into the proceedings, finding our places as witnesses both to Jesus' death and resurrection and to a particular individual life well lived. Even in a monastery, where community is such a central value, "someone was here" matters. The Benedictines got it right; the pastor who retold the story of Barbara and David missed the mark, and Archbishop Myers overreacted.

The triumph of the biographical makes it harder to see that *Preaching to Mourners* is not just "celebrating a life" in a vacuum. There is a community, there is the church as the body of Christ—whether or not one wishes to use the language of "communion of saints." There is the doctrinal heritage of Christian faith and teaching, even when different eras have radically different understandings of this. And there is, somewhere in the midst of all this, the sound of that trumpet in darkness, the presence of God at and after the time of death.

PART IV

What Might Have Been

13

TWO ALTERNATIVES

The genre of "alternative history" has little repute among professional historians. Books based on "what if the South had won the Civil War?" are entertainment, but do not, it is assumed, tell us anything about the real world. Given the North's overwhelming superiority of manpower and materials, the outcome of the war was never really up for grabs. However, we are not convinced that in the realm of ideas and beliefs, things are this fixed and inevitable. It seems that some trends could have gone differently, that people's responses are variable, and that there is at least the possibility of roads not taken. So, in this chapter and the next, we look at several alternatives to what has happened. The alternatives are to actual current Christian views of death and funeral patterns, to the triumph of the biographical and its aim of "celebrating the life" of the deceased. We trace possibilities of responses to the death awareness movement's language and images that might have been. Our purpose is to offer another perspective on changes we have examined, changes that happened without public debate or outcry, without the kind of publicity that accompanied other religious controversies.

All along we have been speaking primarily about mainline Protestants, and that group itself changed during the eras we examine. In 1942 Presbyterian clergyman and funeral manual author Blackwood could assume with great confidence that his style of religiousness represented "mainstream" America. Not just the Presbyterian Church in particular of which he was a member, but the tradition of white, middle-class, nationally spread denominations whose roots lay both in the Reformation and the British evangelical movement of the eighteenth century. Yes, there were distinctive regional differences, and organizational splits left over from the Civil War, but Southern Presbyterians (PCUSA) and Northern Presbyterians (UPCUSA). shared the views of death and afterlife we have discussed, not to mention polity and worship style. Lutherans might still have an "immigrant" ethos about them, but overall we are speaking of a style of religiousness that saw itself, and was seen by others, as in the heartland of American faith and life. It did not have to pay any attention whatsoever to what anyone else (Roman Catholics, Pentecostals, or African Americans) was doing, Indeed, in all the sermon anthologies and pastors' manuals from that era, such groups are absolutely invisible. They might as well have been on Mars.

By the time the death awareness movement brought its new words for death, dying, and bereavement to Americans, in the early 1970s, this situation had already changed. The 1960s was the era of major decline in the numbers and prestige of mainline denominations of Protestantism. In that one decade, the Presbyterian Church lost one-third of its members, and other mainline groups also found themselves floundering and divided over issues such as the Vietnam War. Religious alternatives among Protestants included "nonmainline" groups such as Assemblies of God, while the civil rights movement had drawn national attention to the important role of African American clergy and the black church. Roman Catholics were fresh from Vatican II's reforms, and had also, in this country, lost much of their perceived role as an immigrants' church. Catholics moved out to the suburbs, used English in the liturgy, and in some ways became more "mainline" themselves. And on the fringes of this religious landscape (although not on the fringe of media attention) the counterculture of the 1960s created a plethora of "new religious movements," "cults" to their enemies, which marketed themselves to those who sought a religious alternative to mainstream America. Therefore, the generation of American mainline Protestant leaders who greeted and embraced the death awareness movement were different from Blackwood's generation. They were, in some sense, an embattled establishment, on the defensive but also trying to remain open to new cultural developments and resist what was already seen as resurgent "fundamentalism."

This gave mainline Protestants at home with pastoral counseling experts such as Wayne Oates or (already critical of conventional funerals) Paul Irion the responsibility to welcome the work of Kübler-Ross, the death awareness movement, and hospice. These clergy leaders saw themselves as pastoral counseling experts or chaplains who dealt with dying and grief. By 1983, when Mitchell and Anderson wrote *All Our Losses, All Our Griefs*, there was no doubt that the dominant response of this field to the death awareness movement had been appreciative and enthusiastic. For Mitchell and Anderson, it was Christian theology, with its neglect of "loss" as a category, which needed revision, and each author or editor of a sermon anthology focused on *Preaching to Mourners* would have agreed. Moreover, there was no controversy over how appropriate a focus on death, dying, and grief was for Christian clergy or pastoral caregivers. In other areas, over other topics, pastoral counselors had struggled and been divided. For instance, pastors debated if "encounter groups" should be encouraged, or if these new psychotherapies should be left to the Esalen Institute, and the extreme countercultural ethos that promoted them as the solution for all life's repressions. And debates over sex therapies, divorce counseling, and later homosexuality, all grabbed church and media attention. But pastors and death belonged together; there was nothing strained or unnatural in clergy counseling of the sick, dying, and bereaved. It seemed universally right for clergy to take these tasks and continue their pastoring during the funeral and its sermon, too. Moreover, to follow the pathway laid down earlier by Hiltner, any resources from psychology could potentially be utilized, bracketing some of the atheistic or antireligious personal opinions of the psychologists themselves.

Even beyond this consensus, there was very, very little theological objection to the ideas and imagery of the death awareness movement. To review its primary ideas, these included that death is "a natural part of life" and therefore we should accept it; that dealing with death, one's own or that of others, is a coming to terms with loss, and that dying and grief are opportunities to search for meaning. The death awareness movement, then, opposed what Irion had earlier labeled "vitalism" (life minus death) and militarism, the hope to "defeat" death through medicine or technology. Overall, clergy, pastors, and pastoral care experts could not have quibbled with these claims. The sermons in the anthologies, along with experts such as Mitchell and Anderson, reflect genuine appreciation for the positive work done by the death awareness advocates. All also agreed that some form of public education about death and dying was needed in an America that denied death. Funerals were clearly one occasion for this, even at their most "biographical." In short, silence and denial, when labeled as such, had no champions.

It is worthwhile, however, to look at the few feeble theological objections that were raised, objections that carried little weight overall. These objections certainly did not result in an overall mobilization to restrict the use of death awareness movement ideas and imagery, nor to label them "pagan" or "anti-Christian." Nor does it seem plausible to imagine Christian leaders speaking out against bereavement counseling as "un-Christian," or accuse it of undermining the gospel message. This just seems odd, as an agenda for religious debate, especially if we think of mainline Protestant clergy leading such an attack.

The short answer: this did not happen because hospice and bereavement counseling did not deal with sex, and it is over sexual issues that the most religious furor and media attention continue to thrive. The other short answer is that religious opposition to euthanasia, physician-assisted suicide, and (of course) abortion provided plenty of outlets for those who wished to attack "anti-Christian" approaches to death. The Hemlock Society and Dr. Jack Kevorkian made much better, clearer targets than did the National Hospice Organization, and so the battles of the "culture wars" raged over these specific issues, but not over the basic goals of caring for the dying, or counseling the grief-stricken.

But let us suppose for the moment that this had not been so. Let us imagine that theological energy against the death awareness movement had really mobilized early, so that any of its ideas came to seem as far out and far from Christian values as those of the Hemlock Society, which advocates assisted suicide for the terminally ill. We wonder if this stance of principled fervent opposition even could have been a possibility, a cause around which mainline Protestants rallied.

Our first alternative "might have been" is to look at theological ideas that could have dramatically skewed the stance of mainstream American Protestants away from the death awareness movement. Such theologies might have convinced pastoral counselors and those who trained them that "preaching to mourners" was as dubious theologically as the Esalen Institute's encounter groups were as Christian counseling. Had this happened, then the death awareness movement could have flourished as an alternative, or perhaps—like Masters and Johnson's sex therapy—as a technical specialty that no one without very specialized training (and the right kind of laboratory) should attempt. There would not be books such as *The Pastor and Grief*, or *Hospice and Ministry*, or *All Our Losses, All Our Griefs*. Death and dying would have become a medical specialty, or a flamboyantly secular ideology—but never integrated into conventional theological orthodox Christian faith.

We have already looked at a few potential resources within theology that might have produced such a response. Cullmann's "death as enemy" approach comes to mind, because he wanted to "awful-ize" death beyond all accommodation to it, and to use military imagery to promote its "defeat." Since this was exactly the imagery the death awareness movement found pernicious and misguided when it came to medical handling of dying hospital patients, we suggested a hidden convergence between Cullmann's ideas and the ethos of silence and denial within which Kübler-Ross began her work. She wished patients to "accept" death, to allow the circle of life to close, and did not want this to seem a "defeat." For her, there was a time when the patient's urge to "keep fighting" waned, and then it was indeed appropriate to accept one's own impending death. For Cullmann, this could never have been what Jesus' "Not my will, but thine be done" meant. A consistent Cullmannesque stance in the hospital would have told even the sickest patients that death was still their enemy, never their friend or their ally. While we certainly find patients' families and their doctors thinking along such lines, Protestant mainline clergy rarely seem to join them. Eberhard Jüngel, the German theologian whose idea "[i]n life, man can never resist death enough," came closest to this. His book overloads on military imagery of the battle against death. Yet his statement is completed with the paradoxical, "Dying, he can do nothing at all against death" (136), and he stressed the total passivity with which it is appropriate for humans to meet their deaths. He condemned any attempt at all to prepare oneself as an instance of pagan "works-righteousness" (128). American pastors—including, I am sure, Lutherans—joined with Kübler-Ross and "done something," if not against death, then against the sense of isolation and helplessness that dying in a hospital produced.

Several other voices were raised, albeit feebly, against the death awareness movement's imagery and ideas, from a Christian theological stance. Some clearly come from the more evangelical or conservative branch of American Christianity. For Paul Vitz, in his polemical *Psychology as Religion: The Cult of Self-Worship*, the real target is obviously human potential movement theories and practices (including encounter groups) and the way that psychology, masquerading as "science," has been able to win legitimacy and government support. He takes a sideswipe at thanatology here (108–9), but he quickly turns to sex education programs, which better represent what he finds outrageous. This 1977 book gleefully anticipates the conservative resurgence of the 1980s, but not surprisingly has no sustained discussion of death, anymore than did the psychologies it criticized. Also, recall our first short answer: sex is the topic that galvanizes opposition, that makes religious conflicts newsworthy.

A much more nuanced and well-directed criticism of Kübler-Ross is Roy Branson's essay in the *Christian Century* (1975) titled "Is Acceptance a Denial of Death?" This is the flagship journal of mainline Protestantism, and the tone of Branson is considerably different from that of Vitz. The essay was written during the first triumphant enthusiasm for Kübler-Ross and her "five stages of dying." Branson brings a Cullmannesque view to bear on the death awareness movement, for he argues that in reality, death is not as "acceptable" in itself as the new model of dying insists. To make death into a gentle, harmonious, "natural" event is to ignore the depth of negativity of its true essence. Like Cullmann, Branson believed the authentic Christian teaching is that death was and always will be an enemy of God. However, Branson, unlike Vitz, did not call for a boycott of all hospice programs, or other efforts to promulgate a death awareness movement agenda through government agencies. It was apparent that he admired the actual work done by Kübler-Ross, and believed this kind of service to the dying and bereaved could be continued by Christians who hold a very different set of ideas and images of death. Note too Branson's clever title; the one criticism he knew that fans of the death awareness movement would heed is that their own views constituted "denial" of death. This twist reveals how deeply the death awareness movement's new language had become the "first language" of Christian clergy and other readers of the *Christian Century*. Denial was a term everyone understood, a word theologians, counselors, and ordinary persons shared. There was, we may say, no language left over from that earlier era of before silence and denial that would have suited, and its entire imagery and stock of ideas would have made Kübler-Ross' style of "denial" (if that was what it was) look very mild indeed.

Another example of the Christian theologian's attempt to attack the death awareness movement's alleged rose-colored and romantic ideal of death also shows Cullmann's influence. "Theology and the Darkness of Death," an essay by B. J. Collopy, argues against any attempt to give positive or meaningful content to death. He wrote most explicitly against Karl Rahner, and as a Roman Catholic writing to criticize another Roman Catholic, he did not directly use the "works righteousness" argument of a Jüngel. But he might as well have done so. He did claim that absolute passivity, helplessness, and emptiness are the proper terms with which to even begin a discussion of death. This essay stacks up "awfulness" in a way Cullmann would envy. Death is "an alien growth in the marrow of human experience," "unmanageable, unacceptable . . . awful to the core." "Death is low business" (Collopy, 29, 33, 38, 42). Collopy explicitly contrasts these descriptions with the falsely positive and upbeat imagery of "death as natural event" that he finds at the center of the death awareness movement. It is his obligation as a Christian theologian, he believes, to destroy any such "meaningful" vision of death's place in life. It has no place, it is emptiness and nothingness. "Death's emptiness is common and universal; it holds no hidden theological lode" (49). Even to give it the status of a personified enemy (as Cullmann did) is too generous to it. We can imagine Collopy observing the chess game of *The Seventh Seal*, whose players are the existentially anguished knight and Death. Collopy would certainly agree that Death knows "Nothing." But he would fault the movie's use of the chess game, which has rules that even Death must obey. Collopy would find this too positive; death knows and respects no rules at all.

Suppose Branson and Collopy had joined with Vitz in calling for a Christian protest against all death awareness movement involvement on the part of clergy. Suppose they had persuaded pastoral counselors and caregivers to withdraw support from any "death and dying" organizations, and to renounce all the language of death as "natural event" and as "loss." Suppose that theological awful-izing death had led to lumping Kübler-Ross, and all the other leaders of "thanatology" as no different from Dr. Kevorkian or the Hemlock Society. Any accommodation to death would be an automatic betrayal of the gospel, a sign of secularisim's triumph, or of pernicious Platonism coming back in new psychological guise. Pastoral care training would simply avoid or condemn this body of literature. While Jüngel sounds as if he might be recruited for such a campaign, it is very clear that this is never the agenda of Branson and Collopy, nor of others who tried to critique the ethical "naturalism" of the death awareness movement on philosophical grounds. These voices never made the connection between Cullmann's imagery and Vitz's theologically driven political agenda. They continued to support forms of pastoral care for the dying and bereaved that directly depended upon the new words and images of Kübler-Ross and the death awareness movement.

All of these thinkers focused on the language of "death and dying" as it was developed for hospitalized patients. Now let us imagine how this might have impacted the bereaved. Think what a Christian funeral would sound and feel like, had this road not taken been chosen. A funeral led by Jüngel or Collopy, say. It would clearly not be "preaching to mourners" whose experience of loss needs to be honored. It would not be entirely triumphant, for "death's darkness" is still with us, and Jesus' resurrection has not illuminated it out of our beings. Jüngel and Collopy together stress utter passivity, where any active response of the pastor or congregation would seem suspect. Emptiness and nothingness prevail, in that not even the biographical sermon could compensate for the pervasive futility of saying or doing anything in the face of death. A funeral dominated by the extreme use of "death's darkness" imagery or by total helplessness in the face of death, might even add the implication that all of the work of mourning was somehow "pagan" (just as Jüngel saw hospice-type activities). What looks good on the surface had actually been a sinful proud attempt to perform "works" when God wants only faith, or a self-deceptive high-mindedness when death itself was "low business." No surprise that the ideas of these theologians never made headway, never convinced enough pastors or chaplains, to make a serious alternative to "preaching to mourners." Maybe, given this possibility, "please omit funeral" would have been preferable.

Note how none of these theological critics considers a return to the storehouse of ideas and images from before Cullmann. If any "meanings" given to death are a form of "denial," then it is hard to picture an attempt to reinstate "heaven as home" into Christian preaching, nor to preach natural immortality. What Jüngel and Collopy share is Cullmann's sense that an "authentic Christian view" must be a thoroughly de-Platonized version of the gospel, and that would eliminate the body/soul dualism of all traditional piety. Moreover, any Christian view of death would be solely christological. Jesus' death and resurrection is the only source of true knowledge of death, just as for Archbishop Myers of the previous chapter this is the only correct subject for the funeral sermon. It is Christ facing death "in all its horror" and not Christ promising "mansions" in his Father's house who is the subject of these possible funeral sermons. Gone, utterly gone, are stories of King David accepting the death of his infant son as God's will. Just as gone are the references to children at play in the streets of (heavenly) Jerusalem.

However, let us now turn to a second "might have been" alternative outcome for Christian imagery and ideas about death. Suppose that more of the earlier imagery had endured. Suppose that Barth and then Cullmann had not convinced so many theologians (and those pastors trained by them) that a christocentric focus was the only way to protect the uniqueness of revelation. Suppose the early assumption of natural immortality had persisted, not just on the Internet where "The Rose" poem is still popular for memorial sites, but within the structure of Protestant thinking about death. Here we have almost the opposite of the first "might have been." Imagine a world where death instead of being "awful-ized," is still, as it was in the 1920s and 1930s, made continuous with the images of natural transformations and growth. Not as in the Kübler-Ross version of this (life's circle closes—as we discussed in the previous chapter), but as in "The Rose Still Grows Beyond the Wall," where the transition from shade to sunlight involves no rupture or loss or pain whatsoever. We should reiterate that in what actually "came next," the disappearance of all such images from the post–death-awareness sermons is complete; on this point at least, Cullmann triumphed. But suppose he had not. Imagine that such earlier imagery resisted the theological challenges to it, and inspired a new generation of seminary-trained clergy to continue to preach "natural immortality" at funerals. Allegories of growing roses and metamorphized bugs would continue to illustrate the great universal truth of the soul's "natural immortality." Instead of this imaginable outcome, what actually occurred is that the older, once-conventional, orthodox, and utterly mainstream Protestant Christian imagery is now alien. In the context of *Preaching to Mourners*, it would appear pagan. Or, to update our terms, "New Age."

Yes, that is what natural immortality now looks like, that is where it resides. Somewhere outside of "real" Christianity, in a borderland of "spirituality" along with near-death experiences of the light, reincarnation, and visits from angels. The rose grows from one side of the wall to the sunnier side, upward and onward indefinitely. There is no death as destruction, loss, or darkness here. This is the vision of reality and death that Kübler-Ross herself later adopted, and so Branson may have had a point with his title, "Is Acceptance a Denial of Death?" Maybe "acceptance of death" as a goal was the first stage in an out-and-out rejection of its reality. For the later Kübler-Ross, there was no death, it was just a mistake born of ignorance and fear. (This view is proclaimed in her 1983 book *On Children and Death*.) While the "mainstream" of the death awareness movement ignored her, probably out of embarrassment, Branson, Collopy, and of course Vitz would all find this turn to natural immortality unsurprising and easily predicted. "We knew all along this new language of death and dying was pagan to the core." But the irony is that Kübler-Ross of 1983 was very similar to the Protestant Christianity of the early decades of the twentieth century, of the era before silence and denial. *When Death Speaks* proclaimed a message that is basically compatible with her later "death-denying" ideas. But in 1937 this message was often spoken within a Protestant church at a Christian funeral. Clearly, something had happened.

By the standards of *Preaching to Mourners*, the genre of mainstream Protestant sermons that welcomes the death awareness movement's emphasis on loss, such natural immortality is no longer Christian. It never should have been Christian. It is denial, not given any positive space. It is not given even a nod, let alone a direct refutation, in the funeral sermons of recent decades. It is as if the border between what is legitimately Christian and that which lies outside has been redrawn. We use the term New Age because that has become many recent Christians' catchall for an evil or defective alternative view; "pagan" was what Blackwood would have said. As a positive designation for a specific collection of practices, ideas, and organizations, it may be a very unhelpful category, of dubious use to religion scholars. Never mind; for Christians who want to polemically exclude some alternative possibilities from the landscape of faith, New Age is as good a label as any. New Age is unlike Vitz's psychological enemies; it is definitely not trying to be "objective science" in the conventional Western sense. Nor, for Christians who see it as an adversary, is it truly a different religious tradition such as Hinduism. Once again, scholars might not think the category itself works well, and those who identify themselves with any of the beliefs and practices labeled New Age have a variety of opinions about who they are and how to identify their spiritual choices. But for Christians now, the category New Age designates a defective or evil alternative religious worldview. Within that worldview is a vision of death that corresponds very closely to the "natural immortality" that was once the mainstay of Protestant funeral sermons. That view, as we saw, was once believed to be supported by the Bible, and proved by the resurrection of Jesus. It just seemed so obvious . . . until theological challenges, Cullmann and cultural shifts have now made this same belief "sub-Christian" if not absolutely pernicious. But in an alternative outcome, suppose the boundaries of what is "authentically Christian" had continued as before, and "natural immortality" had retained its place in Protestantism.

One way to imagine this is to take an example of natural immortality imagery from the initial decade of the death awareness movement, the 1970s. (I was introduced to it at a death awareness conference, although the work itself was not part of the official program.) We may wonder if it is as truly incompatible with Christian faith as Cullmann and the authors of pastors' manuals all seem to believe. Perhaps there could have been some space for this within a religious outlook that had acknowledged "denial of death" as a problem, and accepted "acceptance" as a goal for the dying. Paula Trinus' 1972 *Hope for the Flowers* is an allegory of death and transformation. It was published by a division of Paulist Press, which itself suggests a diversity of opinions over the border that separates New Age from Christianity. In this picture book, ostensibly written for children, but meant for adults, two caterpillars live their lives searching for purpose and clear direction. One of the two comes across an elderly caterpillar who is spinning a cocoon. He tells her his aim is to become a butterfly.

> "Tell me, sir," Yellow asked, "What is a butterfly"
> "It's what you are meant to become. It flies with beautiful wings and joins the earth to heaven. . . .
> "How does one become a butterfly?" she asked pensively.
> "You must want to fly so much that you are willing to give up being a caterpillar."
> "You mean to die?" asked Yellow. . . .
> "Yes and no," he answered. "What looks like you will die but what's really you will still live. Life is changed not taken way. . . . You'll be a beautiful butterfly—we're all waiting for you!"
> (Trinus, 23)

Yellow succeeds, and then persuades her friend Stripe to try the transformation. In the cocoon "[i]t got darker and darker and he was afraid. He felt he had to let go of everything. Until one day . . ." (41). The story ends with a picture of two triumphant butterflies, together.

Without butterflies, flowers cannot reproduce, so it is critical not just to their own happiness but to universal natural renewal that the bugs undergo their change. The story permits several interpretations, but it can be read as a manifesto on behalf of natural immortality. Those caterpillars will change because it is in their nature to change, they are born with inner butterflies ready to emerge when the time is ripe. While Teresa of Avila in the sixteenth century used this exact image to emphasize that the little silkworm must truly die in its cocoon (*Interior Castle*, 91–92), the message of *Hope for the Flowers* is that there is barely any "death" at all. No annihilation, no loss; "life is changed, not taken away." This clear statement of a view exactly repeats that of Shepfer, the author of *When Death Speaks*, and many other funeral preachers of the earlier era. Universal intuition and universal natural patterns of change all point toward the truth of immortality. There is no need for a special revelation, a miraculous act of God, or any unique story of Jesus to show us this. This is why even *Death Speaks* was a misleading title; there is no reality behind this personification. *Hope for the Flowers* as a title captures the message successfully.

This example shows "natural immortality" at its genuinely charming best. "Natural immortality" did not require anything more extraordinary than the transformation of caterpillars to support it. It certainly did not depend on the extraordinary out-of-body near-death experiences recounted in many New Age books such as Betty Eadie's *Embraced by the Light*. But even the message of *Hope for the Flowers*, when juxtaposed against all of the anthologized sermons of the post–silence and denial era, now reads as if it must come from another religion, for which New Age is a convenient label. By 1972 the publication date of *Hope for the Flowers*, Christians who preached on death had discovered that no theological attention had been given to loss, and started to offer sermons at funerals with titles such as "Why, God, Why?" Eventually, as we have seen, the preferred pattern became the biographical "celebration of the life" that implicitly ignores the very "immortality" that Trinus' caterpillars can count on. There is no longer room for the message of *Hope for the Flowers* when preaching on death at a funeral, and the absence of such an allegory as Trinus' is noticed only by those who have read through an earlier era's abundance of similar material.

I am not sure this was inevitable. Christians could have more consistently rejected or ignored Cullmann, persisted in the earlier imagery, and kept open the possibility of natural immortality. Note that the symbol of hospice is the butterfly; it is perfectly possible to accept the practical agenda of hospice and the death awareness movement, while also accepting that "death" does not mean the closing of a circle, but the opening of a new phase of existence. Whether or not one thinks this a good or bad outcome, the loss of natural immortality reminds us that this is another road not taken. At least in formal public funerals presided over by Christian clergy, it is a "what might have been."

14

WHAT MIGHT HAVE BEEN—LAMENT

Hasten, O God, to save me;
O Lord, come quickly to help me. . . .
Yet I am poor and needy,
Come quickly to me, O God

—Psalm 70:1, 5

The previous chapter's alternative "might have beens" did not happen. The first of these alternatives, the whole-hearted rejection of the death awareness movement in the name of Cullmann's "death as enemy" approach, would have severed Christians from counseling and care for the dying. It also might have pushed the whole topic into the "culture wars" pattern, so that a discussion of hospice, or grief counseling, would have instantly taken on the adversarial format of the abortion debate. The second "might have been," the continuation of a previous era's natural immortality theology, would have meant the rejection of most of the best twentieth-century theology. Not just Cullmann, but Barth, Brunner, Moltmann, and many others who reframed the understanding of revelation, eschatology, and history would have been disregarded, if Christians had continued to accept a "Platonized" and ahistorical view of the gospel. This possibility also would have prevented or inhibited the refocusing of funerals onto the mourners. Perhaps the split between authentic Christianity and New Age with which we ended the previous chapter is a misleading oversimplification, and that at the level of what people actually still believe natural immortality has as many advocates as does Cullmann. Yet "natural immortality" and its imagery disappear from Protestant preaching at funerals. Banished from these formal and official church occasions, such imagery is no longer considered appropriate or helpful, nor is it deemed theologically worthy for Christian reflection on death. We may say that both "might have been" alternative outcomes we suggested and explored would not have been preferable to what actually transpired. But there could be other, religiously better alternatives that also lost out. These also are alternative "might have been" possibilities that never made it into the sermon anthologies of the post–silence and denial era. In this chapter, we look at one that both had some theologians' support and could have spoken to the needs of mourners and the new understanding of Christian funerals. We explore "lament." But things did not work out that way, and so what this chapter covers remains unusual, idiosyncratic, and jarring today.

Remember, in the recent era of funeral preaching, when the funeral sermon is defined as *Preaching to Mourners*, the congregation is defined as "those who mourn." From this revisioning of the funeral, certain tensions and pastoral dilemmas arise. First, the preacher/pastor knows that not all mourn equally. Some, family members and close friends, will be in the early stages of intense grief (even when the "stages" model no longer is used, some equivalent designation signifies shock, numbness, anxiety, etc.). Others will be in attendance because they are connected in a looser way with the deceased, and want, vaguely to "do right by" him or her. Still others come with the family who mourns, and show up to demonstrate solidarity. For instance, the boyfriend or girlfriend of a grandchild of the dead person will not usually be a "mourner" in the psychological sense, but will be given "honorary mourner" status as part of his or her temporary "honorary family member" status. Today's pastors who plan sermons are very well aware of these distinctions, and also aware that some of those present may not be "mourners" in the normal emotional sense. They may in secret (or in public) rejoice that someone who harmed them in life is now dead and powerless. The newer discussions of "problem funerals" focus on exactly these cases, rather than the Christian character or life of the deceased. Knowing the emotional mix of all these different participants is centrally relevant to how the pastor arranges and presides over the funeral.

Next, the tension between theological affirmation of hope and the pastoral goal of addressing the needs of mourners (the dilemma noted by Mitchell and Anderson) remains and is sharpened when the funeral now becomes "a celebration of the life" of the deceased. Mitchell and Anderson critiqued one-sided emphasis on the resurrection, but this theological issue is not exactly the same as the current pastoral situation. Paradoxically, the one public occasion where everyone should have the right to be sad is now defined as "a celebration," which is normally a happy event. The word itself seems designed to extract whatever "happiness" could be gleaned from memories, stories, expressions of love and gratitude. Nevertheless, the preacher must be truly attentive to the reality of mourners' feelings, and to the deeper reality that a funeral is, alas, about death.

The tone set by the anthologies of sermons from the 1970s on is very definitely not "celebratory" in the sense of a "party." But the tension between pressure to be upbeat and the reality of mourners' grief remains. Their mourning is definitely to be taken seriously, but other pressures and interests have created a biographical funeral where gratitude predominates over sorrow and despair. Remember, in the era before silence and denial, the emotions of the mourners qua mourners were never the focus of the funeral, nor the sermon that was part of it. Today, as biographical "celebration," the funeral sermon's aim is to turn the mourners' attention away from exclusive focus on their grief and loss, back to the good times, and happy memories they share. Once again, think of the sermon that retold the history of Doug and Barbara in the pastor's office, when she learned of her terminal cancer diagnosis. What counters this in the sermon is not "resurrection" but memorial tributes to Barbara in happier times. Each sermon addressed to mourners gets caught in this consequence of making the mourners' emotions the central fact of the funeral situation.

Those who write manuals for preachers at funerals are very well aware that taking grief seriously means to acknowledge that someone has *died*. Barbara is truly gone, separation and loss are real. We are not in the New Age realm where "there is no death," only its illusion. Yet preachers seem also bound by lurking fear of the older criticism of funerals as gloomy and "barbaric." A funeral will be dreary and awful, unless some space is made for "a celebration of the life of" the person who has died; this appears the underlying assumption. But—and here pastors take this very seriously—it must remain realistically helpful to those who mourn. Pastors and authors of manuals struggle with the question, at what point does "celebration" become a new version of "denial"? This is the ambivalence of today's funeral, from the Protestant pastor's perspective (and also from that of the Roman Catholic priests who disagreed with Archbishop Myers' directives to them).

We now take this legitimate and much-discussed pastoral question into the realm of "what might have been." The pastoral agenda of *Preaching to Mourners* might have been better served by an entirely different kind of religious funeral. Suppose the funeral, now clearly defined as addressing mourners, had been transformed into an occasion for a very different kind of biblical mourning. In other words, for lament. Unlike the possibilities in the previous chapter, this one has actually been advocated, has occasionally been tried. But, as we shall see, it did not catch on, it is not the pattern of the contemporary Christian funeral, even if a case can and has been made that it should have become so.

Yes, lament. In the world of biblical scholarship, experts of the Hebrew Bible (Old Testament) discovered that real mourning, expression of sorrow and grief, was a very central part of the biblical outlook. Indeed, one of the favorite forms of Hebrew poetry was the lament. Here, "form" means standard genre, with a set content and structure, not just a poetic form such as a sonnet. Lament is the basic pattern of a huge proportion of the psalms, as well as the book of Lamentations, and major sections of the prophets. What marks the work of biblical scholars and theologians Bernard Anderson, Patrick Miller, and Walter Brueggemann (along with many others) is that they wish to identify and promote a theology they find intrinsic to this "form" of lament. This theology, they believe, presents an excellent and truly "biblical" alternative to many of the traditional Christian ideas, and it would enrich Christian thought, worship, and pastoral practice to learn it and adopt it. "Praise can retain its authenticity and naturalness only in polarity with lamentation" (Westermann, 33). Lament could certainly have changed and improved Christian funerals. Had this happened, there would have been no need for Mitchell and Anderson to complain that "loss" was not a theological topic, or that resurrection-oriented funerals were "pastorally misguided." The "lament theology" these scholars advocated might have become the foundation for a new and different style of Christian funeral, and even a different Christian understanding of God. They proposed this, but one thing is clear: lament did not triumph after the era of silence and denial.

First, the form of "lament" needs to be laid out, as a basic pattern with a specific content and context. The lament has six parts:

1. Address
2. Complaint
3. Petition
4. Motivation
5. Vow of offering
6. Assurance of being heard (Brueggemann, 70; in Miller, *Psalms and the Life of Faith*)

The whole is addressed to the Lord, and even if formulaic has a quality of sincerity and spontaneity Brueggemann et al. insist upon. "Lord, hear my prayer," may be a literary form, but the material that follows will sound, even to us, as if someone really suffers. "My wounds fester and are loathsome" (Ps 38:5). "Ruthless witnesses come forward: they question me on things I know nothing about" (Ps 35:11). "I am overcome by the blow of your hand" (Ps 39:10). The "complaint" can include illness, enemies, depression, isolation—virtually anything, private or public, is subsumed under this rubric. Then, the Lord is asked to do something about this. "Asked" is too weak, and "begged" is absolutely wrong. "Do to them as you did to Midian," "Make them like tumbleweed," "Rise up, O God, and judge the earth" are typical "petitions." One may translate these into "Get with the program, Lord!" or even "Get up off your ass, God, and do something to help!" The motivation is not that *I* the petitioner deserve help, or even that God is merciful and will take pity on me. Most often, the "motivation" is that God's reputation will suffer if he remains silent and inactive. In return, the lamenter promises to fulfill a vow, to offer a sacrifice, and even more significantly to tell publicly how the Lord has come to his aid. "Then men will say, 'Surely the righteous are still rewarded, surely there is a God who judges the earth" (Ps 58:11). Finally, the lament closes with assurance that God has heard;

this was perhaps originally spoken by the priest, but it serves to close the prayer form.

The contemporary advocates of lament believe passionately that this genre needs to be rediscovered and revoiced today. Note, they say, how a dialogue with God does not shirk from asking tough questions, nor are laments written for human doormats. The complaints are realistic, often bitter and despairing. Anger, desire for revenge, the full range of human negativity, are present in these ancient poems/prayers. Significantly, no one is told that sickness or defeat are "the Lord's will" and that passive resignation is the most godly response to adversity. Just the opposite; those who prayed these laments expected much more from God, for God was near, and even more, God was passionately concerned with human problems and suffering. This was before the "Greek" ideal of divine impassivity, so long upheld by Christians, took hold. Maybe the reason for God's concern was not "noble" by our standards; concern for one's own reputation does not strike most of us as "high level" or altruistic enough. But what mattered to ancient persons was that their God cared, and was willing to listen and act in response to their complaints. Moreover, there is an extreme level of honesty and anguish in the psalms that has made them in reality the prayer book for Christians down through the ages. These poems have been prayed both individually and communally, in spite of official theologies that ignored, negated, or undermined their basic content.

This "lament form" is unquestionably found in the Hebrew Bible. That makes lament "biblical," but whether or not it is truly Christian raises another kind of issue. The New Testament seems "lament free," and so Christians could have turned away from this form of prayer. There have probably always been some representatives of this stance. For them, the tone of Christian prayer and worship ought to be joy and triumph, not unhappy complaint. In this view, New replaces Old, and lament gets left behind. It is obsolete, no longer binding or relevant under the new covenant. This is the view of traditional "supersessionism," the belief that the New Testament completely fulfilled and replaced the Old. Biblical theologians such as Miller and Brueggemann have energetically challenged this approach to the Hebrew Bible, at the risk of overglorifying the "Jewish" honesty and directness of the Old (see Brueggemann, 1993, 50). Advocates of lament, they argue persuasively that very valuable dimensions of the "Old" were and continue to be silenced and denied by supersessionist models of interpretation. Lament is surely one such ingredient, and it is not only "biblical," but truly complements some of the New Testament emphasis on triumph and victory, as well as later Christian idealization of "resignation" to God's will.

Moreover, continuous Christian love for the psalms meant that pure supersessionism was impossible to maintain in practice. But the problems posed by some aspects of these same psalms have also been continuous. It did not take modern biblical scholarship or nineteenth-century historical consciousness for these to arise. Some particulars of the psalms of lament have long struck many persons as "sub-Christian." In their authors' desire for revenge, especially, these prayer-poems pose problems. Take, for example, the pious wishes that the children of one's enemies get their heads dashed against the rocks (Ps 137:9), or "May a creditor seize all that he has; may strangers plunder the fruits of his labors" (Ps 109:11). This desire for vengeance must be unworthy of God, and of his people. To the biblical theologians who rediscovered and champion lament, however, calls for divine action are really calls for divine justice. The Lord takes evil seriously and is prepared to deal with it. We are squeamish wimps if we do not want to think that God cares enough about the world to alleviate human wrongdoing. We should expect that God will want to intervene, especially to protect the poor and the helpless. This issue has been vigorously debated (see Jinkins and Zenger), and it is no coincidence that edited volumes on it also include discussions of modern atrocities such as the Holocaust, colonialism in New Zealand, and war in the Balkans (Linafelt and Beal, eds., *God in the Fray: A Tribute to Walter Brueggemann*). These are indeed "lamentable" human situations. To bring religious knowledge embedded in ancient literary forms to bear on them is a significant task, even if it carries with it serious risks.

Brueggemann in particular has worked over decades to teach within both church and academy that this strand of biblical thought is worth recovering. The lack of lament in Christian worship has severed the quest for justice from worship and prayer. Moreover, the absence of public lament has isolated Christians from emotions such as anger and grief and despair. At one point, Brueggemann even found common ground with Kübler-Ross, as he compared the six-part structure of lament to her "five stages of dying." The "Formfulness of Grief" was what mattered; it heals to give structured expression to inchoate emotions, and both the ancient form and the modern psychological model attempted to do this (Brueggemann, in Miller, *Psalms and the Life of Faith*). However, Brueggemann noted, the lament is essentially one side of a dialogue, not an intrapsychic exploration of grief. It ends with an assurance that God has heard, not just with "acceptance." This was in 1977; in his later work Brueggemann de-emphasized "formfulness," and looked instead at the unfinished, ever-questioning stance of the biblical texts that could still speak as *Contested Truth in a Post–Christian World* (ed. Miller, 2000). But the basic claim that our religious life suffers from a lack of lament stands. This is a criticism that could have allied with Mitchell and Anderson's pastoral discovery that there was no Christian theology of "loss." Surely a funeral, already defined as a gathering of mourners, ought to be an appropriate occasion for lament in action.

Imagine what a Christian funeral shaped by lament would be like. Or, to put this in terms already familiar, suppose instead of a "celebration of the life of *x*," the funeral becomes "a time of lament over the death of *x*." Both attempt to "do right by *x*," but the strategy, focus, and emotional tone would be very different. The mood would not necessarily be gloomy or "barbaric," but the rite would definitely begin, as do so many of the psalms, on a negative note. *X* has died. Honestly, we are miserable that *x* has left us. Why did God do this, to him or her? To us? We are angry that things happened this way, that *x*'s cancer was fatal when so many others get cured. While we do not expect God to return *x* to us, we want some action, some direct intervention. We remind God that God has a stake in this situation and in the lives of his people. We promise that when—not if—God intervenes to help us, we will give thanks, doing something concrete to show our gratitude. This will be an act of thanksgiving to God, not necessarily a commemoration of the person who died. At the end, the preacher, after giving voice to these themes, will close with an assurance that God has indeed heard us. And, probably, an assurance that God is not angry because we have been so honest and expressed what is really in our hearts rather than what sounds nice. The music that appropriately belongs at this kind of funeral would not be smooth and easy to listen to. It would be slow, repetitive, and intense, perhaps using "sad-sounding" instruments such as woodwinds to make the point.

This kind of funeral might not immediately seem to "do right by" the dead person. Barbara, now dead from cancer, might not want us all to be so miserable. But perhaps it does, in taking her death as a real blow, emphasize how important we the living know her to be. It definitely intends to "do right by" us as mourners, since we can voice the ancient words of lament psalms and feel how they reverberate with our own less-formed emotions. Remember, we are not just wailing and shrieking in the face of "death's darkness," we are praying to a God whom we seriously trust listens and hears and wants to respond. Lament is possible because of faith, not just because of current distress. There are also all sorts of good psychological reasons why a "lament-based" funeral might be a possibility, to replace the older pattern of preaching to the future dead. This, in fact, just might be a model supported by advocates of the death awareness movement whose concerns include not only "denial" of death, but also the corresponding suppression of anger and guilt and pain. Lament can also overcome the social isolation of mourners, in that shared communal expression of grief temporarily replaces inner rumination. Here, all are encouraged to join in lamenting what is directly and forcefully named as lament worthy. Remember the older view of death as "God's will," including the deaths in the mine disaster; this made any questions of human responsibility unaskable and sinful. Maybe a "lament-based" funeral might do more not just to the feelings surrounding the death, but to the legal and justice issues many deaths raise. Today's funerals avoid these issues entirely.

Because such a lament-based funeral is very far from the examples in the sermon anthologies, and far from the funerals I have personally attended, I tried to solicit examples where the "lament" model was consciously used to structure a worship service. Because of the prestige of Brueggemann, it was not hard to find clergy and church leaders who could understand and respond to this inquiry. Some persons, at least, had tried to include lament as a response by contemporary Christians to the presence of death. Interestingly, the instances of "lament-based" worship I received were from memorial services for children. One particularly vivid example was of a poem sermon read by the pastor at the memorial for a newborn who died.

Nathaniel Dovano,
You came to us across waters
Dark and foreboding.
So long we waited
To see and hear you.
But you came silently,
No crying you made.
Your small unformed mouth
Gasping for air.
Your heart beating strong,
Beginning to fail.

When, O God, will the day come when
An infant will live more than a few hours,
And a great-grandfather will live out his years?

You know broken bodies,
Those stretched on a cross,
Those buried in unmarked graves,
Those disfigured by extra genes,
Those unable to give birth.

Something is awry in this world you have created
When the innocent suffer
When the unborn are maimed,
When some grieve an infant loss
And others yearn for a child.

Is it you Lord?
Is it you who comes to us this day
With cleft palate
And weakened heart?

Yes, resurrected bodies are not whole.
Your nail scarred hands and feet
Are not a perfect body.

Nathaniel Dovano Smith,
Show us the way

To the disabled God you mirror.
Teach us on this sixth day of creation
To say "It is good." (Al Dueck, used with permission)

Note that this is not exactly a lament in the literal sense of exactly following the six-part pattern of the biblical psalms. Nevertheless, it does include complaint, and a petition of sorts ("teach us to say . . ."). This example also ties the specific distress of the family to a wider set of problems and issues ("others yearn for a child") so as not to isolate them more from the rest of those present. There is no expression of a desire for vengeance—for instance, through a lawsuit against the hospital for malpractice. There is also no "assurance of being heard," in the sense of a formal "answer" to the questions raised. Of course, there are also abundant Christian references as well, especially to John 20:27. A suffering, wounded, and even "disabled" God is the God addressed here, unlike in the laments of the Hebrew Bible. God may potentially be all-powerful, but in this age of the world that is not how we can know and experience God.

This unusual example of a memorial service is an exception that proves the rule. Perhaps because the dead newborn had no historical life to "celebrate," there was no possibility of entering the biographical model of a sermon. But in fact, the anthologies and manuals are filled with instances of funeral sermons for dead children and infants. These are now among the standard "problem funerals." None of the anthologized ones are like this example, even when they have titles such as "My God, Why?" They are biographical about the parents, perhaps with an emphasis on their long-term desire for a child. They are "consoling," in a way that this example is not. "Mourning will end, you will be able to live again" may be the promise of consolation behind the specific words when *Preaching to Mourners*. Nothing in the above sermon/poem points toward this idea. In this sense, it is unrelenting in its focus on grief and brokenness now. Nor, of course, in 2000 when this memorial occurred, was the message that the newborn was at peace with Jesus, if not yet able to run and play in the streets of heavenly Jerusalem.

Another example, also from the memorial for a dead child, includes the following responsive psalm-like verses:

Leader #1: O Lord Jesus, God of the lowly and outcast. . . .
You, Lord, are the lover of children,
And we have lost one of our children.

Leader #2: We are comforted that he will know no more pain,
But we are desolate at the loss of the joys he might have known. . . .

People: We ask "How?" We ask "Why?" We feel guilt.
We wonder, "Did God take him to awaken us or punish us?"

Leader #1: No! Our God is not a child-killer. We must not, to answer
Impossible questions, make him seem like one. . . .

Leader #2: Our child did not die to awaken or punish us. He died
because
There is evil in the world, and, temporarily, it has won a battle
Against us.

It is then the people who reply by an affirmation of faith:

In faith we know that Jesus died and rose again,
That in Him death is swallowed up in victory,
And that He will welcome our child into His kingdom.
(Greg Schneider, used with permission)

This second example includes a great deal more resolution than the first; the sense of closure that the original six-part lament form provided is here accomplished by the creedal-like "[i]n faith we know." Jesus' love for children, and even the implied promise of a heavenly afterlife for this child, is part of this second example. Nevertheless, there is much sense of "lament," and direct voicing of anger, sorrow, and guilt even if another voice reframes or replies to these. "There is evil in the world, and, temporarily it has won a battle against us." This is the way military imagery can appear in contemporary lament. Neither of these memorial examples asks that God bring to justice those humans responsible for evil, and do it now, in this age of the world.

These two examples, once again, were both written expressly for memorials for children. Probably the "unnaturalness" of a child's death makes sermons and funerals such as these even possible, since we are no longer in an era when one-third of all human beings die in childhood.

They are not "biographical," which is what American Protestants have come to expect at funerals, and this is not simply because a newborn baby who dies has no life history. The focus is off exclusive preoccupation with the "little story" of the parents, too; it is as much if not more about God and the meaning of this death in light of God's presence and absence in the world. The dead newborn becomes a "sign" of how and who God is, not solely a "someone was here" for himself. Although they are full of references to Christ, it is not the Christ of Cullmann and Archbishop Myers; it is Christ still wounded after the resurrection. Even to mention this is possible because in fact, both these memorials are more theologically oriented than most of the recent anthologized sermons, in that God is the addressee and the focus of complaint. Although "doctrinal" (the older category) is not the accurate term here, these sermons intentionally portray a decidedly untraditional vision of God, a vision that disrupts our ruminations and guilt-ridden preoccupations and fantasies. A God who did *not* will these deaths.

Lament-based funerals, and funeral sermons, do not provide the pathway beyond silence and denial. Biblical, anti-Platonic, focused on the real plight of real persons in the world: they remain an eccentric disturbing oddity that could not compete with "celebration of life." For some Christian readers, the real question may be, how many funerals like these could anyone bear to attend? There is indeed something intolerable about the intensity, the grief, the anger expressed in a public setting, even within a familiar context, surrounded by a faithful and supportive community. We want to go beyond silence and denial, but maybe not so far beyond, not at worship. In a therapy session, or even in pastoral counseling sessions after the funeral, OK. But not in public, even when the stated task is *Preaching to Mourners*. Indeed, some of the advice in manuals for pastors about funerals cautions against too much intensity of emotions, especially since the family will be in shock and probably unable to respond to much of what goes on around them (Hughes, 9; Mansell, 20ff.). Yet it would be a mistake to confuse "lament" with "the screaming room" Kübler-Ross hoped to find in the hospital. That is what all the stress on "formfulness" in lament should have clarified. The two memorial laments, like the ancient psalms, were not simply "raw emotion"; they were carefully crafted, formful expressions of grief. But based on the overwhelming dominance of other models in the sermon anthologies, the lament did not succeed as the pattern for Americans who have turned instead to biographical "celebrations of the life" of the deceased. Lament is too risky, too overwhelming, and just too negative to become a popular pattern for American funerals.

Alas, the real message here may be that silence and denial are more powerful, pervasive, and still with us than we like to think. If the original death awareness movement hoped to overcome these, the anthologized sermons by and large show that it failed to make for integration of negative emotions, of loss and despair, into our formal rituals of death. Christian theologies such as Cullmann's began with Jesus lamenting his own impending death as he prays in Gethsemane. But this was never the way Cullmann's message was rendered in the funerals that unequivocally proclaimed Christ's resurrection victory over death. With the triumph of the biographical, the dead person himself or herself becomes the primary focus, and to "do right by" his or her memory is the important goal for mourners. Therefore any intense focus on God as the one who hears and will respond to our misery, is decentered, even in sermons that rise beyond the story of Doug and Barbara and her cancer. Lament remains a tantalizing "might have been" in an alternative history of American ideas, images, and responses to death.

15

The Eclipse of Poetry

Thank you, Gigi, for laughter and play,
For tears and cheers,
And for teaching me the way
To find light on any day,
Sunny or cloudy, if it may.

—Sara Grace Hole, read at the memorial service for her grandmother (Gigi)

In the era before silence and denial, every funeral manual and *Cyclopedia* included a large section of "suitable poems" to be recited by the pastor at funerals. These poems could bring natural immortality out of the realm of philosophy or doctrine, and make it emotionally, palpably real. The poems played an important role in the funeral, and were intrinsic to most funeral sermons. Our surmise is that they filled in what the Bible could not supply. Although no one at that time would have admitted it, the Bible itself did not include the images and stories necessary to convey natural immortality. Cullmann and others might argue that the reason for this was simple: the Bible did not teach natural immortality, and the relative absence of images such as caterpillar into butterfly should have told Christians to beware reading the Bible through Platonized lenses. But since everyone in the pre–silence and denial era assumed that it did teach the universal intuitive truth of the soul's immortality, the poems that stated this more directly were used to enhance, not contradict, what Scripture and doctrine proclaimed. Poems could support, supplement, and add a dimension of emotion and imagination to the driest "doctrinal" sermon.

When funerals became "preaching to mourners," rather than to the future dead, something happened to poetry. There is still, sometimes, a place for poems at funerals, but it is a tiny place, and their source and function today are entirely different. The child's poem that heads this chapter has a purpose, and indeed was printed on the back of the memorial service program. Yet this purpose is not that of "Crossing the Bar" recited by the preacher at all those older funerals. Thus, rather than choosing to call this section "The Death of Poetry," which would imply its complete disappearance, it seems better, or at least more hopeful, to use the word "eclipse." This intentionally echoes the title of English sociologist Tony Walter's important book on changed English views of death and afterlife, *The Eclipse of Eternity*. "Eclipse" means obscuring; we need to discover what exactly is now obscured, that was once visible. Poetry once revealed, what is now hidden. Maybe what happened to poetry is not just hiding, but a transformation on many levels. For example, the two contemporary "laments" from the previous chapter qualify as "poetry," and were recited by the presiders at the memorials for the two dead infants. Yet both, like the poem to Gigi, were "occasional," written and recited as if for this one event, with a one-time unique focus on this particular situation.

> There is evil in the world, and, temporarily, it has won a battle
> Against us.

The child's poem has rhyme, the others have cadence, but gone are some other poetic features familiar from the examples in the earlier anthologies. There is, for instance, no use of allegory. This too has gone into eclipse.

In the days before silence and denial, poems' images supplemented and expanded those of doctrinal faith, to express what Christians wished to say about death. Preachers found it necessary to reinforce ideas such as "natural immortality" by resorting to Wordsworth, Browning, Tennyson, Longfellow, and others. Before these Victorian authors wrote, there were many poems, and laying the groundwork for them were the poems familiar from hymns. In principle, if the words of the Bible could be supplemented and enhanced by humanly composed songs, then poems without music were no theological problem.

Protestant Christians have long taken hymns for granted. Singable songs were needed, and English Protestants, both Church of England and dissenters such as Quakers and Baptists, produced these endlessly. Isaac Watts and the Wesleys wrote hymns as easily as they had breathed. Charles Wesley wrote over one thousand of them. John Newton, the author of "Amazing Grace," apparently wrote one new hymn a week, on schedule for his weekly prayer meeting. Evangelical leaders, especially those who preached outside of church buildings at large open meetings, must have known that formal church music (English "plainchant") was badly in need of supplementation. Meanwhile in Germany, the Pietist movement also contributed popular singable hymns. Thus, songs for both men's and women's voices (older traditional English choir music was written only for men and boys) were intrinsic to the American Protestant heritage. By the nineteenth century, it seems, every mainline Protestant church was used to singing new, authored hymns. The debates were not over whether to sing, but what music styles were suitably noble and beautiful for the gospel message, and also whether musical instruments should accompany human voices.

Some hymns had been poems before they found the right tune, and became "hymns." (The union of a good poem with the right tune has been compared to a good marriage.) This suggests that there was a porous boundary between "poetry" meant for reading aloud and group singing—a situation very difficult to imagine today. Once the practice of "writing hymns" began, almost any poem from the past could be set to music. This is one reason why the "authors" of traditional songs in the current Episcopal hymnal include Peter Abelard, Thomas Aquinas, and other distinguished religious thinkers from the long-ago past. It is not that Aquinas had a separate career as a songwriter; it is that the crossover between poems and hymns was so easy by the time a published "hymnal" was inaugurated. At the other extreme were what we now call "folk songs" with no single author, but whose words were simple and familiar. These were songs from the start, rather than "poems" first. For example, "Poor Wayfaring Stranger" captures exactly the hope for an otherworldly destination at the end of a hard journey, as did the more "literary" expressions of "natural immortality."

I am a poor wayfaring stranger,
Traveling through this world of woe.
But there's no sickness, toil nor danger
In that bright land, to which I go.

By the early twentieth century, this was no longer listed among "suitable hymns" in the pastors' manuals. But its extremely mournful minor key would have made it appropriate for funerals, and everyone would have known it, too.

Yet even with countless hymns at their disposal, and many persons, male and female, constantly writing more, preachers and congregations at funerals used poetry. Yes, they also sang hymns, but the preacher, as part of his sermon, recited poems or pieces of poems. A good deal of this poetry was of high literary quality, by the standards of that day and also of ours. It did not need music to make it work. No, poetry was recited, read aloud in a special, dramatic tone of voice that preachers were expected to master as part of their homiletics training. Whether this had come at seminary or by apprenticeship, clergy were by definition public speakers. Command over public speaking, and ability to read poems dramatically and meaningfully in public, was part of his job description This, however, was a skill all educated persons were expected to exercise. Men and women could recite poetry in private familial or romantic settings, and schoolchildren learned to memorize and recite it as a routine part of their education (sometimes with unintended hilarious results). Maybe farmers and day laborers never learned how to do this, but those who defined themselves as middle class made a point of reciting and listening to literary poems, as part of the package of decorous worship and a genteel lifestyle.

At a funeral, of course, "decorous" meant that emotional display, extreme weeping or other displays of grief, was forbidden. Although in impoverished backward and non-middle-class Appalachia, the more loudly one cried and wailed, the more one demonstrated love for the deceased (Chrissman, 94), the churches of the educated and middle class shunned such behavior. There is every sign in the earlier anthologies that control of grief was a must, and that this did not appear heartless, but mature and dignified. Of course, for this to work, one must show "control over grief," that is, it must be conveyed that deep grief is really felt, inside. So at the funerals whose sermons we have discussed, no one wails or faints, no one interrupts the service with moans or shrieks, no one is too emotionally "overcome" for things to continue in orderly fashion. This, by the way, is assumed in the funeral manuals. There is no discussion in any of them about problems caused by "out-of-control" mourners; it just did not happen, or the family was expected to deal with it by keeping the at-risk person home.

All this was the setting for poetry recitation by the preacher. The occasion is sad and somber, but not "barbaric." People sit quietly, prepared as the future dead to hear a "doctrinal sermon" about death, heaven, or natural immortality. The poetry, however, is intensely emotive, filled with images and mystery. It speaks often with the voice of the dying or the voice of the mourner, passionately. Even when the message is "and may there be no sadness of farewell" the poem is a message of good-bye. The emotion banned from direct display of grief gestures is rechanneled, or sublimated into poetry. While the theological message did not leave much room for complex grief and good-bye, the poems, somehow, supply this without directly contradicting the doctrines. On the more obvious level, the poems clearly support a theology in which death is really a gentle, natural transition from the shady to the sunny side of the wall. The rose grows:

> As it grew and blossomed, fair and tall,
> Slowly rising to loftier height,
> It came to a crevice in the wall,
> Through which there shone a beam of light.

But, *as poems* maybe they permitted some other undercurrent to find space, even in the middle of the sermon.

Note that we speak here of "poems" not of "poets." "Thank you, Gigi" could have been written only by a granddaughter or other near relative; its author's link with the dead individual is intrinsic to its effectiveness. On the other hand, the individual poets of the earlier era, such as Tennyson, were honored as great and eloquent authors, but not as individual persons. Whether or not they were Christian, with the necessary personal faith in Jesus Christ during their lives, was not important in order for their poetry to be recited at Christian funerals. The faith of Wordsworth may not have been truly orthodox. If not, this did not make a difference to preachers who wished to use his poems as part of their sermons. For this is the wrong kind of question to ask. Poetry of this sort is detachable, up to a point, from the life of the poet himself or herself. Some poets led "pagan" or notoriously sinful and scandalous lives; so maybe there were limits to this detachability. I have found no poems by Lord Byron in the collections of "suitable poetry," probably for this reason. But the other famous poets favored by preachers were simply not high-profile scandalous enough to make use of their material in sermons an issue. For given the way their poems were used, the voice within the poem was not to be confused with the personal cry of Wordsworth or Tennyson the man, bereaved of a friend or beloved. It was a voice that evoked intimations of natural immortality for any and everyone. That was what counted, not personal biography of the author.

But as Protestants in America entered the era of silence and denial, something happened to the poetry. By the early 1950s, the poems are still in the funeral anthologies, but their literary quality has plummeted. Yes, this is an elitist judgment, but there is no other way to describe the change. No major twentieth-century poets of merit are included in any of the anthologies, and the proportion of Tennyson-type authors diminishes. The poems collected for use in funeral sermons by this period may be, like "The Rose Still Grows Beyond the Wall," among *America's 100 Favorite Poems*, but they are not very good as poems. They sound like those on sympathy cards: they are sentimental, simple, decorative, but rarely deeply evocative. I know of no one who buys sympathy cards for the sake of their poems, nor are these the kind of poems anyone studied at school. The term "kitsch" seems appropriate here, if snobby.

Well, perhaps no twentieth-century equivalents to Tennyson and Wordsworth existed. No, that is absolutely not true. My high school English literature classes included attempts to read e. e. cummings, Theodore Roethke, and even some Wallace Stevens, not to mention Robert Frost. Yet these are exactly the poets whose works are never found in any of the funeral anthologies. Perhaps for a more recent generation of high school students, even these names are no longer on the reading list. But the point here is that twentieth-century poets of high literary quality wrote poems potentially available for inclusion at funerals . . . but, like lament, this was a road not taken. Indeed, it was a road that must have been intentionally ignored in favor of sentimental greeting card poems, so long as the minister still did turn to the "Suitable Poems" section of the funeral manual. And eventually, such a section disappears altogether.

When the era of silence and denial of death came to at least a partial end, the death awareness movement gave Americans a new set of ideas and images for death, dying, and bereavement. But it was a downturn for poetry. The changeover from "doctrinal" to "biographical" sermons, which marked the new framework for funerals where *Preaching to Mourners* was the norm, left some new and minimal space for poetry. The family members' tributes and stories, the memories retold as part of "doing right by" the deceased, and "celebrating his or her life" permit some minor space for it. "Thank you, Gigi" accomplishes this. Indeed, tributes will very often include homegrown poems, written by family members or friends, in honor of the deceased.

All of these poems, whether written and recited by the family or the pastor, who may occasionally compose his or her own, are "one-shot deals." They are for the occasion, and that occasion only. Poems at American funerals now are elements of "expressive ritual," they are not reusable, they are not preserved except on the back of the memorial service program. Indeed, we would be outraged if the same memorial poem was trotted out time after time by the pastor; it could not then effectively serve to "do right by" the individual deceased whose life the funeral celebrated. While the two lament poems of the previous chapter seem to have a more universal scope, these also share this "occasional" quality, and neither author saw them as potentially reusable at future funerals or memorials. Neither hymns nor traditional poems were quite so ephemeral, so occasion specific (even when written for a particular event, the poem would have been able to stand on its own afterward).

Today, the recitation of such an occasional poem by a family member is an emotional, not a literary event. Sara Grace Hole as a twelve-year-old was able to read through her poem successfully, with visible effort. In another funeral example, the grown daughter was on the brink of tears as she read her own good-bye poem to her dead father. We in the congregation wonder, "Will she get through it?" not, "Is this poem any good?" It is no longer relevant to measure the poem for anything other than its fittingness in the midst of a biographical funeral, as part of an expressive ritual. The personal biography of Tennyson may not have been known or relevant for those who loved "Crossing the Bar," but a poem today is from one person who mourns the death of another. The poems of the mid-twentieth-century anthologies were bad, of poor literary merit; the poems now heard at funerals escape being judged by any such standard at all. They are sincere, they are expressions of sorrow, gratitude, and love; these are the judgments we can make, if we understand the purpose of the funeral at all. What would invalidate them would be misrepresenting a relationship, or betraying emotions at odds with the sorrow and love demanded in order to "do right by" the deceased. An angry poem by a widow, filled with recriminations against her dead ex-husband, would be morally offensive; its literary contribution entirely beside the point. It would jar and offend in a more direct, gut-wrenching way than even the harsh lines of the contemporary lament poems that we examined in the previous chapter.

> There is evil in the world, and, temporarily, it has won a battle
> Against us

By contrast, the widow's angry outcry would be an actual instance of evil winning a battle against us, here and now at the funeral or memorial service.

But perhaps this situation is due to factors other than the change from one model of funeral to another. Changes in most Americans' literary education have to be taken into account. We have already hinted at this, with references to the "attempt" of high school students to read Wallace Stevens. Maybe twentieth-century literary poems are just too difficult, too unsuitable, to recite at funerals. Perhaps even if they do share Christian images for death that lend themselves to poetry (and this is not the case for some of the authors listed) both the content and the obscurity of more modern poetry (more modern than Tennyson, that is) work against poetry's inclusion today. While the contemporary lament poems are hardly "obscure," they are surely, intentionally, disruptive and disturbing when recited in public. Much contemporary or even early twentieth-century poetry is like these images, dissonant and disturbing. Probably, it is intrinsically unsuited to the kind of funerals Christians post–silence and denial desire. Or the problem is also that we (many of us, at least) have lost the ears with which to hear really good, multi-leveled literary poems.

A fascinating test example for this possibility, a contrast to our American situation, comes from an anthology collected by Liam Swords of *Funeral Homilies* from Ireland. These are modern Roman Catholic homilies; the book was published in 1985 and covers funerals for very ordinary Irish persons. Its editor's purpose was exactly the same as that of the other anthologizers we have studied: to offer the range of suggestions for what works at funerals, using categories such as "For a Disabled Person" or "Death After a Long Illness." Yet these Irish homilies are filled with bits and pieces of poetry! The Irish priest/preachers quote C. Day-Lewis, W. B. Yeats, Rainer Maria Rilke, and Albert Camus (the latter two in translation), not to mention earlier poets such as Donne. There are indeed major twentieth-century poets who had something to say about death. Even more specifically, it was something to include in a Christian funeral sermon, because the priest judged those present would understand the poems and find these relevant to their faith and their grief. Now, some of these poets would very likely have been anthologized in textbooks at religiously run high schools in Ireland. But Camus is also quoted. His personal faith would not have passed muster with the Irish Catholic educational planning board, or whatever school authorities select textbooks. But, in Swords' anthology's homilies, the personal faith of poets is never at stake; Rilke and Camus wrote fine, recitable poems, dealing with death, and related to the content of the priest's message. Even in translations, this purpose and fittingness come through well. Rilke writes of falling leaves, night, and "falling earth" to evoke ending and death (Swords, 22). This works in the middle of a homily at a funeral for a parent.

The difference here is that literary knowledge and education in Ireland are remarkably different from those of this country. Ireland has continued to be a place where this mesh between literature and ordinary people's lives still exists, or at least it did so in 1985. Poems were just not "foreign," not metaphorically and often not even literally. The bits of poetry included in the homilies were meant to sound vaguely familiar, I suspect, just as the biblical quotes were. The Irish of Swords' anthology are in this respect far more like the American Protestants of 1899, than they are like any Americans, Protestant or Roman Catholic, in 1985 or today. They simply know how to listen to complex poetry; it is culturally familiar to them, not something a few college graduates studied in literature surveys. By sharp contrast, one cannot imagine Newark's Archbishop Myers, who banned personal anecdotes about the deceased from funerals in his archdiocese, doing so in order to promote instead the writings of Yeats or Camus! He wanted doctrine alone, or at least the story of Jesus' death and resurrection, to be the sole content of the funeral and its homily. And the furor his policy provoked had nothing to do with use of additional literary materials; it was all about the personal-biographical "little story" of the dead person that his policy rigidly excluded.

This Irish example suggests another "might have been" alternative scenario. Suppose the death awareness movement had not coincided with this eclipse of poetry here in America. Suppose it had allied itself with the poems of major authors, so that instead of stressing the value of "expressive rituals" for mourners, it had taken pains to show how grief could be given form and expression through already-composed truly excellent evocative poems. Just as the lament genre of the Hebrew Bible revealed the positive function of "the formfulness of grief," so too some poetry could really accomplish this, in lieu of "Thank you, Gigi." Suppose books and essays and newsletter articles in death awareness publications were committed to reconnecting the dying and those who mourned with a literary tradition. This alliance, rediscovered link, then could have transferred into the setting of Christian funerals, along with the psychologically based models of grief. Even if pastors were not trained to appreciate poetry, they could have gained awareness of its potential from reading death awareness materials offered in the pastoral counseling courses, which were saturated with poems. Nor does this sound automatically too "elitist." Remember that the Irish examples included funerals for farmers and housewives; to assume only an "elite" can "appreciate poetry" is itself the problem, which the death awareness movement has done nothing to overcome.

But the reappropriation of poetry did not happen. It is indeed another "might have been." The psychologists' models for "the grief process" were appropriated and adapted by pastors *Preaching to Mourners*. But without poetry, because in fact the death awareness movement as a whole has a remarkable blank spot for most literature. I mentioned in the introduction the importance of Tolstoy's "The Death of Ivan Ilych." But it is hard to name one other work of literature that has played any role in the death awareness movement's agenda. Not just the literature of the past, but that of the present, is simply missing. Not just poetry; all the major novelists of the nineteenth and twentieth centuries, the ones we did read in high school, are not resources, go unmentioned altogether in death awareness writings. The lack of poetry is just the tip of the iceberg.

There is, significantly, one giant exception to this eclipse of literature in the death awareness movement: personal memoirs, narratives of dying and grief. These *are* resources, these *are* cited, some of them are famous. *A Grief Observed*, by C. S. Lewis, is well known, familiar; it is mentioned and recommended in death awareness writings, and not just by Christian chaplains or pastors. The rise of this genre of *First Person Mortal* writing is one of the remarkable by-products of the death awareness movement (see Bregman and Thiermann). Lewis' narrative came before the movement began, but once it offered new ideas and images for dying and bereavement, a flood of other examples followed. These deal centrally and directly with the experiences of interest to the death awareness movement, they are not "fiction," they have the enormous advantage of being "real people," enduring "real situations." (Although some examples of "fake memoirs" have received a lot of publicity, none of the favorites of the death awareness movement have had their reality questioned.) And some of these are actually by persons who can write well. Stewart Alsop, Max Lerner, Madeleine L'Engle, Philip Roth, and Alan Paton, all professional writers, authored memoirs of bereavement, or of their own dying.

But these autobiographies are memorial tributes and personal testimonies in book form. They serve some of the same purposes as expressive rituals within the biographical funeral, such as the good-bye poem read tearfully by the daughter at her father's funeral. While Alan Paton's *For You, Departed* is a wonderful memorial tribute to his dead wife, and a vivid document of life in white society of South Africa, it celebrates the life of one unique person. It could not be excerpted and recited for anyone else's funeral or memorial service. The high quality of the books by all of the above writers is important, but at their funerals, even poor writing by Alsop and Lerner would have been more appropriate than excellent pieces by and about strangers. We are a long way from "Crossing the Bar," where the voice of the poet was *not* the historical individual Alfred, beloved husband and loving father, and so on. Today, it is much more important to hear the voice of those who mourn for *this person*, or hear his or her own posthumous words read by mourners, than to enter the realm of literature, which includes literary anonymity.

We in America have lost the ability to move there, at least in the context of funerals. We can move into cyberspace, we seem to be able to move into fantasy worlds without entirely losing our sense that they are "fantasy," and we can accept "reality television" while knowing that it is not quite literally "real." But literature in funerals, no longer. We do not think of this as a loss, we do not even notice it. It has become invisible, in total eclipse. Were it not for the Irish counterexample, we could blame this on the changed qualities of literary poetry itself. But that is simply not fair; the shift is due to us.

With this change, or loss, comes diminished ability to explore imagery for death. Imagery, that is, which we can share or that communities can find meaningful as images or allegories of that which will retain its mystery. We have new words for death and dying, we have biographical funerals, and we have theologies of loss, but these lack the expression of more general, universal imaginative renderings that could have replaced "Crossing the Bar." Archbishop Myers' solution, a focus solely on the Christian "big story" of Jesus' death and resurrection, may be theologically defensible, but it is more than just pastorally misguided. It is imaginatively empty and abstract, disconnected from more than just the mourners' private emotions. The images that accompany the big story are frequently the wartime analogies and metaphors of Cullmann: D-day and V-day, military victory over death. These are never fleshed out by contemporary war poems, and indeed the tone of sermons that rely on Cullmann is too triumphant to permit any actual experiences of warfare—in poetry or any other form—to enter. This is definitely a road not taken; not by Myers, not by any of the Protestant pastors whose Cullmannesque sermons appear in anthologies. Myers did not want poetry or literature; he wanted theology. But it appears to be theology stripped of the emotional, pictorial, and imaginative possibilities that made older "doctrinal" sermons rich and engaging.

"The Rose Still Grows Beyond the Wall" is, in my opinion, kitsch. Its view of death is false; as a poem it is shallow and almost hits the reader over the head with its assurances that the rose continues to grow upward forevermore. But it does accomplish what both Myers and biographical sermons fail at: it offers us an image of death, evokes our response of wonder and hope, in a manner that does not demand our formal intellectual assent to doctrine. It gives the reader or hearer something to ponder, beyond Doug and Barbara's visit to the pastor's office, something that reaches toward a "big story." In this case, I am convinced that it is not the same "big story" as that of Christian faith, where suffering and dying and death are real, even if followed by resurrection. But this is not the reason this poem has disappeared from Protestant funerals. Not because of its New Age philosophy, but because all poetry that serves this important purpose has now vanished, gone into eclipse. Today, it seems, we barely recognize that this is a loss, for although we have gone beyond silence and denial, our new language for death and bereavement has obscured this dimension of Christian funerals. "To do right by" the deceased is not sufficient; the funeral ought also to open us to reflection that makes death mean something, that connects us emotionally and spiritually with a full vision of Christian faith. Such a vision includes death. Poetry, once the vehicle for this, is now gone, part of a "before" we have forgotten.

PART V

Conclusion

16

What Christians No Longer Want to Say about Death

In these chapters, we have questioned some of the popular assumptions about the Christian past. It is not necessarily a "resource" for persons today. Our expectations that it should be need to be held in check. While the death awareness movement tells us "people used to see death as a natural event," this statement may be useful as a rhetorical device in an argument about the present, but it misleads as a real description of what held true for persons one hundred years ago. As we looked back to the ways Protestant Christians once spoke of death, on the formal occasion of a funeral, during the decades of the twentieth century, we should instead let their own ideas and images be severed from our own needs and hopes. These Christians' views on death were internally coherent, supported by what they believed the Bible taught, and by their own traditions and sensibilities. But that does not make them suitable for appropriation by us today.

Suppose we reverse the perspective of these questions. Imagine that the people of the past received a glimpse of our present. Some things would surely surprise them about our lives, views, and attitudes. Some of our ways would delight them, while other beliefs and assumptions would disappoint or even horrify them. We are not speaking here of the people from biblical times, but of persons a few generations back. Those who sat at the funerals of their families and friends, and heard

"Are you living under the power of the world to come?" or listened as the pastor recited "Crossing the Bar" to them during the sermon. When it came to wisdom about death, they would surely feel they could teach us something. Perhaps they would smugly sit in judgment on our preference for tacky sentimental biographical anecdotes over solid and profound doctrinal truths. Or they might be bewildered by our abundant use of "death as enemy" language, when they knew their faith taught that heaven was a home, and death a journey. They could be delighted that, finally, mourning was being taken seriously as a Christian theme, or they would believe this was both theologically erroneous and pastorally misguided (to twist Mitchell and Anderson's statement). In short, they might admire and envy us for what we have learned on these topics, or pity us for what we have forgotten.

Some answers to these "maybes" seem beyond dispute. The Christians of the past would not have denied that "death is a natural event." But by this they did not mean what we do. They would have included immortality of the soul as part of "natural" universal truth, and therefore death as transition rather than annihilation would have been the most "natural" understanding of it. Not "there is a time to be born, and a time to die," but other imagery, especially of transformations such as caterpillar into butterfly, would have been best to illustrate this vision of death as "natural event." Birth and death are not paired together, and all our imagery of the life span or "circle of life" is foreign to them in this context. Most of all, they would all have agreed that this vision of "natural immortality" is behind the message of the gospel, and so Christ's promise of eternal life with him in the mansions of his Father's house is not based on anything utterly unique. It is not based on his own one-time miraculous resurrection, although this offers historical proof of the general reality. It is based on universal intuited truth. The message of life everlasting, then, does not need to be christologically focused or christocentric. Barth, Brunner, Cullmann, and Archbishop Myers were all wrong. Christian faith does not rest on any such narrow, miraculous, historical or quasi-historical foundation. Jesus offers us salvation, his death redeems and restores us to God's favor, but it does not become the entire foundation for the entire edifice of doctrine. "Are you living under the power of the world to come?" could make sense without this. To accuse such a stance of being "sub-Christian" or "Platonist," as some of the theologians just named did, would have made no sense at all to those earlier generations of clergy and their people.

To us, the problem is rooted in the generic "otherworldliness" of their faith's focus. Perhaps the term "otherworldly" is too vague, covering too much; it could include Dante's Inferno, Purgatory, and Paradise, and the *bardo* realm of the *Tibetan Book of the Dead*. But for American mainline Protestants of the early twentieth century, it did not. It meant a certain more restricted picture, sharply defined, which they took for granted as what the Bible revealed. "The world to come," heaven, and natural immortality just dominated their thinking about death. *When Death Speaks*, that is what it said to them. It said it over and over again. Consequently, it sounds to us as if they did not take embodied, historical life seriously. It sounds as if they had ignored or disregarded this world as God's creation, the beauty and meaningfulness of life now, in this world, even in a world where death and loss are real. Nicholas Wolterstorff lamenting his dead son speaks for us when he says,

> In our day we have come to see some dimensions of the Bible overlooked for centuries. We have come to see its affirmation of the goodness of creation. God made us embodied historical creatures and affirmed the goodness of that. We are not to yearn for timeless disembodiment. But this makes death all the more difficult to live with. (31)

When read as Wolterstorff reads it, the Bible does not teach "natural immortality," and gives far more space to "lament" than it does to any depictions of a personal afterlife. Whether or not Christian faith ought to be entirely christocentric—a belief all the theological advocates of "lament" dispute—whether it must hinge 100 percent on Jesus' death and resurrection, it must not become otherworldly in the Platonic mode. That now appears as the mistake of persons in the past, in the age before silence and denial. We who live after silence and denial cannot retrace our steps back along that same path again. Wolterstorff here speaks for us.

Indeed, when the issue is put this way, the amazing thing is that Christianity survived at all, to preach a message of hope now for mourners. As *A Trumpet in Darkness* for us, it does not require natural immortality or "the world to come." The people of the past would have been astonished (horrified?) that a form of faith could be proclaimed, only a few decades after their own time, which ignored or eliminated so many of their favorite doctrines and images. The sermons and manuals of the post–silence and denial era show an ability to accommodate not just to psychology (here, all the psychological models of bereavement and grief) but to people's own changed sensibilities. Grief matters, *All Our Losses, All Our Griefs* need to be related to God's presence and purposes in ways more direct than had been the case in the recent past, or much further back than that. Christianity in America has survived what English sociologist Tony Walter called *The Eclipse of Eternity*, and whether in its liberal or more conservative forms, it has managed to do so while jettisoning much of the stock of ideas and images that were so recently its main sustenance. In this case, it has accomplished this without public outcry, protests, or indeed, without anyone seeming to notice much of a shift. Perhaps in this it differs from Christianity in Western Europe, even though the two continents share similar religious roots.

We should clarify these assertions. It is not that the people in the pews no longer accept "natural immortality" at all, in any form. I counted at least seventy-five Internet sites that included "The Rose Still Grows Beyond the Wall," and almost all were memorials for someone who had died. But not one was connected directly to a mainline Protestant sermon. When in public, Protestant Christians now want to say something about death, the message of the ever-growing rose is no longer their message. It may well be that beliefs such as this form of "natural immortality" will persist for a long time, regardless of how many seminary-trained clergy label them Platonism, New Age, or pagan. It is even possible that what pastors now sharply distinguished as New Age rather than "authentically Christian" (back in chap. 13) is what an increasing percentage of ordinary persons actually believe. The religious "nones" of surveys, or those who declare themselves "spiritual but not religious," may be happy to embrace those ideas that we have segregated out of Christian teachings, under the category of New Age. What we focus upon, however, is what Christians say and have said on the formal, public occasion of a funeral. There, something must be said, and a message is conveyed through the sermon—whether doctrinal or biographical—of what death means for Christian faith. This is where the line between New Age and "legitimate" Christian views has been drawn, narrowing the boundary of the latter when contrasted to the past.

Although New Age in this sense has its champions, for many of my students—representing here the younger generation of Christians—it is a given of their faith that "God defeats death," and that Christians always are on the side of "life." Therefore, agreeing with Wolterstorff and taking his stance to the extreme, death is always anti-God and anti-Jesus. Medical decisions should be made so as to insist that "life" is the primary Christian value. Life is sacred. It is always wrong to "give up," and although they have none of them read Cullmann, their use of military imagery linked to Christian faith makes death into an enemy God can and will defeat. They like Kübler-Ross, except that they complain that even some of her "acceptance" patients ought to have kept fighting, since God is always on the side of life. Some of these Christian students may eventually buy the counterargument that there comes a time when it is appropriate to forego the use of life-prolonging technology if the patient is on the brink of death and such treatments are futile and costly. But they none of them invoke "the world to come" to justify such a decision. Protestant and Roman Catholic together (and these categories are less meaningful to them than would have been true a few decades ago) they would agree with Henri Nouwen:

> Death does not belong to God. God did not create death. God does not want death. God does not desire death for us. In God there is no death. God is a God of life. (75)

The difference is that Nouwen struggled to come to a different view; he wanted initially to "befriend death," but found he could not (29). The deepest meaning of Christ's death and resurrection—and this quote comes at the end of an intensely Christ-centered book—prohibits this as a final goal. For the students, it is simply obvious that the choice is between a Christian view that fights against death because "God is a God of life," and a secular one, where ultimately the autonomy of a Hildegarde Dolson makes suicide, abortion, and "please omit funeral" all perfectly acceptable. And for the vehemently secular, Hildegarde Dolson was absolutely right, and personal choice is the only value worth defending.

But this brings us to a second surprise. Christianity survived its loss of older natural immortality and otherworldliness. But the attacks on traditional funerals and the theology of death that seemed to go with them could have produced much more dramatic changes in practice, to match the dramatic disappearance of key religious ideas. This has not been the case. "Please omit funeral" has not been the prevailing trend, although what are now called "traditional funerals" are proportionately fewer than before. "Doing nothing," rationalist Dolson's solution, has not won over the population, even in a mobile and busy society. Memorials may have replaced funerals for many, and cremations replaced burials. But the Dolson rationalist hope for a funeral-less world where death was so "barbaric" it could be ignored entirely, has not materialized. Indeed, a funeral director assured me that it is much less usual now to hear people say "Do nothing" than it was a generation ago. Perhaps it was Dolson's generation who wished this extreme rejection of ceremony and tradition. Certainly my secularist students, those who make no secret of their hostility to religion and tradition, do not express such a desire to have deaths go uncommemorated. Dolson underestimated people's need to memorialize, to say something. She underestimated the need to "do right by" the deceased, a duty that emerges so prominently only when the older meanings of funerals faded out. She would have been no happier with Doug and Barbara's story as the topic for the sermon, than she was for an earlier era's messages. In the terms of our study, silence and denial could not entirely control what people did or decided not to do, even when their ideas and images for death shrunk and faded. What came next in no way resembled the rationalist minimalist stance of Dolson and those who along with her found death too unacceptably morbid to deal with, period.

If Christianity survived the death of otherworldliness, and funerals survived a rationalist and/or denial-based attack on their meaning, these developments have ambivalent consequences for Christians. Up to a point, the death awareness movement's message did prevail. The new words for dying, death, and bereavement did succeed in reshaping Christian thinking about death and mourning, even when a few voices such as Vitz's were raised against it. (Very few, as we saw.) But how much it succeeded depends on what one considers the core of the movement's message. For Kübler-Ross, it was that death was both natural and "acceptable," an intrinsic part of life. For Mitchell and Anderson, it was that loss should be taken as a central and religiously meaningful human experience. For some anthologizers of sermons and authors of pastors' manuals, it meant that at last Christian funerals could focus on mourners, on their need to cry out to God and be heard now, in the midst of grief and confusion. For Brueggemann, it meant that grief itself could be made "formful" and that ancient Hebrew lament psalms were prayers that Christians ought to voice once more. For all of the above, it meant an end to the era of silence and denial, which had brought misery and loneliness and deception instead of happiness.

So far, so good. Even Vitz would really not have had a problem with much of this. After all, a psychology of mourning or "the grief process" implicitly critiques the exuberant expectations of the human potential movement, which was his real target. But the death awareness movement's message was not basically that a funeral should become "a celebration of the life of *x*." Maybe its goal of "acceptance of death" translates better into the New Age mantra "there is no death" than to any Christian message about resurrection. That thought, after all, mirrors Kübler-Ross' personal progression of beliefs. Moreover, Christians today are left to ponder how congruent is any extended focus on mourning, however pastorally sensitive, with the message of "the big story" of Christ's death and resurrection. Thomas Long's fine study of funerals is the most recent voice to protest against the reduction of the Christian message about death to the focus on the emotional needs of mourners, and the memorializing of the individual deceased.

> Of key importance here is the movement; this is an event that goes somewhere. It goes somewhere not only because a dead body must be buried, but also as a sign that a saint of God is "traveling on" in faith. A baptized Christian who has been on a pilgrimage of faith and has now come to the end of the earthly road is going on toward God. (Long, 88)

For Long, Mitchell and Anderson's plea for a theology of loss was too much of a corrective, in other words. Yet these are questions for Christian persons today; they continue to be threshed out among chaplains, pastors, funeral directors, and ordinary Christians when family members die. Unless one accepts the hierarchical authority of an Archbishop Myers, they will continue to be negotiated and debated by all these parties. Nevertheless, none of these choices, nor even the terms of the discussion, would have made much sense to the people in the age before silence and denial. Long's vague "going on toward God" would have felt almost as incomplete, vague, and unsatisfying to them as an exclusive focus on the resurrection felt to Mitchell and Anderson.

For the real conclusion we have reached is that the older situation is gone. Their past is not a "resource" directly for us, we cannot leap back to it and hope to appropriate it undigested and unfiltered. As I realized time and again when I read through the sermons of that era, no one now, not the stodgiest, most conservative Christian congregation, could sit through these sermons. They would rise up and throttle the preacher, if not literally, then metaphorically at the next worship committee or board or vestry meeting. The ideas, the style of delivery, the choice of poems to recite, the whole atmosphere of the funeral, would be impossibly distressing if not absolutely offensive to us. It would not just be the confident assurance that the dead child was better off now, playing in the streets of heaven, than he or she would have been as a sinful adult. Nor the message that Christian resignation was the only appropriate stance to hold in relation to a death that by definition would be "God's will." It would have been the entire dreary, otherworldly atmosphere. Christian funerals were to be "hopeful," but little of what they took as signs of "hope" would strike us that way.

Even some of their most cherished "hopeful" ideas would backfire, I suspect, if we were to hear them now. Take, for instance, the endlessly expressed sentiments of domestic piety, where heaven was a home, our real home, the residence of our beloved dead. We would not be reassured by this; we would be obsessed by the loss in our own homes here and now. The empty room, the hospital bed no longer needed, the closet full of clothes to be sorted and given away: who cares for a "home" that has no connection at all with these? Therefore, poems whose central message is "may there be no sadness of farewell" would strike us as heartless. Or make us guilty because we seemed to fail to do right by the deceased whether we mourned in spite of his or her command not to, or whether we refused to mourn and felt like traitors not just to our own emotions, but to our deepest awareness of the power of human attachment. Even before we were told that the fourteen-year-old boy who drowned while fishing did so because God willed this, the ideas and images of the older era would grate on us, outrage us, and fail to inspire hope or comfort. If not for the reasons Dolson gave, "please omit funeral" might seem like a very good idea.

This admission revives the problem of how if at all the past should be remembered, used, or forgotten. The shortest answer is that this exercise of looking back before silence and denial makes us cautious about those clichés regarding the past that pervade not only the death awareness movement but many of our cultural perceptions. We now suspect nostalgia about "old-time religion" and old-time attitudes toward death. It can make us much more aware that what Christians used to say about death is not what Christians ought to say again. The future of Christian thinking about death may not lie with Cullmann (I personally hope it does not), but it will definitely not lie with what Cullmann reacted against. Yes, Christian preaching at the time of death ought to be able to improve over biographical anecdotes about Doug and Barbara and her cancer. There are real resources beyond this, even in the pastors' manuals that stress *Preaching to Mourners*, but these do not lie in the relatively recent past of the early twentieth century.

Possibly there is something that can be retrieved from that era before silence and denial. Not the specific ideas about death and afterlife, and not in their clergy's insistence on "doctrinal" sermons, at least given their understanding of "doctrine." But as we saw in the discussion of "The Eclipse of Poetry," a vision of death for Christians may be not just a matter of "doctrine," but of imagination and vision. Some imaginative capacity was once called forth by the poems of the past, but seems to lie dormant in us. This may be how we can reach out toward a sense of divine involvement with life and death, of God's presence and majesty and passionate involvement with all dimensions of our world and our lives. The eclipse of poetry, in both its lessened quality and its eventual transformation into family memorial testimony, is a loss for Christian faith. Were there a way to rediscover its underlying function, without its specific ideas (such as natural immortality or "may there be no sadness of farewell") then the choices left by silence and denial, Cullmann, and the death awareness movement would be substantially enriched and deepened. Instead of a "big story" stripped of all imagery except military victory over death, and disconnected almost entirely from anyone's "little story," we might have a bridge to link these together.

Such poems exist, but lie outside of the current world of *Preaching to Mourners*. Not in Ireland, as we saw, but for us here, and so I am not recommending that the pastor's funeral sermons include recitation of

Wallace Stevens or T. S. Eliot. Perhaps visual media will today work better for many of us, as well as music. The use of these should not be primarily to become part of biographical, memorial tributes, but to open the imaginative ears of all to hear something wider, deeper, and higher about Christ, God, and death. That was the accomplishment of the funeral sermons from the era before silence and denial, and that is what their best legacy for us can be.

For this might restore a fuller sense of "worship" as the purpose of the Christian funeral. If we, like Blackwood, still contrast this goal with focus on the deceased person or on the pastor, we will in the end seem to have opted for "one size fits all," a choice that does not seem to succeed, even with an Archbishop Myers to enforce it. Moreover, Blackwood and many Christians today would constrict "worship" into something positive, hopeful, upbeat, although his standard of hope would never work for us. This leaves no room for "lament" as worship, and I am convinced that this "might have been" path not taken deserves more consideration. Yes, it seems to make funerals more unbearable, to obscure the message of resurrection in favor of angry complaint against God. Yes, it leaves space for revenge fantasies, in a way that almost all Christians will find problematic. But it is worship of a God who cares about us, who cares about life on earth, who never heard of "impassivity," and who does not offer natural immortality as a way out of pain and loss. It is also definitely "worship" in a sense that Doug-and-Barbara anecdotes are not. If the message of the death awareness movement was that we need to include death and loss in our full picture of human existence, then lament will fulfill this far better than the kind of "life celebrations" that seem to have become the norm even for anthologized funeral sermons.

In the church I belong to, the former clergyperson at one point decided it would be a good thing if all the members above a certain age were to leave instructions for their funerals. Mostly, of course, this meant phone numbers, preferences about funeral homes, and existing arrangements regarding burial plots. But it was also to include some things about the funeral service itself: which Scripture passages, which hymns, and who should be invited to participate as readers. This exercise was not a great success. We did get into a good discussion when one elderly parishioner voiced her wish for Eric Clapton songs at her funeral. I got as far as certainty that I did *not* want the John 14 "many mansions" passage read at my funeral. But then I realized there was one passage I definitely would want read. It would not be because my funeral would be "a party for myself." But, as I thought about this, this event would be an occasion where others present could "do right by" Lucy. This required not loads of biographical anecdotes, but a representation of who Lucy had been that would make sense to them. For that purpose, Psalm 19 fit:

> In the heavens he has pitched a tent for the sun
> Which is like a bridegroom coming forth from his pavilion
> Like a champion rejoicing to run his course.
> It rises at one end of the heavens, and makes its circuit to the other;
> Nothing is hidden from its heat. (Ps 19:4-6)

This is not about death. It does not even seem at first to be about God, although the second half of the song sings the praises of "the law of the Lord." This, like the sun in the Middle East, can be harsh and forbidding, but in the song it is "sweeter than honey, than honey from the comb." What links the poem's two halves is the sense of awe, of transcendent presence, and of omniscience. The sun surveys all, and rejoices in its own movement as well as in what it sees. This is not the doctrine of natural immortality, it is nature as metaphor, a wonderful image of Planet Yahweh. Nor is it "Christian hope," but it is a prelude to or preparation for such hope. Although it may evoke memories of Lucy, and her love of the outdoors, its more direct effect is to evoke wonder at the scope and stretch of God's presence in and over the world. In short, it is there for worship, and it helps place a single individual's death in the widest possible setting. There are other passages that are "about death," but this is one I want read at my funeral. It points not back before, but truly beyond silence and denial.

Bibliography

Anderson, Bernhard W. *Out of the Depths: The Psalms Speak for Us Today*. Revised and expanded ed. Philadelphia: Westminster Press, 1983.

Augustine. *Confessions*. New York: New American Library, 1963.

Aulén, Gustav. *Christus Victor*. Trans. A. G. Herbert. New York: Macmillan, 1967 [1930].

Bailey, Lloyd Sr. *Biblical Perspectives on Death*. Philadelphia: Fortress, 1979.

Bane, Donald, ed. *Death and Ministry: Pastoral Care for the Dying and Bereaved*. New York: Seabury, 1975.

Barth, Karl. "The Strange New World in the Bible." In *Word of God, Word of Man*. Trans. Douglas Horton. New York: Harper & Row, 1928, 28–50.

Bellah, Robert. "Civil Religion in America." In *Beyond Belief: Essays on Religion in a Post–Traditional World*. New York: Harper & Row, 1970, 168–89 [original essay 1967].

Bergman, Ingmar. *The Seventh Seal*. Sweden: Janus Films, 1957.

Bernardin, Joseph Cardinal. *The Gift of Peace*. New York: Image Books, 1997.

Billman, Kathleen D., and Daniel L. Migliore. *Rachel's Cry: Prayer of Lament and Rebirth of Hope*. Cleveland: United Church Press, 1999.

Blackwood, Andrew W. *The Funeral: A Source Book for Ministers*. Philadelphia: Westminster Press, 1942.

Bowers, Margaretta, et al. *Counseling the Dying*. San Francisco: Harper & Row, 1981 [1964].

Branson, Roy. "Is Acceptance a Denial of Death? Another Look at Kübler-Ross." *Christian Century* 92 (1975): 464–68.

Bregman, Lucy. *Beyond Silence and Denial: Death and Dying Reconsidered*. Louisville, Ky.: Westminster John Knox, 1999.

———. *Death in the Midst of Life: Perspectives on Death from Christianity and Depth Psychology*. Grand Rapids: Baker Book House, 1992.

Bregman, Lucy, and Sara Thiermann. *First Person Mortal: Personal Narratives of Illness, Dying and Grief*. New York: Paragon, 1995.

Brown, Sally, and Patrick Miller, eds. *Lament: Reclaiming Practices in Pulpit, Pew and Public Square*. Louisville, Ky.: Westminster John Knox, 2005.

Browning, Don. *The Moral Context of Pastoral Care*. Philadelphia: Westminster Press, 1976.

Brueggemann, Walter. *Deep Memory, Exuberant Hope: Contested Truth in a Post–Christian World*. Ed. Patrick Miller. Minneapolis: Fortress, 2000.

———. "The Formfulness of Grief." In Miller [first published 1977], 84–97.

———. *Praying the Psalms*. Winona , Wisc.: St. Mary's Press, 1993.

Brunner, Emil. *Eternal Hope*. London: Lutterworth Press, 1954.

———. *The Mediator*. London: Lutterworth Press, 1946 [1927].

Brunner, Emil, and Karl Barth. *Natural Theology*. Trans. Peter Fraenkel. London: Geoffrey Bles, 1946.

Cabot, Richards C., and Russell L. Dicks. *The Art of Ministering to the Sick*. New York: Macmillan, 1936.

Chrissman, James K. *Death and Dying in Central Appalachia: Changing Attitudes and Practices*. Urbana: University of Illinois Press, 1994.

Christensen, James L. *The Complete Funeral Manual*. Westwood, N.J.: Fleming H. Revell, 1967.

Collopy, B. J. "Theology and the Darkness of Death." *Theological Studies* 39 (1978): 22–59.

Conwell, Russell. *One Thousand Thoughts for Funeral Occasions*. New York: George H. Doran, 1912.

Cooper, John. *Body, Soul and the Life Everlasting*. Grand Rapids: Eerdmans, 1989.

Cullmann, Oscar. "Immortality of the Soul or Resurrection of the Dead?" In *Resurrection and Immortality*. Ed. K. Stendahl. New York: Macmillan, 1965, 9–53.

Curley, Terence P. *Console One Another: A Guide for Christian Funerals*. Kansas City, Mo.: Sheed & Ward, 1993.

Daniels, Earl. *The Funeral Message: Its Preparation and Significance*. Nashville: Cokesbury Press, 1937.

Deford, Frank. *Alix: The Life of a Child*. New York: New American Library, 1986.

Dolson, Hildegarde. *Please Omit Funeral*. Philadelphia: Lippincott, 1975.

Douglas, Ann. *The Feminization of American Culture*. New York: Avon Books, 1977.

Dueck, Al. "Personal Lament" from a service for a dead baby. Sent as e-mail, July 5, 2001. Used with permission.

Eadie, Betty. *Embraced by the Light*. New York: Bantam, 1994.

Episcopal Church. *Book of Common Prayer*. New York: Church Hymnal Corp., 1979.

Evangelical Lutheran Church. *20 Funeral Sermons*. Minneapolis: Augsburg, 1952.

Feifel, Herman, ed. *The Meaning of Death*. New York: McGraw-Hill, 1959.

Fowler, Gene. *Caring through the Funeral: A Pastor's Guide*. St. Louis: Chalice, 2004.

Freud, Sigmund. *The Future of an Illusion*. Ed. James Strachey. Garden City, N.Y.: Doubleday, 1964 [1927].

Frink, A. L. "The Rose Still Grows Beyond the Wall." Numerous websites, of which http://www.inspirational-words-phrases.com is typical. This poem appears to have no copyright.

Gorer, Geoffrey. *Death, Grief and Mourning*. Garden City, N.Y.: Doubleday, 1965.

Gunther, John. *Death Be Not Proud*. New York: Harper, 1947.

Hallock, Rev. G. B. F. *Cyclopedia of Funeral Sermons and Sketches*. New York: George H. Doran, 1926.

Henderson, J. Frank. *Liturgies of Lament*. Chicago: Liturgical Training Publications, 1994.

Herberg, Will. *Protestant, Catholic, Jew: An Essay in American Religious Sociology*. Garden City, N.Y.: Anchor Books, 1960.

Hiltner, Seward. *Preface to Pastoral Theology*. Nashville: Abingdon, 1958.

Hole, Sara Grace. "Thank you, Gigi." From "Service of Celebration and Thanksgiving for the Life of Sara Elisabeth Thiermann." January 16, 2010. Used with permission.

Holifield, E. Brooks. *A History of Pastoral Care in America: From Salvation to Self-Realization*. Nashville: Abingdon, 1983.

Hughes, Robert. *A Trumpet in Darkness: Preaching to Mourners*. Philadelphia: Fortress, 1985.

Huxley, Aldous. *After Many a Summer Dies the Swan*. New York: Harper, 1939.

Irion, Paul. *The Funeral: Vestige or Value?* Nashville: Abingdon, 1966.

———. *Hospice and Ministry*. Nashville: Abingdon, 1988.

Jinkins, Michael. *In the House of the Lord: Inhabiting the Psalms of Lament*. Collegeville, Minn.: Liturgical Press, 1998.

Joyce, Jon L. *The Pastor and Grief*. Lima, Ohio: CSS Publishing, 1973.

Jüngel, Eberhard. *Death: The Riddle and the Mystery*. Trans. Iain and Ute Nicol. Philadelphia: Westminster, 1974.

Kelsey, David. *The Uses of Scripture in Forms of Modern Theology*. Philadelphia: Fortress, 1975.

Ketcham, William E., ed. *Funeral Sermons and Outline Addresses: An Aid for Pastors*. New York: Harper & Brothers, 1899.

Krieg, Robert. "The Funeral Homily: A Theological View." *Worship* 58 (1984): 222–39.

Kübler-Ross, Elisabeth, ed. *Death: The Final Stage of Growth*. Englewood Cliffs, N.J.: Prentice Hall, 1975.

———. *On Children and Death*. New York: Macmillan, 1983.

———. *On Death and Dying*. New York: Macmillan, 1968.

Laderman, Gary. *Rest in Peace: A Cultural History of Death and the Funeral Home in 20th Century America*. New York: Oxford University Press, 2003.

———. *The Sacred Remains: American Attitudes towards Death 1799–1883*. New Haven: Yale University Press, 1996.

Lewis, C. S. *A Grief Observed*. New York: Bantam, 1976 [1961].

———. *Reflections on the Psalms*. New York: Harcourt Brace, 1958.

Lifton, Robert. *The Broken Connection*. New York: Simon & Schuster, 1979.

Linafelt, Tod, and Timothy K. Beal, eds. *God in the Fray: A Tribute to Walter Brueggemann*. Minneapolis: Fortress, 1998.

Lindemann, Erich. "Symptomotology and Management of Acute Grief." *American Journal of Psychiatry* 101 (1944): 141–48.

The Liturgical Conference. *Preaching on Death*. Minneapolis: Color Printing Specialists, 1997.

Long, Thomas. *Accompany Them with Singing: The Christian Funeral*. Louisville, Ky.: Westminster John Knox, 2009.

Malcolm, Andrew. *Someday*. New York: Harper & Row, 1991.

Mansell, John S. *The Funeral: A Pastor's Guide*. Nashville: Abingdon, 1998.

May, William F. *The Physician's Covenant: Images of the Healer in Medical Ethics*. Philadelphia: Westminster Press, 1983.

McDannell, Colleen, and Bernhard Lang. *Heaven: A History*. New Haven: Yale University Press, 1988.

McWilliams, Warren. "Divine Suffering in Contemporary Theology." *Scottish Journal of Theology* 3 (1980): 35–53.

Mendenhall, George E. "From Witchcraft to Justice: Death and Afterlife in the Old Testament." In *Death and Afterlife: Perspectives of World Religions*. Ed. H. Obayashi. New York: Praeger, 1992, 67–81.

Miller, Patrick D., ed. *The Psalms and the Life of Faith*. Minneapolis: Fortress, 1995.

Mitchell, Kenneth R., and Herbert Anderson. *All Our Losses, All Our Griefs*. Philadelphia: Westminster Press, 1983.

Mitford, Jessica. *The American Way of Death*. New York: Simon & Schuster, 1963.

Moltmann, Jürgen. *The Crucified God*. Trans. R. A. Wilson and John Bowden. New York: Harper & Row, 1974.

———. *Theology of Hope*. New York: Harper & Row, 1965.

Moody, Raymond. *Life After Life*. New York: Bantam, 1975.

Moreman, Christopher. *Beyond the Threshold: Afterlife Beliefs and Experiences in World Religions*. Lanham, Md.: Rowan & Littlefield, 2008.

Myers, John J., the Most Reverend. "Reports on Policies for Funeral Liturgies Need Clarification." Roman Catholic Archdiocese of Newark. http://www.rcan.org/archbish/jim_articles/sit103-02-05.htm. February 5, 2003.

Neumann, R. *Sowing in Tears, Reaping in Joy: A Collection of Funeral Sermons by Lutheran Pastors in America*. Burlington, Iowa: German Literary Board, 1912.

Nickelsburg, George. *Resurrection, Immortality and Eternal Life in Intertestimental Judaism*. Cambridge, Mass.: Harvard University Press, 1972.

Nissenbaum, Stephen. *The Battle for Christmas*. New York: Vintage, 1997.

Nouwen, Henri. *A Letter of Consolation*. San Francisco: Harper & Row, 1982.

Oates, Wayne. *Pastoral Care and Counseling in Grief and Separation*. Philadelphia: Fortress, 1976.

Paton, Alan. *For You, Departed*. New York: Charles Scribners, 1969.

Pattison, George. *Anxious Angels: A Retrospective View of Religious Existentialism*. New York: St. Martin's, 1999.

Pelikan, Jaroslav. *The Shape of Death*. Nashville: Abingdon, 1961.

Phelps, Elizabeth Stuart. *The Gates Ajar*. Ed. Helen Sootin Smith. Cambridge, Mass.: Belknap, 1964.

Pinnock, Sarah. "Atrocity and Ambiguity: Recent Developments in Christian Holocaust Responses." *Journal of the American Academy of Religion* 75 (2007): 499–523.

Richmond, Kent D. *A Time to Die: A Handbook for Funeral Sermons*. Nashville: Abingdon, 1990.

Robinson, John A. T. *In the End God*. New York: Harper & Row, 1968.

Schneider, Greg. "A Responsive Reading for Hans Peterson, Nov. 21, 1978 to May 24, 1986." Used with permission.

Schuh, Rev. L. H., ed. *Funeral Sermons*. Columbus, Ohio: The Book Concern, 1925.

———. *Funeral Sermons by Lutheran Divines*. Columbus, Ohio: Lutheran Book Concern, 1918.

Schwartz, Hans. *On the Way to the Future*. Minneapolis: Augsburg, 1979.

Shepfer, H. Reed. *When Death Speaks*. Burlington, Iowa: Lutheran Literary Board, 1937.

Southard, Samuel. *Death and Dying: A Bibliographical Survey*. New York: Greenwood Press, 1991.

Swords, Liam, ed. *Funeral Homilies*. New York: Paulist Press, 1985. [First published in Ireland, 1985].

Teresa of Avila. *The Interior Castle*. New York: Paulist Press, 1979.

Thielicke, Helmut. *Death and Life*. Trans. Edward Schroeder. Philadelphia: Fortress, 1970.

Through the Valley of the Shadow: An Anthology of Select Funeral Sermons. Lima, Ohio: CSS Publishing, 1976.

Tolstoy, Leo. "The Death of Ivan Ilych." In *The Death of Ivan Ilych and Other Stories*. New York: Modern Library, 2004, 1–60.

Trinus, Paula. *Hope for the Flowers*. New York: Newman, Paulist Press, 1972.

Urban, Linwood. *A Short History of Christian Thought*. New York: Oxford University Press, 1985.

Vitz, Paul. *Psychology as Religion: The Cult of Self-Worship*. Grand Rapids: Eerdmans, 1977.

Wallis, Charles L., ed. *The Funeral Encyclopedia*. New York: Harper & Brothers, 1953.

Walter, Tony. *The Eclipse of Eternity*. Houndmills, UK: Macmillan, 1996.

Waugh, Evelyn. *The Loved One*. Boston: Little, Brown, 1948.

We Are the Lord's: An Anthology of Select Funeral Messages. Lima, Ohio: CSS Publishing, 1989.

Webb, Marilyn. *The Good Death: The New American Search to Reshape the End of Life*. New York: Bantam, 1999.

Westermann, Claus. "The Role of Lament in the Theology of the Old Testament." *Interpretation* 28 (1978): 20–38.

Wolterstorff, Nicholas. *Lament for a Son*. Grand Rapids: Eerdmans, 1967.

Wyschogrod, Edith. *Spirit in Ashes: Hegel, Heidegger and Man-Made Mass Death*. New Haven: Yale University Press, 1985.

Zenger, Erich. *A God of Vengeance? Understanding the Psalms of Divine Wrath*. Trans. Linda Maloney. Louisville, Ky.: Westminster John Knox, 1996.

Index